STONES INTO BREAD

GUERNICA WORLD EDITIONS 9

*Published with the help of funding
from the Department of Humanities,
University of Calabria*

STONES INTO BREAD

Vito Teti

Translated by
Francesco Loriggio &
Damiano Pietropaolo

GUERNICA
World
EDITIONS

TORONTO—BUFFALO—LANCASTER (U.K.)
2018

Michael Mirolla, editor
Cover design: Allen Jomoc, Jr.
Interior design: Jill Ronsley, suneditwrite.com
Guernica Editions Inc.
1569 Heritage Way, Oakville, (ON), Canada L6M 2Z7
2250 Military Road, Tonawanda, N.Y. 14150-6000 U.S.A.
www.guernicaeditions.com

Distributors:
University of Toronto Press Distribution,
5201 Dufferin Street, Toronto (ON), Canada M3H 5T8
Gazelle Book Services, White Cross Mills
High Town, Lancaster LA1 4XS U.K.

First edition.
Printed in Canada.

Legal Deposit—Third Quarter
Library of Congress Catalog Card Number: 2018941937
Library and Archives Canada Cataloguing in Publication
Teti, Vito, 1950-
[Pietre di pane. English]
Stones into bread / Vito Teti ; translated by Francesco
Loriggio & Damiano Pietropaolo. – First edition.

(Guernica world editions ; 9)
Translation of: Pietre di pane: un'antropologia del restare.
Issued in print and electronic formats.
ISBN 978-1-77183-338-7 (softcover).–ISBN 978-1-77183-339-4
(EPUB).–ISBN 978-1-77183-340-0 (Kindle)

I. Loriggio, Francesco, translator II. Pietropaolo, Damiano,
translator III. Title. IV. Title: Pietre di pane. English.
V. Series: Guernica world editions ; 9

PQ4880.E864P5313 2018   854'.914   C2018-902358-9
                                                 C2018-902359-7

Table of Contents

Translators' Note

IF IT WERE at all possible, translators would rather remain invisible when it comes to the texts they've made legible for those who don't have access to the language of the original version. They would prefer not to be thought of at all, to remain anonymous. Ideally they hope readers will believe that what they're reading is how the author wrote it and will forget about them altogether. But as Italians say, *traduttore traditore,* translators are betrayers; they can never—by definition—fully cover their tracks.

That this is so, that it must necessarily be so, is most evident, in this book, with the interludes. They're transcriptions of lullabies, nursery rhymes or other occasional rhymes sung or recited in a particular locality of Calabria and in the peculiar, particular local variety of the *calabrese* dialect, itself quite a marked departure from standard Italian. Needless to say, there is no English—Canadian English or North American English or British English—that would render that specific *calabrese*-ness. We've stayed with standard English, trying instead to capture at least the orality, the rhythms of the verses.

As for the rest, we've endeavoured to remain as faithful as possible to Vito Teti's prose and its discrete mixture of spoken and "cultured" Italian. We've deliberately and directly interfered only in the "Bibliographical Note," where we've added references to works first written in English but listed in their Italian translation or to available English translations of some of the works that first appeared in other languages and of which, again, the "Note" mentions only the Italian edition.

Finally, for full disclosure, although we've checked and corrected each other's translation, each one of us has focussed on different portions of the book. Francesco Loriggio is most directly responsible for "Prologue: Of Remaining," "Angelino's Turn," "The Road to Vallelonga," "The House of the Thirty-three Loaves of Bread," "Figs in Toronto," the interludes pertaining to them, plus the "Note on the Texts" and the "Bibliographical Note"; Damiano Pietropaolo for "The Shadow and the Sewing Machine," "Murat's Nets," "Clouds and Back Streets," "The Stones of My Cousin Giò," "The Emperor's Funeral," "Village Mother" and related interludes.

Foreword: On Exile and Return

Damiano Pietropaolo

Translation is the other side of a tapestry.
—Miguel de Cervantes

I'M ON A flight from Rome to Toronto. It's late September. I've spent the summer in the village of Maierato, in Calabria, the land where I was born and raised until, barely into my teens, my father moved his family to Toronto, where we made our home in Little Italy. Toronto's Little Italy figures prominently in the book that's sitting on my lap: Vito Teti's *Pietre di pane*, the original version of this book, with which I'm engaged in an ongoing dialogue, both as reader and as translator. As the airplane rises over the Mediterranean, I'm visited by a familiar anxiety, common, I think, to most immigrants. I'm not quite certain of my destination: Am I returning home? Am I leaving home? Or am I simply longing to re-live, if only on the printed page, that ancient drama of exile and return so prevalent in the literature of the Mediterranean? *Pietre di pane* bills itself as an essay on the anthropology of *remaining*, on the cultural and existential impact of immigration on those who were left behind when fathers and other relatives moved to *lamerica*. It's also Teti's deeply felt personal and poetic *nostos* with a modern twist: There is no home to return to—his father took it with him when he moved to Toronto's Little Italy in the 1950s.

As a reader, I'm captivated by Teti's seamless weaving of personal storytelling, poetic evocation of village life, and anthropological observation of the daily lives of villagers who had been bereaved by emigration, into a single unified tapestry hanging in the crevasse opened by emigration, a two-way mirror in which those who had *left* and those who *remained* are reflected as a single community. As a translator I'm reminded, that at best, the English language version of *Pietre di pane* is the other side of this tapestry: two sides of the same story, or a single story? A few days ago in the village of San Nicola Da Crissa, Teti's birthplace and the place where he has chosen to remain, *Pietre di pane* was presented to the community.

It was a festive late summer gathering of people from both sides of the Atlantic. In this piazza overlooking a valley of ancient olive and fig trees, many in attendance were immigrants, like myself, who make a point of returning to the place of their birth every summer. *Pietre di pane* had brought all of us, those who remained and those who had moved away, to this piazza, in celebration of our togetherness.

As a translator of the book I read, in English, a fragment in which the author reflects on his visit to Little Italy as he meanders along its streets visiting long lost friends and relatives, on Beatrice Street, Grace Street, Montrose Ave, looking for houses that his father had called home. He has brought gifts of figs from the old country as a reminder of the taste, feel and smell of the land of their birth, their homeland. He's unaware that in many of the back yards of his friends and relatives fig trees flourish in the harsh Canadian climate and will yield a respectable crop.

As I read my translation I was struck by the fact that for many of the younger visitors in the Piazza, the Canadian-born children of immigrants, English was not the language into which the experience of their parents had been translated: It was their mother tongue. In *Pietre di pane*, as in many of his other essays, Teti delves at length into the theme of the double: the San Nicolese community in Toronto is but the "double" of the community that remained. In the piazza that late summer evening the geographic distance between the doubles had vanished; they were one and the same. Translation seemed redundant. There was no need for a middleman. English was the other side of the mirror, a *doppelganger* reflection of the original.

The Canadian-born accepted English, not as some foreign language, but as the "double" of their mother tongue, much as the fig trees growing in the back yards of the community were but the "doubles" of fig trees back in San Nicola da Crissa. It dawned on me that, as the translator, I was the "double" of the author, and not only in linguistic terms. I'd left the valley and settled on the other side of the mirror.

In the back yards of Little Italy there is an abundance of fig trees. In my father's back yard a young sapling of a fig tree, whose mother thrived in the valley below us, served as the daily reminder of a faraway world that had morphed into an intangible memory of another place and another time. As a hermeneutic bridge across the chasm of immigration, the fig tree is not symbolic of our *history*; it is the embodiment, the transplant and translation of our *story* to be passed on across the generations and across languages. Teti's journey into the New World is really a return to an Old World transplanted onto a new land.

In smuggling a sapling from the old world and planting it in the new, my father, like countless other immigrants of his generation, was not driven by nostalgia, but by the burning desire to create a new world: not the translation of the memory of the old world into the new, but the creation of a new flesh and blood reality, a *double* of the world left behind, to be sure, but a *double* whose gaze was firmly focussed on the future. For those of us who left this valley when we were children, the fig trees in the back yards of Little Italy represented the *locus amenus* of a happy childhood broken asunder by a tsunami of emigration that depopulated not only Teti's and my own villages but the whole region of Calabria.

On my first reading of *Pietre di pane* I was moved deeply by the mirroring of my own experience of an interrupted, wounded childhood. I was overtaken by a Proustian longing for a vanished world. Later I came to understand that the children who had remained in villages that were turning into ghost towns suffered the same fate. Immigration had opened up a chasm that we have been attempting to bridge through storytelling.

When my father took us away from Calabria to make a new home in Canada, I did not think I would ever return. Setting sail to Canada felt to me like the beginning of a permanent exile from this valley of olive and fig trees onto which the villages of Maierato, San Nicola, Filadelfia, Monterosso opened up their shuttered windows every morning. At twilight the flickering lights of San Nicola and other villages on the hills across the valley marked the horizon of the known world. On the margins of Medieval maps of the Old World, before Columbus opened up the channels to emigration beyond the Pillars of Hercules, it was customary to place a warning: *hic sunt dragones*— here be dragons. When we ventured away from this valley beyond the borders of the known world, the dragons of immigration, speaking in an incomprehensible language, were waiting for us with open jaws.

Vito Teti journeys to Toronto in search of a world that moved away; we return from Toronto to search in vain for worlds we have left behind. Our attempts to abolish the distance of time and space that separates us lead to the only possible common destination: a theatre of memory in which our *history* becomes the source of a mythopoeic performance of our *story*. *Pietre di pane* is a narrative of emigration poised between scholarly research—the anthropology of remaining— and literary creation.

This contamination of anthropological observation by the poetic processing of memory makes of *Pietre di pane* a sort of bridge between the two sides of the crevasse opened by emigration. Read from this perspective *Pietre di pane* is its own doppelganger, the *double* of itself: an anthropological research that is refracted—translated—by the fictionalized poetics of those who have remained and those who have left. Like Frank, who meanders through the streets of Toronto looking for his father's home, those of us who left, return to the narrow streets of San Nicola and Maierato looking for a place between poetry and reality, for a narrative we can call home.

As the never-ending flight cross the Atlantic is reaching its destination, I'm haunted by the famous question asked by Northrop Frye just as Canada was turning one hundred:

> *It seems to me that the Canadian sensibility has been profoundly disturbed, not so much by our famous problem of identity, important as that is, as by a series of paradoxes in what confronts that identity. It is less perplexed by the question "Who am I?" than by some such riddle as "Where is here?"*
>
> ("*Haunted by Lack of Ghosts*")

Where is here, indeed? It's a question that haunts each and every immigrant. *Pietre di pane* is haunted by the same question. Ultimately Teti's anthropological journey into the historical reality of exile and return takes him, and us, to our final destination: the translation of our daily experience as immigrants into a poetics of belonging, a narrative that abolishes distances of time and space and plants itself into the ground like the fig trees of Little Italy to affirm the essence of what it means to be here.

Prologue: Of Remaining

"I HATE TRAVELLING AND explorers. Yet here I am proposing to tell the story of my own explorations." The opening of Claude Lévi-Strauss' *Tristes Tropiques* is one of the most celebrated and compelling lines in all anthropological literature, and it reminds us that voyages and displacement are among the founding traits of anthropological experience.

Nothing could then seem more foreign to the history of anthropology than the idea of remaining. Remaining appears to us as the antithesis of voyaging, of self-questioning, of the willingness to face disorder, the encounter, or the effects of the discovery of what is new for us.

But are the idea and the practice of remaining really incompatible with anthropological experience? And, above all, can we think of travelling separately from the idea of remaining? Should remaining really be associated with immobility, with the refusal to meet the other, to come to terms with one's shadow, with one's double, with alterity as such? Is to remain to defend the feeling of being at home in a place? Or is there also a form of remaining that displaces, that at times can be as troubling as travelling? Here, through the various narratives I'll be recounting, what I'll suggest is that we need to reconsider both our conceptions and our practices of remaining in the light of the new ways by which we can articulate the idea of "here" and the idea of "elsewhere."

In the Western tradition nomadism has been more alluring than sedentariness or attachment to place, errancy more than permanence. Awaitals and the nostalgia that goes with them have been the topic of narrations far less often than the adventures and the nostalgia of those who have left. And yet the two experiences are interrelated, and in quite a profound manner. Ulysses' voyage would make no sense without Penelope's waiting. In his *Per l'alto mare aperto* [*On the Open Sea*], where he reflects on the beginning and the end of modernity, Eugenio Scalfari reminds us that the portrayal of Ulysses in *The Odyssey* coincides with that of four female figures: Circe the sorceress, Calypso the woman in love, Nausicaa the trembling virgin and Penelope, who is both spouse and queen.

To complete the picture Scalfari mentions the Sirens with their beguiling song and then a fifth character, Athena, whose presence towers above that of the other women and whose task is to show human beings their limits, so that when they are forced to confront the mysterious in life they won't lose their self-control. "Without those female figures, which are part and parcel of the Odyssean myth, the modern hero would not have existed, and the myth would have had a very short life." It takes the sorceress, the woman in love, the virgin, the spouse, the sirens/temptresses, the wise goddess to delineate the contours of the feminine, whereas only one hero suffices to recapitulate the various male types: the warrior, the navigator, the husband, the seducer, the trickster, the avenger.

Modernity arises together with the myth of the hero who travels and returns and with the myth of the woman who waits. But waiting shouldn't be confused with passivity, with resistance to change, or with apathy. Waiting is pain and purposiveness, hope, patience, the ability to continue and to renew one's existence, in spite of everything. Waiting is concentration, attentiveness.

I was born in a land in which departure and waiting have contributed to the making of a new mentality, a new identity. Migration is made of the pain that comes with leaving and of the pain that comes with staying: It's made of the waiting, the hope, the failure, the success of those who haven't gone anywhere.

The story of the "men without women" who have populated the many cities of the world is completed in its full sense by the story of the "women without men" who remained behind in the many villages or the surrounding countryside. But the waiting of the women of the "Americans," as the migrants were invariably called, translated into organizational ability, into the acquisition of new roles, the construction of new selves. The waiting was often voided by the departures that weren't followed by a return. But the mobility of traditional spaces rested, for better or for worse, on the contribution of those who left, very often without returning, and of those who remained, very often without waiting.

The flight, the mobility, the anxiety of people who live or who have lived in Calabria constitute the other side of the sedentary, rooted portion of their lives; they're attitudes and choices that send back to a long history marked by catastrophes, the abandonment and the refounding of places in which to live.

Would the voyage retain its meaning without anyone waiting for the return of those who left?

The voyage of the anthropologist is also intrinsically bound to the need to return, the need to explain to those who remain behind, or, perhaps, before anyone else, to oneself. In anthropology writing and narration come into play—as impulse and as obligation at least—before one leaves for the field. The Ulysses who narrates his adventures and, in narrating them, gives meaning to his anguish and his experiences is the prototype of the traveller who finds himself compelled to tell his story, to narrate.

When the voyage is final, a voyage without return, what will be narrated, explained, and perhaps founded anew, will be the place from which the voyage originated, the culture that the traveller left behind and to which he belongs. But just as the voyage doesn't necessarily require a mental displacement, the waiting can involve major external and internal change. The voyage can become a false displacement and staying back, vice versa, result in significant alterations to one's way of life.

Travelling and remaining, leaving and returning are experiences that can't be kept altogether separate. Migrations have entailed the end of a universe but also the proliferation of stories and places, of shadows and doubles.

On the way

During the Romantic period—but we could go back much further in time, the themes of the shadow and the double, of the risk of losing oneself and of the need of finding oneself seem to be linked both to the experience of travelling and to the experience of remaining. *The Wonderful Story of Peter Schlemihl* by Adalbert von Chamisso, which appeared in 1814, narrates the tale of an individual condemned to a perpetual wandering but who nonetheless in his travelling without a direction seeks to find some sort of salvation. Joseph Joachim von Eichendorff in his *Memoirs of a Good-for-Nothing*, of 1826, tells us of voyages undertaken without going anywhere, a genre that Xavier de Maistre had inaugurated in his *Voyage Around My Room* (1794).

There is, especially in the English 19th century, a whole series of narrators and wanderers, of narrator-*flâneurs*, who make the most extraordinary discoveries and leave the door open to the most sensational changes to their way of life by straying only a few kilometres from home. Some of the great authors of the European tradition (from E.T.A. Hoffmann to Baudelaire and then to Joyce, Kafka, Musil) come to terms with their selves, the places they live in, their time, their world, often without leaving the sites of their birth or even without setting foot outside their room. This introspection is fundamental for anthropological thought, so much so that these authors and their works have become an integral part of the cultural baggage many anthropologists now carry with them.

During this phase of history what begins to take hold is an idea of travelling that intersects with the idea of the stationary, with the kind of movement that requires little effort and unfolds in a small space. To repeat, it's an idea that, although often underestimated, has proven to be crucial for the history of anthropology and ethnography. Scholars who study local traditions, collect oral texts and record local customs, folklorists and ethnologists are now able to uncover an elsewhere in the locale they have been inhabiting. The native village becomes the field in which to conduct research, and the "others" are individuals with whom one is in everyday contact.

The result has been a blossoming of studies, of explorations and documentations, the discovery of the diversity and alterity of the native and the familiar that was to reveal itself crucial for the perception of the self and the other in the history of anthropological thought. Ernesto De Martino's revisitation of the urgings by the Italian Jesuits of the second half of the 16th century, to pay more attention to the "Indies in our backyard," marked the beginning of the anthropologists' "return home."

The criticism levelled at traditions that have been too local-oriented are well known, but there exists a substantial amount of research in folklore and ethnology, in Italy and Europe, without which the history of anthropology would appear to be written in a very biased, one-sided manner. Sir James Frazer, the prototype of the "armchair" anthropologist, was able to construct his impressive narrative thanks to data and documents coming to him not only from the world of "savage," "primitive" peoples but also from European antiquity and the European lower classes.

When all is said and done, folklorists, in their most refined versions, prefigure the kind of *flâneur* who strives to reinterpret the local context in a more refined manner. Giampaolo Nuvolati has noted that "the domestic, native *flâneur* re-envisages the locales of his everyday meanderings but filters that reality by way of a number of instruments, both descriptive and narrative, that allow him to grasp the most recondite meanings." The 19th-century *flâneur* who visits burgs and their surrounding countryside with an attitude that is often anti-modern and nostalgic is followed by the better-known *flâneur* who visits the city in which he lives and discovers it, interrogates it or narrates it. From Charles Baudelaire to Maxime Du Camp, from Walter Benjamin to Marc Augé, the eye has lingered on the city, viewed now as labyrinth, as a place where some loss can't be avoided, now as a living body, now as a field of study, an area wherein to observe transformations or continuities.

The urban voyage is a basic component of modern and postmodern anthropology. Often the distinctions between the "view from afar" and the "view from close by" have to do only with the need to produce easy classifications. No doubt the two ways of looking, the two types of surveying, the different modes of approaching places and people differ, and they do change both the narration and the writing. The basic problem regards the question of how it is that one observes, with which ends in mind and what degree of participation. As well, it's important to determine whether geographical distance corresponds to interior, psychic distance. One must always ask: "Far away from where?" And: "Far away from whom?"

The fascination with the elsewhere or some elsewhere doesn't presuppose a physical voyage but a mental experience that may permit alternatively, and sometimes simultaneously, long-sightedness and short-sightedness. The ordinary and the extraordinary are constantly hybridized and redefined. Freud and Heidegger had in common an interest for the condition that the German language calls *Unheimlich*. Something that previously was familiar suddenly presents itself as foreign, as unknown: It's the condition we associate with displacement. The Italian writer Claudio Magris reminds us that "the well-known, always rediscovered and enriched, is the premise on which rest encounters and adventures …. The most fascinating voyage is a return, an odyssey, and the places that belong to some habitual itinerary, the usual microcosms traversed day after day for many years are a challenge worthy of Ulysses."

Observing one's own world entails responsibilities and risks: It puts one into play differently than when one observes a far-away world. In his *The Metro Revisited*, Augé has spoken of this a sort of splitting:

When I wrote *An Ethnologist in the Metro* I really didn't intend to do an ethnology of the metro. I was just observing as an ethnologist the ethnologist that I was, that had just returned from Africa. I observed that ethnologist and posed questions to him. He answered as best as he could, with the references and the terminology of an ethnologist. In other words, I was trying to put myself in the shoes of an indigenous person, but I was that particular indigenous person. From this perspective, I didn't have to make such a great effort, where imagination was concerned. The difficulty, rather, consisted in finding the questions to ask of this indigenous person, since I had to ask the questions as an ethnologist. I shouldn't be accused of too much fastidiousness: It was the ethnologist I was dividing in two to make him understand (to make me understand) what it meant to have to answer questions by someone like me.

We're beyond the narrations of interpretative anthropology. Ethnology overlaps with literature, introspection, memory, although without merging with them. The anthropologist now is both the observer and the observed. He fixes his gaze on others while being himself part of them. He collects information and finds that he is himself an informant. He asks questions to others but also, at the same time, to himself. Hence the difference lies not in the distance but in the motivation. Which doesn't mean taking the writings of an ethnologist to be literature but that the two types of writings are contiguous and complicit.

In the contemporary global dimension of things, it is possible in some way to re-construe the return, the familiar, even if within a dynamic no longer circular but multidirectional, comprising multiple internal and external trajectories. During the last few decades anthropology has gone beyond the assumption whereby the elsewhere is its only and exclusive object of enquiry, the only acceptable type of "distance." It has begun to also concern itself with the endotic, the known, to practice cultural criticism, bringing about what George Marcus and Michael Fisher have defined as a "return home," a "repatriation." Needless to say, in this case too, one never returns exactly to the point of departure, the place one had left behind.

In a world of non-places, of spaces that are not yet places or no longer places, what meaning are we then to attribute to staying back today? At a time in which anthropology has had to come to terms with the crisis that has invested its object of study, we're called upon to once more ask ourselves whether such a decision, such an act can also be part of anthropological practice. The anthropologists who remain and encounter those who, like them, have not gone away experience directly, in their lives, the new cultural dynamics. They see those who leave and can analyse the ways by which separation occurs; they see those who arrive burdened with new problems and can, in each of the cases they are faced with, interpret the hybridizations, the conflicts, the surfacing of new processes by which identity is affirmed and confirmed.

By staying where they are, these anthropologists can ponder the circumstances of post-emigration, can re-envision the territory they live in as it transmutes into a frontier territory and can reinterpret the unease that goes with the changes, the suffering, the restlessness, the "what am I doing here," the remorse, the cultural shock of those individuals who may feel they belong to an unchangeable tradition, whereas, in all effects, they are caught in the maze of globalization. Finally, in remaining on home grounds, these other anthropologists can analyse and narrate both the emptying out of the villages around them and, simultaneously, the processes by which those villages become re-inhabited by new people.

Moving about in cities, scouring on foot the outskirts and the marginalities that constitute them, crossing villages and the surrounding countryside, looking at the newly-arrived and getting to know them requires that one be versed in the art of walking slowly, quietly, often in solitude and with circumspection. I know people who have travelled much and seen nothing. I've met others who have been all over and have never walked, and yet others who have always stood still where they are and known the world. Now that the far-away is no longer far but nearby, "easily negotiable perhaps even domestic," as Antonio Prete writes, and "can be found at home, on the computer monitor, the display of cell phones, the sound that reaches us in the headphones we have on," the undiscovered and the unexpected are perhaps to be found in places apparently closest to us, at times those we inhabit and that perhaps have become the most distant, the most far away and unrecognizable ones.

Walking, even for those who have stayed behind, is an exercise by which to come face to face with what is true, just as it once was for those who had chosen distant places as their field of research and for whom the voyage was discovery, salvation, therapy, the widening of their horizon. *Solvitur ambulando*, the solution lies in walking, as Bruce Chatwin used to write in his notes.

Solvitur ambulando

The salvational concept of walking can be found in all religions. It features also in the traditional cultures of my homeland. The act of walking, as numerous oral texts attest, appears as an element on which truth, novelty and justice are founded. The Christ of Calabrian legends and tales "travels throughout the world," by himself or accompanied by Peter or other disciples, affirming all the principles of justice and truthfulness among human beings. The most venerated saints and madonnas in our portion of Italy come from lands outside it, and from even farther away the traveller saints that, besides truth, have brought with them peace and well-being.

In his life story, Saint Francis of Paola, one of our most beloved saints, combines asceticism and walking: He is both a saint rooted in our region, in a place, and a traveller. Not by chance he has become the patron saint of those who have to take to sea and of emigrants. Emigration itself has been an exodus of a religious kind, the search for a "new world," a "new life." The Calabria of bygone times is crisscrossed by countless "songlines," to use Bruce Chatwin's term. The religious voyage, which involved the region's population, was a way to counter the monotonous, afflicted life, a space of freedom, a yearning for salvation and healing. "On and on they walked," say various folktales in which the protagonists free themselves or try to free themselves from poverty, hunger and injustice. To walk is to know, to understand, to improve one's condition.

The "old ambler" folktales tell us about the man of experience who knows the ways of the world, a quality we're called upon to view as the ability to make better sense of the place in which one lives. But we have lost the old habit of walking. Today we move about via internet, on the Web. We surf. To remain is now to journey to some antipode in a world of fake transportations.

According to the calculations of the University of North Carolina, May 23 2007 was an important date in the history of humanity. On that day was born the child that made the number of the inhabitants of cities larger than the number of the rest of the planet. Three billion plus one. The population of the big cities was greater than the population of the rural areas, the villages. Within the next forty years, it has been further calculated, there will be at least 27 mega-metropolises reaching the threshold of 20 million inhabitants, some of them with more than 36 million. Tokyo will be the most densely populated, with over 30 million, but many of the mega-metropolises will be in China, India and Africa, which together will hold almost a fifth of the planet's urban population.

A child born in the city has thus far had one probability out of three of being born in its shanty towns. Today almost a billion-and-a-half people inhabit slums, the ecosystem of the future, human rejects who eke out an existence in areas made out of rejected urban materials: cardboard, plastic canvas or tin plates. In about thirty years three-quarters of humanity could find itself in that universe of cement-steel-glass plus shack-like hovels.

For some years I have been trying to come to grips with the emptying out of the villages around me, with the delocalization of the region in which I was born: The largest Calabrian cities are somewhere else, abroad. And in the last few years this land, a land of flight, a land from which to depart, has become a place of arrival, where newcomers are welcomed and sometimes expelled. The great shifting of peoples makes me live with unease and bitterness, with distress and uncertainty the problem of the fate of my region's hinterland, the end of the villages, of the villages resembling Christmas nativity scenes.

In the meanwhile cities clone themselves; they become like one another all over the world, with the same streets, the same shopping malls, the same department stores. Already two-thirds of British cities can boast the same High Street, the street of shopping, equivalent to the American Main Street. But, one store at a time, one street at a time, even the cities of Europe and Italy now tend to resemble each other.

Nostos and algos

"Nostalgia" is one of the most beautiful and enticing terms coined in the modern era. It evokes the flaring up and the breaking down of times and places, individual and collective lacerations and dispersions, departures, flights, returns, losses, rebirths. It brings about a happy combination between *nostos*, return, and *algos*, pain. In European vocabularies it appears for the first time in the *Dissertatio Medica de Nostalgia* presented on June 12 1688 at the University of Basel by Johannes Hoffer, a young Alsatian student of medicine.

Later, at the end of the 18th century the attention nostalgia attracted shifts from medical treatises to the writing of exiles, wanderers or refugees and becomes a sort of feeling to nurture and to cherish. The anguished hero cursed by fate of the Romantic period is both nostalgic and melancholic. Nostalgia and melancholy become a sort of habit, a custom, a way of being. Nostalgia ceases to be obsessive behaviour, "a delirious idea," melancholy that paralyses, a nagging thought, or detachment from the present. It becomes one of the manifestations of the ability to wait, of hope, remembrance, changes into the narration and invention of a new identity, an open identity no longer clinging to a homeland which is definitive and distant.

The double and the shadow of those who have left contribute, in a problematic fashion, to redefine the identitarian attitudes of those that remain. The "grievances" of the migrants that return—their disappointments—are well-known. And in those who have remained resentful, bitter answers come to the fore in no time. Together with the rhetoric about how migration leads to success there is the rhetoric of those that have stayed back. The misunderstandings between the two sides arise from a misplaced notion that identity is static, that it is akin to granite, that it must be preserved and transmitted in its "purity," its "original form" and in its fullness.

In reality those who leave and those who remain can't do without each other, even if what binds them is often based on mistaken views, distorted images, projections and expectations. Life is always elsewhere. Flight, wandering, apprehension are traits that in times past have characterised the anthropology of Calabria and the Calabrian people. It shouldn't be forgotten that their history has always been marked by the mobility of people, things, animals—a "nomadic tribe," as Corrado Alvaro used to say—by the withdrawal of inhabitants from living spaces and the refounding somewhere else of those same sites. And we must also not forget the passing through or the long stopovers of foreign rulers and their armies that never failed to leave an imprint.

Migration has accentuated those aspects of mobility, restlessness, precariousness and incompleteness that were already part of the frame of mind of the people of Calabria. The sensation of being here and elsewhere, the nostalgia for the village that one has lost and the ability to get by in another world, regret and hope are traits inherent to a certain form of wandering that concern also the individuals who have stayed behind. Calabria has become dilated, delocalized; it's "besides itself."

Ernesto De Martino has written important texts on territorial anxiety, the sense of bewilderment and distress that takes hold of Southern Italian peasants when they are no longer able to see the bell tower of their village. The disappearance of the "bell tower of Marcellinara" from the line of sight which he described in one of the most celebrated pages of his *La fine del mondo* [*The End of the World*] is a metaphor for anxiety, for the fear of losing the centre, the point of reference that individuals in traditional societies have in common. At times this territorial uneasiness could come upon individuals even in those locations inside the village considered foreign, or in the less frequented rural areas or other sites with few inhabitants.

Exacerbations of and deviations from modernity have in recent years imagined a sort of individual fully free of nostalgia, a kind of dweller living permanently in non-places, a cosmopolitan without roots and without a sense of belonging. The absence of nostalgia would be to non-places what nostalgia is to places. One could come to believe that to non-places, to the "end" of places as they have been known historically corresponds the end of the "feeling of place," the negation of any possible sense of belonging. The non-nostalgic person of our time would thus be endowed with no sense of place, would have no connection with any site, because supermodernity creates anthropological non-places, places which are desacralized, the same, uniform place.

In life things aren't so simple. Giovanni Ferraro, in his unfinished notes, writes that "modernity betrays places but then condemns itself to frantically reproduce their simulacra. Modernity forgets places but at the same time fosters the nostalgia and the search for them." Places continue to affirm their demands on non-places. According to Augé himself, places and non-places are in effect slippery polarities that communicate with each other. The one is never completely erased and the other never completely fulfilled. Places and spaces, the places and non-places of actual reality permeate each other; they oppose and evoke each other.

It's worthwhile asking if the so-called non-places, however anonymous and unliveable they may be, are undefinable spaces, spaces that can't be controlled and that depersonalize individuals, or whether, instead, they don't impose on individuals itineraries by which to forge a different identity, to claim a different presence in the world. In several of his writings, Franco La Cecla has shown what kind of efforts people of different cultures undertake to not lose their way, and he reminds us that even the inhabitants of the most undistinguished, informal sites, whether they be in the modern metropolis or the *favelas*, continuously find it necessary "to wrap their thoughts around a site" in order to create new centres, new forms of social life and dwelling.

Are train stations and airports really non-places that generate no emotion? Or do they not, rather, give rise to the need for new ways of relating to places? The sensation is that in places of transit travellers come to terms with their condition, their doubles, their shadows and bring into play different modes of recognition. Emigration itself has its own seaports, its train stations, its airports.

Besides, even if in a complementary manner and in opposition to homologizing tendencies, today as never before there is greater attention towards local cultures and small-scale homelands. Naturally there is the danger that this attention can translate into localism, in foreclosure towards other levels of culture and place, in attitudes such as those of Italy's *Lega Nord* [*Northern League*], or others like them, more or less explicit or more or less camouflaged.

One of the risks of much literature on this topic (or on such notions as identity, tradition and memory) is that it may slip towards metaphysics, towards place fixed in its immobility, in an ahistorical condition. To counter this risk, often looming also when we talk of the "spirit of place" or "the feeling of place," we need to reaffirm the mobility of places, even as it relates to our own mobility.

On the geographical scene of both the old and the new world are now beginning to appear individuals and groups that need to invent "the village," the origins, the small-scale homeland as the site of a diversity to reclaim, of a superiority to flaunt. But the need to relate to a place shouldn't be reduced, finally, to the affirmation of one's particularity or one's privileges, to the desire to distance oneself from others, to a separation sometimes also physical from them.

Despite a tradition that has privileged the negative connotations of nostalgia, other views have come to the fore, such as the one articulated by Ralph Harper, which have discerned in nostalgia a "moral dimension," "a regenerative sense of presence" that can help protect from the emptiness and the uprootings of our era, hence "providing a counterpart to all the negative aspects of our life."

Some authors have insisted on the need of individuals living in the modern era to find a place, to belong somewhere, to be part of a space they can call home, a space that doesn't have to be the one they have abandoned but can be anywhere. Nostalgia highlights the need of some presence as an answer to the yearning for displacement and uprooting. Not for nothing, there are essays that emphasize its role in times to come: It has to do with the desire to be elsewhere, to be able to imagine another existence in another space and another time, the desire to get away. It's the mental, psychological state of human beings who seek emplacement, human beings in transit who risk losing themselves: a difficult, laborious trajectory undertaken in order to assert certain aspects of one's personality, certain "energies" and ways of being that the narrowness and the limits of the place of origin denied. Even the nostalgia of migrants has been envisaged as a way to regain one's bearings in the new world where one arrives, not as an inconclusive, sterile bemoaning for times past but as a resource through which to build a new life. As well, our own nostalgia helps us to recognize and appreciate other people's nostalgia, to consider it as also useful to us.

On this much can be learned from the intellectual and existential circumstances of Pier Paolo Pasolini. He lived most of his adult life during a period in which Italian society was facing the full brunt of modernization. As a poet he drew away from an intellectual tradition too servile towards cultural fashions, too anxiously ready to cut all links with the past, a tradition that founded whatever it proposed on forgetfulness, on psychological repression and the dream of an economic development forever unstoppable. In Pasolini's *Scritti corsari* [*Corsair Writings*] the nostalgia of the past, of an agrarian civilization appears to us now as a rebuttal of the modernist rhetoric that was permeating Italian society in the 1970s, a lucid critique of the violent destruction of local cultures and other alterities, a rejection of the modernization enforced by the dominant classes, and only in the form of assimilation and homogenization. To "break down the barriers of an Italy with too restricted a vision," to adhere to another world, the world of the peasantry, of the sub-proletariat and the working class, was for him the most radical denunciation of the petty-bourgeois world, the provincial, vulgar, consumer world.

In the light of the events of the 1980s, the 1990s and the present, Pasolini's *pietas*, with its religious desire to preserve the voices, the gestures, the faces of those at the bottom of the heap presents itself to us in all its prophetic force. Pasolini found himself in the paradoxical condition of someone who no longer belongs to a world that has already disappeared and simultaneously feels estranged from the world that is imposing itself.

To avoid a standardization falsely cosmopolitan one must learn to observe and to interrogate places. Perhaps the risk we're facing, that we may have reached the end of the idea of place, that places may now be desacralized, the risk both opposite and complementary to localism and particularism, can be averted by way of a nostalgia that looks not behind, to the past, but to the here and now. By way of a nostalgia that views itself, in accordance with intellectual traditions of a utopian-critical bent, as a refusal of the present but also as one that looks to the future, that includes a sense of the future. Not for nothing there have been works entitled *The Future of Nostalgia*. If, as Augé writes, non-places are the contrary of utopia ("they exist and don't harbour in them any sort of organic society"), it's places, finally, places that with their tenacity stand for a utopia, which can bring about change. By the same token, it's this utopia that makes it possible for new places to exist, for new locations in which modern modes of emplacement, of rootedness can arise.

The new immigrants tell us that places haven't disappeared but are constantly re-invented and redefined. Those who now leave their original homes travel with a nostalgia of the place they have left behind and with the desire to recognize themselves when they are elsewhere. In their search they may often have to face the threats of the inhabitants of the sites they try to settle in, who fear that they may be expropriated. We fluctuate between the need to find ourselves once again and the fear that others may harm us. We're fascinated by our origins, which are both mythical and invented, and are often terrorized by other people's origins, which are far away and unknown to us. The problem then is how to ensure that there be dialogue between the different streams of nostalgia, between the nostalgia of those who arrive and the nostalgia of those who are the hosts.

Remaining

Neither an act of weakness nor an act of courage, remaining is a factual reality, a condition. It can become a way of being, a vocation, if lived without subjugation or subalternity, without arrogance, complaisance, narrowness and closure of mind, but with, instead, a propensity for self-questioning and restlessness. To remain is to go through the painful and authentic experience of being always "out of place." There is also a total uprootedness of those who stay put.

And so mixtures, hybridities, *métissages* can't be considered gratuitous gifts or inevitable outcomes. They have to do more with persuasion, in the meaning Carlo Michelstaedter gave to this term: "The road to persuasion points only in this direction: do not adapt yourself to the adequacy of what is given to you."

Against rhetoric and for persuasion has had something to say the Calabrian poet Franco Costabile, who, like Michelstaedter, committed suicide:

> There
> me and you, Southern Italy,
> must have a talk sometimes
> must argue really calmly, without hurry, quietly
> by ourselves
> without telling each other fairy tales
> about our land.

If Kant had warned that there is no such a thing as a return, Rimbaud pointed out that "One never leaves." The world has become too small (as villages once were) for us to be able to think that we can experience the otherness the travellers and anthropologists of yester-year had accustomed us to, the otherness they contributed to dissolve, among other things. Even today the stream of anthropology known as *Urgent anthropology* and the idea that some cultures may disappear inspire the launching of ethnographic expeditions.

Taking this sort of thinking to its extreme consequences we should say: "No-one should stay back," because in a world in perpetual motion the individuals who remain at home are travelling. And perhaps leaving, returning, staying, have become—or have always been—different modalities of voyaging. If we don't feel to be prisoners of any place or to be the proprietors of some place, it means that we're free to meander anywhere we wish.

The adventure implicit in staying—the labour, the harshness, the beauty, the ethics of remaining—is no less decisive and foundational than the adventure that goes with travelling. The two experiences are complementary, need to be thought of and be narrated together.

For many people, then, staying back hasn't been a short-cut, a symptom of laziness, a comfortable choice. On the contrary, it has been an adventure, an act of foolhardiness and, perhaps, of bravery, something presupposing both toil and pain. We shouldn't give in to rhetoric or hyperbole but remaining is the extreme version of voyaging. It's an art, an invention, a practice that undoes all bombast about local identity. It's a different way of relating to places and a different experience of time, a reconsideration of the rhythms and the seasons of life.

As Mario La Cava has phrased it: "It's not necessary to leave the land of one's birth to affirm the value of one's creativity. In the end those who decide to travel can only look at the world, whereas those who have solid roots in a place can come to better understand the meaning of the surrounding reality. They can interpret it. It's ideas that should move, more than the legs of human beings."

Angelino's Turn

NGELINO WAS HAPPY to play among the agave plants and the bramble bushes, in those sandy grounds where prickly pears and gorsy shrubs grew. He entered abandoned houses searching for objects that would allow him and Nicola to build "something or other" in the open space in front of the church. From when he was two years old, he had witnessed with great patience the departure of people who left, hugged each other, made their suitcases, cried. The village was always more and more empty, but he wasn't sad. Some friends still remained, and in any case there were the sand banks to jump over, the shut-down, barren houses to visit, the countryside with its red, yellow, green colours, depending on the season, and further back, almost as if he could touch it from his window, the blue sea where his father had brought him sometimes in the summer or even in winter, when they had gone down to buy some everyday goods in the new village. With his friends Nicola and Marina and with his two brothers, Giorgio and Pantaleo, they looked for bird nests, climbed trees and scrambled up the sand. Only in front of the old tower would he pause, enraptured.

One day, as they were playing with the pebbles from the sea, Marina said: "In a month we'll be leaving. My father says that it's better to go to the new village." Angelino felt a knot in his throat and that evening he didn't eat anything. The day after he went to the river with Nicola. He realized that he would become used also to the idea of Marina's departure. And, who knows, some day he would run into her again and they would marry, as did grown-ups who are friends as

19

children, don't see each other for a long time and then meet again and stay together forever.

Once in a while he would go to the river bank to look at the women who were washing clothes or those other women who came from one of the areas by the seacoast to gather firewood. There was one of them who always astonished him with her ability to climb anything and with the way she would load a bundle of wood on her head and walk away, hands holding her flanks.

From somewhere very far, there would be letters from his older brother, who had gone away to study in some boarding school. By the fireplace, his father would read them and he would listen quietly, next to his mother, his grandfather and his other brother. He was happy to receive news from Giuseppe, of whom he was very fond, but he feared that those letters might actually take him away forever. All those who had left had said, in tears: "I'll write you."

His father would stroke the nape of his neck and would say: "One day perhaps we'll go where your brother now lives, or by the seacoast, in a village nearby." In doing so his father thought he was making him happy but Angelino would become serious and would stop playing. He didn't want to go elsewhere; he was happy to stay in that place, where everyone went away and he remained as a custodian, pensive, steadfast, like what was left of the ancient castle. His house was just by the side of its tower. In returning from the fields, his father often would stop and drink from the pitcher the wife handed him and then he would offer the water, so very fresh, to the children. It was a water that came from a spring called Pregna and was good for the health.

The gesture, that the father repeated all the time, pleased Angelino. And he also liked hearing the stories of when the house welcomed all sorts of visitors. More than once he was there when the father offered some hearty meal to some important writer from some other distant place who was interned in their village for political reasons. His father told him that the young man was quite good-looking, that he read a lot of books and was always walking around with a notebook in his hands. He also would say that he thought the young man would stay in the village and never go back to the city. Where they lived, he would add, reminded the young man of his own far away village.

During those evenings, Angelino listened to the stories about the flood that had struck the whole nearby area a year before he was born. It rained day in and day out, the women, above all, recalled. God, did it rain. The sky's sluice-gates opened and the water poured noisily among the dirty alleys and then broke into the houses. The sea was in a bad mood and grumbled, almost as if it wished to rise up and up, until it reached the older part of the burgh. Women sent prayers to Saint Barbara and Saint Leo, lighted candles and threw salt from their windows. Then the rain stopped, the sky cleared up, a sun and a sky as never seen before appeared.

Nobody would have thought that the rain could cause all that damage, invade houses, taking with it walls and entire plots of land, sweeping away animals and furniture and, above all, causing a land-slide that, older people claimed, sooner or later would have brought down the houses near the Castello, especially those right at the edge of the cliff, among which was the one of Angelino and his parents. Someone said: "It's better if we leave with our own feet; otherwise next time we'll be going away carried away by the water." And some families that had friends by the seacoast began to make the move.

From the tales he heard his father and mother tell, Angelino learned that his own birth was accompanied by rain and thun-der, that it occurred in the dark, as in the folk songs in which one bemoans one's bad luck. But the story was told calmly and with a somewhat amused tone, and Angelino took it as a good omen that he arrived in this world in the dark, while his father had gone down in the cellar to pick up a bottle of wine. Even his mother told him that it was a good sign.

And then one day in the spring Nicola's family also left. Angelino looked from behind his window as if dazed. When Nicola lifted the eyes towards him, he motioned a "Good-bye" with his hand. Though they wanted to, they didn't cry. After all, they had said to each other: "In a short while we'll see each other at school, down there, by the sea."

For Angelino the days of spring flew by as in a dream. He would go in the small fields, one after the other, all with their trees in bloom, pick flowers and bring them to one of the votive images of the Madonna in the streets. He meandered around the tower. He was almost always by himself, sometimes with his brothers. Now and then, relatives or friends of his father and mother from the seaside villages would come up and, during that time, the small square of the village looked like it was when the village was still full of people. And in any case, Angelino would say to himself, it wasn't bad living there.

He was especially happy for the fact that he was now six years old and in the winter he would be going to school every day, including when it rained. His father would be with him until they reached the plain at the foot of the village, and from there he would make his way to the school of the seacoast destination, where he would be able to meet Nicola and other friends, maybe see Marina again.

"At the end of the summer we'll leave," said his father with sorrow and gentleness one evening after they had finished eating. His mother answered that it was better like this, they couldn't stay by themselves in a place which was now without other people. Angelino's brothers looked at each other with glee. He fell silent, as if faced with a calamity. He knew that sooner or later they were going to leave but he hoped it would be as later on as possible.

In the month of August he sought the company of some of the children of the families that had returned to re-inhabit some of the older houses, children who went around the side streets and some of the smaller alleys. He heard them speak of houses that had fountains inside them. The women didn't have to go get water with their jugs on their head. They didn't go to the river but, instead, to the beach. Some of them also went in the water. Trains passed by, with people inside them waving even to those they didn't know. The children of rich people had bicycles and those of poor families would build for themselves some sort of two-wheeled contraption with the ball-bearings of trucks.

Angelino entered the old uninhabited houses that had unhinged doors. In some of them fig trees had grown, with fleshy figs which he didn't touch, feeling that it would be like stealing. He went in the fields and gazed at the scarecrows with bewilderment; maybe it was their turn now to look after not only the fields but the entire village, for the day the inhabitants would return. Yes, because as his mother would say, many of those returning would understand that it was better to live up in the old part of the village, where at least one knew everyone and could exchange some words with the others. Not like it was in the villages of the coast, where people came from many different places and when they spoke no-one could understand them.

Angelino pledged to himself to leave the village in the best possible way. He started by cleaning the open space in front of the church with a broom made of brier. Then from his father's storage cabinet he picked up nails, a roll of string and some wire. He made the rounds of all the houses that were open, that still had a door, and closed them. Here Nicola had lived, he would say; here *compare* Rocco had run into the dead who came back at night, one after the other as if in a procession and he had fallen sick; and there was Marina's house with its basil plants and the long, hot, red pepper still hanging from the window sill.

He would sit in front of the houses as if to fix his thoughts on the faces that he had known, to remember the stories he had listened to, to see once again people who ended up who knows where. Everything seemed possible and the smile hadn't yet disappeared from his lips. His mother and father were happy because the children had taken well the news about the family's departure. Angelino tried to keep himself busy with always new activities; he invented new pastimes, pretending to be playing hide and seek with friends who were no longer in the village. It seemed to him as if everything had remained as it was before, and at times he didn't even feel any sorrow.

One day he stopped in front of a house that he had seen always shut. Most likely, the people who had lived in it had left before his birth or before he had begun to roam around the side streets. He was struck by the pinkish colour of the front of the house, by the balcony, which was on the first floor, and by the stone portal. It wasn't a house of rich people, but it resembled the ones of the better-off, leisured people that had moved to the seacoast.

He returned home to his mother and asked: "Who lived in the house right in front of the one in which Ciccillo used to be?" His mother was a bit surprised by the question. She knitted her eyebrows as if to remember, opened her mouth as if to say: "What strange things come in your mind"—and then answered: "That house is the house of Vittorio, an *americano* who came back when he was on with his years. His wife no longer recognized him because while waiting for him she lost her mind and his son, who had become a lawyer with the money the father had sent, didn't want to have anything to do with him, didn't even want to enter his house. Like his wife, the *americano* also went mad. One morning he started shouting, to curse America, the mountain, the villages on the coast, as well as the more ancient villages, and then disappeared. The house was closed by the authorities and now appears to be the son's property."

Angelino listened intently, looking toward the sea, trying to imagine that place called America. In his mind would crop up the stories told by the adults, stories about gigantic fruit, dishes full of macaroni, and meat that would drop down from the trees, but also those other terrible stories about people who died on the ship and were thrown in the water. Then he said to his mother: "When we will have gone away, what will happen to these stories? Who will remember the people who lived in those houses?" Teresa embraced her son and said: "People have their history even if no-one remembers it, and all stories end even if there is someone to remember them." She spoke as one adult spoke to other adults. And she thought that Angelino had grown up too quickly and had already become a man, what with all the stories he had heard and the stories his father had read him at night time.

Then came the evening before their departure. Angelino made the last round of the streets. He entered the church and looked at the statue of Saint John, as if to say to him: "Not even you were able to protect the village." Then he returned home, where the preparations were feverishly under way. His mother, his father, his brother were all taking steps to keep something aside. There was the busy to and fro of feast days in that home, although the atmosphere was that of the days of mourning.

"Don't forget your things," said his father. Angelino put in a plastic bag the wooden recorder from the fair at Polsi, the book entitled *Guerin meschino*, the album with the pictures of soccer players, some issues of the *Corriere dei piccoli*, and sat on the bed, tired, as if he had hoed a large piece of land. He looked out of the window and saw that the sea was still, as if it were the top of a table. It was hot and the flies showed no mercy as they landed on his little legs. He looked at the glass of the cupboard with the pickles and the memoriam card of his dead grandmother.

He went out and walked towards the tower adjacent to his house. The elders used to say that it had been built so that the pirates could be spotted when they were arriving from the sea but it had to be always rebuilt, like anthills, that always crumble and always magically rise up again. For him, it was imposing, so tall that it would almost brush against the only white cloud of the clear sky, clear as it can be only at the end of September. He felt that now was the right time. Now or never. Now and forever, he thought, and as he climbed he pushed away the thorns stuck in the red sand of the wall. Halfway up he became afraid of falling. He thought he would die and no-one would find his body. He almost liked the idea of disappearing, of fading away in the sweet smell that came up from the fields full of jasmine, down there by the seashore. It was only a moment, then he continued inserting his fingers in the spaces between the stones and the bricks.

When he arrived at the top he was sweating all over and his heart was beating fast. He saw the top of the houses from above. Where he lived seemed quite small to him now. Everything looked different from up there. The cemetery with its crosses was like one of those fences make by ramming into the ground tree branches and bits of reed. He could barely distinguish the tomb of the baroness who, as the elders told it, was buried alive and standing up. The villages by the sea had never appeared to him so clear as now. A strange sensation of well-being went through him. When he closed his eyes, he was happy. Wherever he would live, he would never forget that place. He reopened his eyes and lifted his arms high in the air, as if to fly.

This text is one of the many tales of "the last inhabitants" that I listened to in my research in the field. It was inspired by the story of Gianni Carteri, the last child to leave Brancaleone Calabro in 1958, which was abandoned due to the floods of 1951. I dedicate the text to him, a sensitive, refined scholar of the works of Corrado Alvaro and Cesare Pavese, and to his mother, whom I met in the cemetery of the old part of the village, towards which she maintained an almost religious attachment.

The Road to Vallelonga

Stanotte quando jia mu pigghju sonnu
Mi vinne la Madonna a rivigghjare.
—Rivigghjati divota! No dormire!
La strata de Bonserrata hai de pigghjare—.

Mi partivi de 'na strata longa
E arrivai dirittu a Valelonga.
Poe quando arrivai e 'ntra la chiesi trasivi
'Ncantata restai: Oh! Chi bejizzi vitte!

A mmenzo la chiesi c'era la Madonna
Seduta supa na colonna
E lu Bambinu chi 'mbrazza tenìa
Tuttu lu mundu benedicìa.

Li pellegrini benenu a pede
Si rifriscanu la faccia alli funtani,
Ca hannu mu fannu la vegglia a li sue pedi
Ca lu vennari la ficeru li paesani.

La dominica quando fa jorno
Si mentenu a sonare li campani
Li tamburinari si fannu lu giru
Ca poe nc'è la missa a lla pontificali.

Poe quando nesce la processione
Gira pe' li strati principali
E li barcuna su' parati a festa
Cu' li damaschi chi stiparu apposta.

Li vergineji jettanu li hjuri,
Ca l'avianu cogghjutu cu' d'amuri.
Poe 'ntra lu voscu nc'è la litanìa
Sutta la cerza chi scegghiu Maria

De li Capistanoti este 'ntonata
E de la banda este accompagnata.

E quando è l'ura de l'Ave Maria
Ognuno si 'nde torna pe' la via;
E 'ntra lu cori si porta Maria
Dicendu lu rosario e la litanìa.

Last night into slumber I was about to drop
When the Madonna was there to wake me
Do not sleep, she said, o you my devotee
It's on the way to Monserrato you now should be.

I began walking on a long, long road
And Vallelonga quite directly I then did reach
Upon arriving I soon the Church did enter
To be fully entranced by the beauty before my eyes.

In the middle of the Church was the Madonna
Seated high above on a large tall pillar was she
And the child that in her arms she held
To all around did his blessings dispense.

The pilgrims on foot had one by one arrived
And their faces at the fountain soon refreshed
For it was their turn now to be at wake at his feet
Just as the villagers had on Friday there stood.

On Sunday at the very early break of day
All the bells begin to ring and ring
The drum players do all their many rounds
To announce the high Mass and the Bishop.

Then when procession from the Church starts
And one by one into all the streets it moves
The balconies for the feast are fully adorned
With the damask drapes for that day well stored.

The young girls all in white throw the flowers
They with full love and care had gathered
Then into the grove the litany is intoned
Under the oak tree the Virgin Mary had picked.

It's the people from Capistanoti that lead the chant
With the band supplying full accompaniment.

And when the Angelus begins to fall
Each and everyone on their road return
Into their hearts the Virgin Mary bringing
The rosary and the litany all repeating.

(*Religious song sung by devotees, probably dating back to the end of the 18th century*)

Ni partimme de tantu luntanu
Vinnemu, Madonna mia, mu ni vidimu,
'Ntra chista chiese mu vi salutamu
A Bui li grazi mu vi li cercamu.

Vi li cercamu e Bui ni li dunati
Ca siti santa e ni li cuncediti.

La Providenza mu ni la madati
Ca simu figghji e peccaturi 'ngrati.

We left from places far far away
Coming, o dear Madonna, for here to meet,
In this church you to greet
Your blessing and good grace to seek.

We beseech you and you do this afford
For you are saintly and can all accord

May Providence be what you do us send
For children we are and sinners who need to mend.

(*Chant of pilgrims travelling to Vallelonga*)

Voices from a humanity on the move

Suddenly, in the night, I would hear the sound of steps, the voices of women talking to each other across some space, the unmistakable language of horses, pigs, sheep, cattle. The animals wouldn't let themselves be led easily up the slope of Via Campanella, in San Nicola da Crissa, where I lived as a child, and it had to be negotiated by anyone who wished to take the shortcut for the fair held during the feast of the Madonna of Monserrato, at Vallelonga.

I don't know how much of what I now hear is due to the prestidigitations of memory—memory not only remembers, it forgets and not infrequently invents, reorganizes the past, lets it emerge differently from how we actually lived it—but now I seem to be able to distinguish the different forms of speech of the various groups of pilgrims, merchants, fair regulars coming from the villages of the Poro area or the Mesina area, from the seacoast, from Pizzo.

In the heart of the night of the second Tuesday of July, all these people walked and walked to secure a spot in the woods of Vallelonga to rest their livestock and lay out knick-knacks and merchandise or just to buy early on and then return home when the temperature had again cooled down. I listen once more to the religious chants of the women, to the sound of a tired mouth organ accompanied by tambourines, of children crying, or to the imprecations of those who had to deal with animals less than docile after many hours of travelling.

My childhood is full of echoes of distant sounds and voices. "Come see, come see, best pots anywhere. Here's your friendly pot maker"; "Tinsmith at your service, here and now! Any pots to repair? I'm at your door!" The voice of the *codderaru*, the tinsmith, who came from far away, reached my ears as if from a fairy-tale world or as if in a dream, when it was still dawn. I would soon realize that it was Sunday, and, true, it would have been nice to sleep a bit more, but Sundays and feast days was when the itinerant humanity went on the move.

The voice of the tinsmith, however, was particularly familiar to me, as was the voice of the women from the mountain villages, who addressed the "pretty ladies" of the houses for " a drop of olive oil" or a handful of olives in exchange for their savoury *damoncelle* apples or their lupini beans, their chestnuts or potatoes that grew where they came from. Well-known to me too was the voice of the seller of textile and clothing materials, who kept yelling out the names of what he had to offer, carrying on his shoulder underwear and other garments rolled into a cube covered by greenish-coloured cloth. "Gorgeous stuff, gorgeous stuff"—and "Gorgeous Stuff" is how we children called him when we ran after him.

Then in the Fall months there was the *crastaturi*, the man who went from village to village castrating pigs, to ensure that they grew fatter. From time to time the *sampavularu*, a worshipper of Saint Paul who acted as if he had the same powers as the saint himself, came by with the serpents hanging from his neck, producing a mixture of amazement, curiosity and terror among us children. There was the voice of the knife grinder who cried: "Knives and scissors sharpened!" Or the umbrella mender would pass by, shouting himself hoarse with his: "It's raining, it's raining. God, how it rains!" As well as the salt seller with his: "Yes, they've salted him, they've salted him. God, how much salt they put on him!"

We didn't miss the full drift of their language, with its irony and self-irony, carnivalesque, allusive, metaphorical, full of double meanings, and pronounced in many accents and colourful intonations. All forms of speech that have now disappeared but then made us laugh were a kind of sound track for our games, one that initiated us to village life and now goes hand in hand with our memories. All of this happened only fifty years ago, which could just as well be centuries. And it's why we feel out of place and we seek new forms of emplacement, of rootedness.

"Where is Ceravolo the *sampavularu*?" "Where is the *crastaturi*, the gelder?" "Where is the *coddaduri*, the tinsmith?"—we would say, us children, as we ran behind the errant figures, teasing them, trying to attract their attention, so great was our fascination with them or our fear of them and our desire to reabsorb them back into some kind of domesticity.

Familiar voices closer to us were those of the *ciucciari*, the peasants who moved about on or with their donkeys, of the women who went to pick olives, of the men and women who would go to work also on Sunday and returned at night. I still remember very well the voices, the sounds, the rhythms, the pauses that in statutory holidays came to me from musicians, pilgrims, sellers of livestock, male or female gypsies who went around with their metal spatulas, their lanterns, with other utensils, and passed by right in front of my room, which abutted on the street.

I not only distinguished the voices but from their steps would know who the people were. The voices, the sounds were characterizing traits of the old village and allowed one to be recognized, perhaps even more so than the faces or other physical aspects. One might no longer be able to identify individuals not seen for many years by looking at them, because they had aged, had changed, suffered some sort of physical decay, but as soon as one heard their voice, they became familiar again.

Sounds, voices, the yelling, the names being shouted out loud, refined my aptitude to listen, and when I was a grown-up I would distinguish the steps of friends who were about to do a serenade, of the women going to the fields, or of the travelling vendors who had become motorized and went around selling brooms, roosters or chickens, *zibibbo* grapes and melons. The memory of these voices and of the sounds of the village, of the big church bells and the other less strong little bells whose ring summoned us to Mass or to school, for feasts and the breaking out of fires, for deaths and marriages, have always been a great boon to me in my search for times lost.

That clamour of steps, of human voices, that hotchpotch of noises is no longer available in today's villages. Silence, not the silence one wishes for but the silence now associated with the emptying out of the villages of the Calabrian hinterland, the many departures from other larger locations nearby with a more abiding and more central history, is something we view with great poignancy, those of us who were born and raised there, in places that were thick with noises and sounds of all kinds, full of toil, happiness and life.

On Saturday evening, the day before the tinsmith would make his rounds in our village, my grandmother and my mother would review the condition of pots, pans and other copper paraphernalia. Often they would get up early, eager and careful, to ask for repairs where holes or dents had appeared. They would look out of the window and ask: "Hey tinsmith did you bring me my pot?" until the precious container made it back to the kitchen, nice and ready for use. I have quite a vivid memory of the tinsmith who came from the seacoast area, from Pizzo, and worked his way up towards Vallelonga and the inland area known as the Serre. His name was Ciccio, and he had an intense look, a musical voice, and a patience that never ended. He listened, was used to it and seemed always resigned, in full accordance with the rites of selling, buying and bargaining, with the protests that went with them, the requests for discounts and credit on the part of the women. He acted as if he were upset and unremitting and then finally gave in. He would leave smiling, with his "Look, look, you'll never see more beautiful pots! Your tinsmith is here!"

Waves of sound would reach my ears also during the days of the feast of the Madonna of Monserrato, leaving me in a pleasant drowsiness, a sort of trance, from which I emerged thanks to the complicity of my grandmother Felicia and my mother as soon as dawn arrived. I would go to the balcony of the house and watch for hours the throng of men, women and children that marched on—as in certain stories by Corrado Alvaro—with livestock, objects of all kinds, foodstuff, as if they were a primitive, nomadic tribe in an inhospitable land. I tried to count the sheep, the pigs, the cattle, the people, the children: I would reach one hundred and then would have to begin anew.

That stream of voices, noises, sounds, colours would continue all day, altering the usual landscape of the *ruga*, the side-street, which was called Cutura. Now and then I would go down outside, to observe from nearby, together with other children, that "mobile, open-air theatre." An unrestrainable nostalgia of the road would take over me. It was the childhood restlessness that at other times would compel me to follow the shepherds who passed by right in front of our house when they took the herd to the pastures in the countryside near our village, as if by following them I could conjure strategies of escape. Our mothers didn't approve of these impromptu excursions and upon returning home some of us would get a good whacking.

At the fair of Monserrato

For the fair held at Monserrato everything was different, everything was permitted. Children and youths waited for the trip with the impatience, the curiosity, the happiness of those who would be travelling to some wondrous elsewhere. I still hear the generous, warm voice of my grandmother saying: "Get ready, because we're going to the fair." But by then I would have been ready for some time, waiting for those words from at least the beginning of July. We would leave, my grandmother, my mother and I, together with our neighbours, at the first light of dawn, on the day the fair began, or at other times on Saturday or Sunday, when at the fair there would be the procession. The light breeze that blew up the slope with which our trip started would complete the waking up. The journey wasn't an easy one: We would have to be alert in order to fully satisfy our inquisitiveness, to observe the details, the little things that saw as protagonists people on the move who talked and gossiped, told stories, sang, prayed. I listened carefully to the news, the stories, the prattle, the legends. I already sensed that people are also words, narrations.

In walking, I held the hand of my grandmother or my mother. As did all the other children with theirs. The fathers and the older adult men weren't that many. Like my father, they had already undertaken a more difficult journey for a much more distant land. It was Canada, about which, however, we knew everything we wanted to know through what the women would say and the letters with the coloured edges containing dollar bills and photos that the mailman would bring from time to time. I now think that I've grasped the historical continuity between the religious pilgrimages whose aim was grace and salvation (but which were initiated also for economic reasons, in order to establish new contacts and promote new exchanges) and the voyage of salvation and hope that ended beyond the ocean and which by the end of the 1950s had decimated the population of villages such as San Nicola and Vallelonga.

I remember shadows, trees, fountains, the *cone*, or street icons, the pathways of that journey of happiness and discovery. In front of the icon of the Madonna, near our village, when we were already at the end of the slope, there would be a pause. From the *sporte*, the large drooping baskets, from the *faddale*, the ample aprons women tied around their waists, or the bundles being carried, someone would take out the *frittate*, or home-style omelettes, the salami, the olives, the sardines and the cheese. As Alvaro noted (in his youth he had been in a pilgrimage to the sanctuary of Polsi he never lost memory of), when the *Calabresi* started off on a journey, even a short one, they always brought food and water with them. For them there can't be any sort of physical move, whether it be journey or pilgrimage, without these last two elements, which aren't just nourishments but also symbols of communion, of closeness to others, of prosperity.

There were parts of the route that we children lived both with some anxiety and with amused disenchantment. In the areas that were *mancuse*, or somewhat sinister, that is, areas quite humid and muddy, where, because of the high trees and the high hedges, even in the summer months there would be *tajii*, or ground that remained clay-like due to the abundant winter rains, we had to be careful not to dirty our shoes or our new trousers. We would jump on the large, flat stones that some well-meaning person had placed there, or on the spots of grass that were still miraculously dry. We were accompanied and protected by the hands, the attention, the incitations of the women.

Those passage-ways, and especially the one after the *cona* of the Madonna, were for all intents and purposes tests we had to go through: it's as if they were rites of initiation to the world of the adults. From time to time I still happen to pass by the place where women would stop to say a prayer and to have something to eat and drink, thus segmenting the journey, a place now physically divided in two by one of the many roads that cut across the nearby farmland. All of this, that then seemed to me large and mysterious, now appears extra-small, far away, out of focus. And yet it was along that unrepeatable, interminable itinerary that my awareness of the trek as toil, truth, salvation began to take shape. Or, to put it differently, walking as a metaphor of life.

Those trails, those footpaths, those trees—I remember especially the oaks and the seacoast cherries—were the "songlines" of our people. The pilgrimage to Vallelonga involved inhabitants of a number of villages, both near and far, the communities of the areas near the sea and the communities of the hinterland. It was a journey that would lead to a "centre" where these groups would come together, and thus, along with the feast days, the fairs, and other pilgrimages taking place in that part of our region (Torre di Ruggiero, Serra San Bruno, Chiaravalle) helped to draw the multifarious, colourful map of the economic, cultural and religious trajectories of a "land in motion." Flight was the other side of sedentariness. Mobility, the return, that very particular experience of remaining in the village but with the awareness of what it is to go away, were all aspects of a restless, anxious people.

I had the fortune to observe the vivacity, the conviviality, the desire to hit the road and to better itself of a population that was always on the move, that had already, by necessity and by choice, become extremely mobile. I was experiencing the last flashes of a universe at its twilight. When as an adult I was to read research that based its argument on the closure, the isolation, the social immobility, the lack of communication of Calabrian villages, I didn't have to go far to find proof of the partiality of such views: It was enough for me to dig down in my childhood memories, those of the members of village music bands, of the *ciucciari,* the men who moved about on their donkeys, the itinerants we knew, of the pilgrims who went as far as Seminara and Dinami, in order for me to acknowledge the ancient fate of populations that would wander here and there for work, for contact with other people, for religious devotion. If today we were to trace the routes of the traditional pilgrimages of the Serre and of Calabria as such the result would be a map embracing all the hamlets, the valleys, the mountains, the hills of the region.

After walking up the slope and going through the dark and slimy part of the route, we would arrive in a plain where wheat, corn, potatoes grew and where the sparse oak trees reached high towards the sky. I remember the yellow of the morning and of the fields that had just been tilled. As if by some magic when we began the stone-filled downhill road in the territory of Vallelonga the sounds of the fair began to reach us: Men, livestock, sellers, microphones, bells, record-players, merry-go-rounds would be always closer at hand. The downhill portion was steep but comfortable. Only for a moment would we stop and think that on the return it would be the way up that would be taking us back to everyday life.

At the bottom of the valley, there was a small torrent to cross: We would stop at a fountain to quench our thirst. Today I know that for the devotees the water they drank was a source of purification; it stood for a desire of renewal. There are no pilgrimages and sites of cult without water, rivers, caves. Then, after a last stretch, we were already in the inhabited areas of Vallelonga, behind the church, which today has been elevated to the rank of sanctuary.

The rounds we made with my grandmother, my mother and other persons began after we quickly paid our respects to the Madonna. The statue, the devotees around it, the prayers, the songs, the gestures, the offerings, the candles, the paper images, the throng that entered and exited, the beggars at the door, all reminded us that the church was one of the centres of the world, a site where demands, needs, expectations, hopes converged. As all the other children, I couldn't wait to run among the stands between noisy crowds, in the wood with the large oak trees where we could find the fountains with the large spigots and the drinking troughs so high up that they made one want to bathe and where there was a little basin with little red fish.

Together with all this, there were the sellers who, in accordance with pre-established, unavoidable rituals, discussed the prices of each of the goods, the *zanzani*, or mediators between seller and buyer, with their fascinating theatre of gestures and language, the women who looked at the clothing or at the shoes, touching them, commenting on them, and asked the price or started bargaining about it with the seller if they were interested. Then in some corner there would be terracotta pots, ropes, string, ribbon, whistles, caps of all sorts.

Thanks to the generosity of my grandmother, I never returned home without at least a *pagghietta*, a cap that, naturally, I would never wear after that day, and without a wooden whistle that I would break in a day or so, and the hard biscuits which I wouldn't eat because I thought they were only for poor people, the *vozzareju*, or small jug that I would fill with water on the way back, or the *caruseju*, the little piggy-bank that I brought back with me, shaking it to hear the sound of the coins I had already been given.

When I look back, I still see the man who shouted: "With this one you win, with this one you lose," quick and magical as he illustrated the game of the three cards, young and old following with their eyes rather worried—which card to choose?—as they witnessed that so very swift movement of the hands. And there was, too, the roulette, where people tried their luck, hoping to hit the jackpot with a few *lire*, and the man with the air rifle who, when paid, allowed one to shoot. Or there was the merry-go-round that would turn and turn, and which was the best metaphor of the pleasant dizziness the fair would cause.

And, finally, there were the chairs of the very improvised cafés, the ice lemonade, the gelati, the shacks with their smell of goat meat or tripe or wine, the racket of the drunkards in the morning, the unending requests, the push-and-shove and the protests of the customers. After many hours, we would go back to the church to once again pay our respects to the Madonna. Grandmother would leave some paper money this time and would pick up some images that at home we would place next to the images of saints and the photos of dead relatives or relatives who had migrated. As for me, I returned home satisfied with what I had "purchased" and with my dreams. And with the certainty I would be returning to the fair and the atmosphere that went with it.

Ontario 1994

That universe no longer exists. It's gone forever. The coming of modernity, even in the most isolated hamlets, and the great exodus have brought about the twilight of an ancient rural culture. That feast, I would never live it again at home. And instead one year I experienced something like it, about six thousand kilometres away.

A large tract of green that at the horizon meets the clouds of a sky decisively low. A hot humid Sunday of the July of 1994. In Vallelonga this was the day of the feast of the Madonna of Monserrato. But here too in the immense province of Ontario, a few kilometres from Toronto, along Highway 50 North, the same rite is being celebrated. I observe while walking with my cousin Franco and my fraternal friend Ciccio Bellissimo, ancient lineaments, faces, gestures. I listen to familiar expressions and modes of address invented and learned far away from here. The people welcome me with great cordiality, in tune with the ancient rules of hospitality, all of them well versed in the pleasure that comes from meeting someone from the same village.

I feel a sense of dislocation the very moment I find myself in front of elements that remind me both of community and village life. This place is the double beyond the ocean of the woods at Vallelonga. Just as the feast is the image of the one celebrated where we lived, and the *jarda*, the backyard, is the double of the small plot of land back home.

Vallelonga has lost big chunks of its population; it has about half the number of people it once had. But it hasn't vanished. It has just changed location, moved elsewhere. It's reborn in the New World. What has occurred is a grandiose anthropological amplification. The original community has dilated beyond itself: It's now also "beside itself," become other than it was.

We approach an elderly gentleman. His name is Giovanbattista Rizzuto, of the generation born early in the 20th century (1904, in his case). He migrated in 1949, thanks to the sponsorship of Joe Pileggi, becoming then himself sponsor of many individuals from Vallelonga. I had wanted to meet him for a long time, having heard of him through my father's stories and his nostalgia. Before I'm even introduced, he gives me a big hug, and so does a nice lady, one of his seven children, and her husband, a very affable, cordial person who is also from Vallelonga. I'm touched by all this. I know that Rizzuto and his family are greeting and hugging someone else, not actually me. In front of them they see my father, whom I'm told I resemble in a surprising way and whom they remember because he lived for a long time in their house.

Rizzuto begins to tell of his life back home, of his departure in 1949, when he was already 45 years old, of the slow, progressive settling down in the new country, of the goals achieved. And he speaks to me of my father, of the room that he shared with my uncle Tommaso, of my father's habits, his pleasant, jovial disposition. That house, I saw it from the street many times, as if waiting for someone to come out. I feel as if I am my father and think how surprising it is that I have to undertake a journey beyond the ocean to attempt to re-compose the fragments of a broken identity, to better know myself. As, in a different manner, had happened with the Calabrian Vallelonga, the Vallelonga of Toronto helps me to re-appropriate myself of a history that belongs to me but that I haven't lived in person.

When I was discovering a small yet large ancient world at Vallelonga without my father, my father was entering another world without me and without my mother. Migration is a world that explodes and whose fragments disperse, look for each other, find each other without ever fully reuniting. Those who stay back and those who leave remain always linked to each other, even if they should never happen to meet again.

The journey of the Madonna

The procession with the statue of the Madonna, which is a wooden copy of the one in Calabria, has come out of a little chapel, the work of individuals from Vallelonga. The statue is preceded by boys and girls who walk one after the other. The bearers of the statue and the persons nearest to it sing hymns of the Calabrian village tradition. After them come a musical band and the greater portion of the faithful. I look in all directions, take some pictures, and feel a kind of vertigo, as I did when I was on the merry-go-round in Vallelonga.

The behaviour and some of the gestures of the people give one the impression that a bit of the peaceful, intent, intimate world of the Calabria of the 1950s has been transported and transplanted by some deity in a time outside of history and in a kind of non-place. Other faces, other sounds and colours let one sense that all around are also the throbbings of a great metropolis, of which the protagonists of the rite now fully partake, without having given up their history, their religious traditions and their origins but, rather, founding on them their new reality.

I listen to the litany sung by men and women to the accompaniment of the band. The statue of the Madonna is facing in the direction of the place in Italy where it came from. It's been a long time since I've listened to voices so moved, so fully engaged, so thoughtful, so aware of the beauty of renewing one of the rituals of the parents, who hoped to pass on their tradition to the children born in another world. In those songs and sounds that are rising towards the glorious Canadian sky, clouds of nostalgia, of memories, of regrets, of hard work, of hopes and good omens run into each other. They're clouds that ride high, and thanks to the force of the emotions and the devotion link the two Vallelongas.

These sites belong to us who haven't migrated, just as Vallelonga and San Nicola belong to the young men and women that have known them through the recollections and the tales of the fathers and the mothers. And suddenly, for a few moments, as if by some miracle, I feel as I am without time and without space, everywhere and nowhere, innocent and happy as when I was a child. I think of the paradoxical implications of emigration, of the displacements and the disruptions it has provoked, how it makes it possible for you to recover, if for a brief instant, the dimension, the fullness of childhood in a location where you have never been but in which someone else has lived for you.

Another turn on the merry-go-round

In our part of the world, stories never end. They go on, like the yarns of drunkards who just keep talking from dusk to dawn, I walk with you, you walk with me, no-one wants to leave the other, and when it's daylight they're still walking around. There's never, really, an end. Everyday things never end, but how time slips by. As my mother says, everything, ultimately, passes on. And it does with the indifference of places. In the sense that places leave traces and memories only if someone looks for them. Otherwise they're silent or noisy, vacant or full without by themselves indicating they are.

I've returned to Vallelonga and the feast of the Madonna of Monserrato during the last few years, after a long time. Only for the feasts does the village still show signs of liveliness. Emigrants by now have reached the third or fourth generation and the ties with that reality are rather occasional and rare. The woods are very beautiful. And deserted. "How beautiful they were," says my mother. "Now I believe nobody uses that part of the landscape anymore; back then in those groves there would be animals, now they say they're nice and clean. There are the merry-go-rounds. Before there were the shacks. I remember the many types of oaks, small and large. How time goes by!"

The vendors are now people of colour who sell goods that you can find anywhere else in the world. Tripe and the stew are still quite in demand. And for the children it's still a great holiday. I embrace the children of yesteryear, on which time has left its mark. The shacks are no longer there and there isn't the man with his "this card wins, this card loses" but there are the games and the bumper cars. Children have their pockets full of tokens. I look around. I'm the oldest and I try to see myself as I would be if I were much younger. I didn't like the rides that were too fast and seemed to rise towards the sky, while someone eager to get on pushed you from behind. My mother had convinced me that it was possible to fall off and I had to contend with bouts of real giddiness.

As a child I went to the fair on foot. I had little money and could buy only a few things. I was never bored. I was happy. But was I happy or am I inventing this happiness in the past tense? I avoid, this evening, acting like the elders of my youth who told only accounts of hunger and grief, wars and departures. Those who have walked their way to the sanctuary to pay a visit to the Madonna and to see the stands can't talk about their terror of the end of things, can't keep harping on their old age. I should instead perhaps say that I've become a child with my children. But I would be lying. We all have our childhood in our own time, our Vallelonga to live and to remember. We can't take over the time of other people. One doesn't return. If not with writing and memory. From some distance away, I see the fireworks zooming up towards the sky. A thousand colours and shapes. I'm going around with my son in the automobile that I've always driven and never driven. When the bumper cars arrived on the scene at the fair I was already too old.

Interlude

Venemi sonno e non addimurare
Lu picciriju meu mu dorme vole.
Lu picciriju meu mi ciange a vuci
Ca vo' la naca sutta li sambuci
Lu picciriju meu ciange a gridati
Ca vo' la naca sutta li granati.

Lu picciriju meu de pochi jorni
De Napuli nci arrivanu li addorni
Lu piccciriju meu de pochi misi
De Napuli nci arrivanu li abbisi
Lu picciriju meu de pochi anni
De Napuli nci arrivanu li panni.

Dorme, dorme, facci di rosa
Ca la mamma fa corcosa
Ti la cuse la cammiseja
Dormi, dormi, facci beja.

Lu picciriju meu l'avimu zitu
Napuli e Roma è tuttu cumbitatu
Mo 'nci lu levu 'nu bellu presente
'Nu vacilotto chjinu de dinari.

E chi è bellu lu picciulu meu
Quandu a Roma si nde va
Si fa 'nu bellu studente
E si 'nde vade pe' li città.

Come sleep and don't delay
What my baby wants is to sleep today.
My baby who keeps crying out loud
Wants to be rocked under the elders and their shroud.
My baby who cries and shouts wants to be
Rocked under the pomegranate tree.

My baby only a few days old
From Naples will receive trinkets untold.
My baby when a few months old
From Naples will receive cards manifold.
My baby when a few years old
Will receive clothes in Naples sold.

Sleep, sleep, o face like a rose
Your mother for you won't repose.
She will sew you a shirt of lace
Sleep, sleep you beautiful face.

For our boy a girl we've found
Guests will come from all around.
I'll surely a worthy present bring
A barreful of coins will be the thing.

What good looks has my little one
As to Rome he is set to go.
A great student he'll surely become
One who knows the city head to toe.

(*Lullaby sung in San Nicola da Crissa*)

The House of the
Thirty-three Loaves of Bread

Mangiai, mangiai, mangiai:
Vurdu mi fice,
A 'nu sordu de pane fumme dece.
Chiju chi mi restai 'mbitai l'amici
E l'atru nci l'unai alli povereje.

I ate and ate and ate
As full as can be I became
A penny of bread was enough for more than eight
With the rest I invited friends who were game
And the other penny I gave to the most needy in sight.

(*Nursery rhyme from San Nicola da Crissa*)

Bread crumbs

We would exit the house running, with the *fettazze*, the big slices of crispy white bread just out of the oven, in our hands. We would run in the street with the slices just a bit moistened and spread with sugar, or with bread and olives, bread and cheese, or with bread and *sopressata*, the sausage of meat cured with white salt, pepper and spices. The crust, specially cut, that my mother would give me knowing my preference, was like a fairy tale about life. We would eat, us children who grew up in the 1950s, playing and running in the back streets of our village or in the vegetable plots full of people.

My grandmother and my mother would remind me not to go in any place where there were children who didn't have enough to eat. The two most important women of my childhood always showed great compassion towards others, but at that stage of my life I took the warning to be just an attempt to have me stay put, because I was always on the move, without a moment of rest, *senza rigetto,* as the expression went, then as much as I am now.

With bread as food, most Calabrian villages, though not all, managed to go beyond hunger, to overcome centuries of deprivation. Later, when in writing my dissertation I began reading essayists and writers of fiction in order to better decipher oral and written autobiographical sources, I understood, finally, that the bread and the rest we received from our parents was a luxury. Villages were still hungry for bread. In 1959, Saverio Strati sets the novel *Tibi e Tascia* in one of these Calabrian hamlets and tells a story in which the two hungry children of the title would pick up the crumbs left by better off people and would dream of the food of the rich: eggs and sausages, chicken and goat meat, *prosciutto*, cheese, wine.

Corrado Alvaro in his *Un treno nel sud* [*A Train in the South*] tells of how the intercity buses "transport perpetually, without confusion, without hate and almost without grief, a population that has become nomadic, that carries its heavy bundles, its bread, the pocket knives to cut it with, bit by bit, dreaming of tomorrow's bread ... A *Calabrese* eats his bread with his little knife as if it were from a fine piece of wood, sitting with his sack of things in railway stations, waiting for trains going to Milan, Rome, Turin, Aosta, for any destination where he may seek his fortune."

And during those same years, Leonida Repaci in his *Calabria grande e amara* [*Calabria, a Great and Bitter Land*] leaves some unforgettable descriptions of the hunger of the Calabrian peasantry. Hunger was the word that recurred over and over again in those stories of the elders. To flee hunger, above all the hunger for bread, and to find bread for their children, many left for Canada, Germany, the United States.

My father had left for Toronto shortly after I was one year old and in his letters with the coloured lines arrived the dollar bills with the image of the Queen. We needed them to buy bread and, later, the satchel for school, my black corduroy shorts and the white shirt that my mother would sew with the help of a *maestra*, a real dressmaker. It was perhaps due to this modest well-being that, when it came down to it, I couldn't catch the drift of the tales my grandmother Felicia would tell me. One such tale that still at times surfaces in my mind is the one which admonished not to throw bread crumbs on the ground. It was a sin; Jesus didn't approve. And after we died we would be sent back to earth to pick up all the bread crumbs we had squandered. I didn't quite believe my grandmother's stories but when eating I would look around where I was sitting somewhat worried.

The romance of bread

Bread—but perhaps we should use the term in the plural, since bread has many forms—has its landscapes, its archives, its mills, its tales, its legends, its saints and its ingredients, its myths, its folklore, its museums. And yet the great novel about bread has still, in large measure, to be written.

White bread, brown bread, black bread, dark bread, yellow bread, corn bread, rye bread, oat bread, of rye mixed with oat, chestnut bread, potato bread, of herbs, of acorns, of barley, of barley and rye, of lentils, of chickling, bread mixed with a thousand other substances, with lupini beans, millet, vetch, hay. Hard bread, sour bread, a sign of the extreme poverty of those who bought it, is full of lower quality bran, with discarded flour, heavy, inedible, cheap because of poor quality, of sorrowful cereals from sorrowful lands, of wretched stuff for wretched people, delicate, white bread, fresh bread, blessed bread, of superfine flour, scented, fragrant bread for the ladies of the gentry, bread used in the Mass, in celebrations and feasts, *ammogghiato* (that is, soaked), or dry, bitter, stale, mouldy, rock-hard, bread that doesn't go down, bread to chew, which requires really sharp teeth.

In the second half of the 19th century, various observers, starting with Vincenzo Padula, showed their embarrassment in describing "the horrible bread" composed of all sorts of mixtures with which the peasants and the hired hands of the poorest Italian regions, such as Calabria, satisfied their hunger. It was a bread so dry that, as Leopoldo Franchetti observed during a trip to the Italian South in 1874, to eat it labourers "had to scrape it with their knives in the hollow of their hands and then pour it in their mouth in the form of crumbs."

As Luigi Bodio writes in 1979, of the bread made of a mixture of rye and corn flour, which was often their only nourishment, people in the Reggio Calabria area said, with quite a bit of irony, that they were eating "bread and knife," as if the knife was the accompaniment of the bread. And as notes one of the contributors to the Jacini Report, "the bread normally available was made of a flour of wild lentils called *fraca*. When the dough of this flour is baked in the oven it becomes of a colour so dark that it resembles a blend of dirt and minced wood." And this is what, with obvious disappointment, Lionello De Nobili recounted in 1908: "To a mayor of a small village in the mountains near Reggio I asked how the peasants around there were nourished: 'To the servants, to these half-beasts we give a bread of millet and corn.' And to show me, I was brought some buns, black and mouldy and hard as stone."

A bread of *mischio*, a mixture of "lentil flour, flour of chickling and barley, with an acid and bitter taste," that Umberto Zanotti Bianco finds at Africo in 1928 and sends to friends in every part of Italy to attest to the condition of that village and to raise sufficient funds to build a nursery school there. Loaves that "demonstrate none of the physical traits of bread made of grain and which are for the most part musty." Giustino Fortunato writes to Zanotti Bianco that he had seen this bread, of which memory had been lost, before 1860 in the regions of Apulia and Basilicata. Corrado Alvaro remembers "the bread with hay kneaded into it" of Africo and in the novel *Gente in Aspromonte* [*Revolt in Aspromonte*] he tells of a shepherd who goes to the house of a rich man and explains to the son that what he smells is the aroma of "white bread," a bread he has never seen.

Witnesses of the past have written an ample and colourful dictionary of bread, of the many types of bread. The drastic contrast between the well-to-do consumers of white bread and the poor consumers of black bread remains strong in Calabria and seems more marked than the contrast between the rich as carnivores and the poor as herbivores.

Hunger is a hunger for bread. Dreams at night and reveries during the day have to do with white bread. Nicola Misasi, the novelist, one of the interpreters of the psychology of those who dream of that bread, writes in 1883: "One becomes a glutton on one's deathbed. Then one wants the tidbit, the dish of scrumptious food, yearning to go in the other world with a sweet taste in the mouth; the dying peasant would, him too, like to taste this ineffable happiness of the rich 'gentleman,' a piece of bread white as snow, light, porous, soft, with a browned crust. For so many years he fed himself with bread made out of *lupini* beans, of barley, of chestnuts, a hard, heavy, dry, rough bread that scratches the mouth, hurts the teeth, and weighs like lead on the stomach."

During my childhood, of a person who was on his deathbed people would say: "They've put him on white bread" because only when the poor were seriously ill could they taste white bread, which not by chance was called *pane de gnura*, or bread of the rich ladies, while, vice versa, rich ladies were called "women of white bread."

How many times I heard stories of nostalgia for white bread and expressions of revulsion for the dark, uneatable bread! I would try to share the feeling. It wasn't easy. By that time we had too full a stomach to understand the sensations and the vocabulary of forced fasting, of those individuals who had dieted not to fulfill some current, new-fangled vogue but because they had nothing to eat.

In the novel entitled *Fontamara* Ignazio Silone was able to give voice to the hunger of the peasants from the Abruzzo region and from the Italian South. "Bread and children, a hundred jumbles," reminds us a proverb from Basilicata. In Calabria it appears in several variations, which hark back to practices common to the whole Mediterranean that involve the blending of foodstuffs and the coupling of bread not only with other cereals but with many other products, such as fruits and herbs.

Proverbs are ambivalent things, and ambivalent are the readings that, through them, can be made of the past. Some people recall the hundreds of mixtures to underscore the imagination, the skill, the culinary talent of the women of previous times. Others, instead, ac-knowledge those mixtures to point to the dreariness of those times, when hunger was alleviated by turning into bread whatever edible entity was available. There is some truth to both of these interpre-tations. Necessity and imagination, deprivation and ability, poverty and inventiveness did go hand in hand. The memoirs or the accounts of Calabrian writers, of travellers, observers from elsewhere are first-hand, direct attestations. They are forceful, well-told, bitter, realistic and quite effective. They throw light on the rhetoric about the good old times and make us realize how recent an affair the gastronomic melting pot of Calabria really is.

Hunger is the word most often recurring in the stories of the elders. It was a hunger for bread, and not by chance a proverb admon-ished that "better dark bread than dark hunger." This situation was to last until the 1960s, until the period in which the slow vacating of the villages began, because people flee from the hunger of bread, the disconsolation caused by hunger, and go in search of a piece of bread.

Saints of bread

One could outline a geography and an anthropology of the land in which I was born by making a list of all expressions that have to do with bread and the various types of flour or by compiling an inventory of the various saints whose life and cult is connected to bread.

Southern Italian local saints, and above all saints of Calabrian-Greek background, make miracles dealing with bread. Saint Fantino of Tauriona, who died around 336 c.e., "a humble and poor servant" known also as *Il cavallaro*, the stable man, at night, during the period of harvesting, would grind the sheaves of grain of the poor using his master's horses. Of Saint Saba, from the 11th century, who from Sicily moved to the area of Mercurio, on the right side of the Simi river, are worth noting the multiplications of wheat, fish, wine and two different kinds of oil, all in favour of the starving poor.

Saint Nicodemo (10th-11th century), who was born in Sicrò, in the valley of the Saline, lived an ascetic life in the wooded mountain known as Cellerana: "Every day from dawn until 9 AM, he would prepare bread on stones he split with his own hands, to feed all the needy, using a flour that he had milled. Instead of bread, at dusk, he would nourish himself with a decoction he obtained by boiling chestnuts, to which he sometimes added the fish that fishermen freely donated."

Saint Leo (10th-11th century), who lived an austere but industrious life in the mountains and the groves between Bova and Africo, is depicted in images that show him with an axe and a ball of resin, a reminder of the miracle he performed when in a period of famine he transformed pitch into bread. Even to Saint Bruno (11th-12th century), the founder of the order of the Carthusians, a 17th century hagiography attributes a multiplication of bread.

Saint John Theriste (10th-11th century), known as "the harvester of Stilo," makes his best known miracle near Robiano, where he was headed one day in June to visit a benefactor of the monastery. Along the way he met some men busy harvesting wheat, who upon seeing him began poking fun at him. The saint stopped and offered to share with them the bread and the wine he was carrying. The workers accepted, and the bread and the wine miraculously was enough to feed everyone. While bowed down on the ground to thank God, a violent storm broke out, with the workers hurrying to take cover under the trees. When the saint rose from his prayers, he noticed that the wheat had been cut and arranged in sheaves. In the images about him, Saint John of Theriste appears with a sickle in his right hand and a flask of wine in the left. During processions in his honour, the faithful offer him small bunches of ears of wheat or other types of grain. His miracle is still quite vivid in folklore and his name is invoked whenever storms and floods take place.

Miracles by which waters that had swept aside everything in their way were stopped or by which rains were induced to come after long periods of drought were miracles for bread, intended to favour the production of wheat. At the beginning of the 20th century a peasant from Rossano says to Francesco Nitti: "Here we have a God that when it rains everything goes into the sea and when it doesn't rain everything dries up. This year it hasn't rained for six months and we're all without work and reduced to poverty." And Francesco Perri in *Emigranti* [*Migrants*] writes "once the rains started no-one knew how it was going to end, because in Calabria either the weather is dry, which means that we have to bring all the saints out of the churches to see a bit of water; or it rains, and especially when it rains with the scirocco, it never ends."

It was "a religion of water," according to Corrado Alvaro, for a people that suffered thirst in a land floating on the sea or that watched as the rains and the raging torrents devastated cultivated lands, houses, neighbourhoods. Water was never enough for drinking needs, was always far away, and the woman carrying the jug is a recapitulating symbol of traditional societies. Together with the nostalgia for bread, there was the nostalgia for water.

Wheat and bread have been the perennial torment, the daily preoccupation of the populations of the Mediterranean basin. How promising is the harvest? It's been often the most pressing question on everyone's mind, for poor people, obviously, more insistently than for the rich, who always have their sacks full in their granaries. Fernand

Braudel, to whom we owe the consideration just mentioned, adds: "And one needs always to hurry, to take advantage of the last rains of spring or of the last ones of the fall, of the first or the last of the good days. All agrarian life, and thus the best of Mediterranean life, unfolds under the sign of hurriedness, with the fear of winter always there; granaries and wine cellars must be filled up."

The employers, the owners, the gentry give no respite; workers are called upon to hoe the land or cut wheat until late at night. *Da scuru a scuru,* from dark to dark, peasants laboured from before dawn to well after dusk, before returning home, tired and weary, to eat a bowl of soup and put themselves to bed so that they could wake up early and go back to the fields. All for a piece of bread. Quite other than the mythology and the rhetoric of slowness! Slowness is a need, a dream, an invented notion, a possibility for the men and women of today; it can't be associated with the men and women of other periods, who were always in a rush and worked the whole day eating "bread and knife," bread and nothing else.

They weren't a choice, those light meals always on the fly and with only dark bread on the menu. And so it's no surprise that as soon as conditions permit it, peasants leave behind, without regrets, the corn bread or the bread made from chestnuts in order to nourish themselves—finally—with bread made from wheat. Already in the 1960s Roland Barthes was writing that the move from white bread to dark bread "reflects a change in social markers: Dark bread has paradoxically become a sign of refinement." The available varieties of bread are each "signifying units" and ought to be evaluated within a specific "alimentary system." Unfortunately, Barthes' considerations haven't spared us confusions between the integral dark bread of the individuals fully satiated within our society, which is a sign of refined taste, and the dark bread that the hungry peasants found too hard, sour, often inedible. The "local, typical" food product is one of today's inventions; it rightly no longer forgets traditions but at the same time it cleanses them of their less edifying aspects.

The age of bread

In his *Lettera aperta* [*Open Letter*] to Italo Calvino, dated 1974, Pier Paolo Pasolini stated:

> The rural universe, to which belong the sub-proletarian urban cultures and, until a few years ago, belonged those of the working class minorities, is a transnational universe that doesn't even recognize nationhood. It's what is left of a preceding civilization (or of a number of preceding civilizations, all more or less similar), and the dominant, nationalistic class has modelled these remnants according to its own interests and its own political aims … It's this peasant world without borders, pre-national and pre-industrial, which had managed to survive until a few years ago, that I mourn … The men and women of this universe didn't live in some golden age, just as they had no involvement, if not an informal one, with the Italy Italians refer to as *Italietta,* the Italy with perennially provincial, second-rate horizons. They lived in that phase of history that Felice Chilanti has called the age of bread. In other words, they were consumers of goods absolutely necessary. And it's this, perhaps, that rendered equally necessary their humble, precarious life. While, by contrast (just to be rather elementary about it and to close this line of argument), it's clear that superfluous goods also render life superfluous. That I may regret or not regret the disappearance of this agrarian world remains my personal affair. But this doesn't in any way stop me from expressing my criticism of today's world, *as it is.* Indeed I can do so all the more the more lucidly I feel myself detached from this world and the more stoically I choose to live in it.

All those *panettoni,* the Christmas vanilla-flavoured bread-like cakes allowed to go bad, frittered away, the dozens and dozens of Easter eggs broken hurriedly to look for what was inside, while the chocolate was ignored, discarded, forgotten in some drawer—all this embarrasses me and causes even some dismay since I can't explain or vouch for other forms of behaviour. Why is it, as a proverb tells it, that "only forbidden bread generates appetite," while the bread available in abundance breeds only indifference and little respect for food?

In the past the preparation and consumption of bread were accompanied by numerous prescriptions and interdictions. My grandmother and my mother, who gave bread to our neighbours, used to say that it was a bad omen to send yeast after the Ave Maria, when it was dark, and one could run into the errant souls of the dead. I was happy about their generosity in giving but it took me a long time to understand why the *levatu*, yeast, had to be passed on when there was still daylight.

When a new batch of bread was put in the oven I would participate. I enjoyed seeing the movements of the women, their skill, the art of working the flour into dough and the delicateness with which they cleaned the oven or would lay the smaller left-over pieces of bread. Before putting the dough into the oven, grandmother would say: "*A Deu sia lodato*," "All praise to the Lord," while mother or one of the women closest by or who chanced to be at the window to say hello would reply: "*Oje e sempre*," "Now and always." Then they would cross themselves and would pray: "*San Martinu pane cotto e furnu chinu; San Vincenzu lu 'ncenzu; Santa Rosa la bella rosa; Santu Nicola tuttu chizu chi ci vole.*" "Saint Martin, bread well-cooked and oven full; Saint Vincent and incense; Saint Rose and beautiful roses; Saint Nicholas and all we need." Then they would close with the Lord's prayer and a Hail Mary and would again cross themselves.

The oven was the centre of the house, of the village, of the agrarian universe. Still today in many villages the consumption of bread is never without gestures, prayers, rites of thanks. Bread had to be put on the table on the flat side, because the round side stood for the face of the Lord and it would have been a sign of scorn towards God's graces to overturn the loaf. For the same reason, it was considered a grave sin to insert the point of the knife in the bread. The nostalgia for the "civilization of bread," during which a lot of care would be given to left-overs, to discarded pieces and the soft part of bread, isn't a senseless and improbable return to the good old times but a refusal of waste and excess.

I've listened so many times to the story of the house at 245 Lisgar Street, that emigrants used to call "the house of the thirty-three loaves of bread." During the first years after their arrival in Toronto, thirty-three people lived there. Among them was my father. Vincenzo Bellissimo, or Giotto, as he was known, who in our village was a peasant, would go by the house every morning and would lay in front of the house a bag containing a loaf for each of the tenants, who would pick them up in the evening, upon returning from work. Those were years of hardship but also epic years, the years of the construction of the double of the village, there in the new world. The foundation of the new site was accompanied by gestures and activities borrowed from the culture of the origins. I've gone in pilgrimage to that street on several occasions, stopping in front of the house of the bread. I knew that what I had become and what I was continuously being offered I owed to the world of the parents. I could feel that there was toil in just inheriting their toil.

Giotto was born in 1926 and was twenty-two when on a ship full of fellow villagers he left for Toronto, and, due to his ability to cover walls with white paint, with that nickname which would follow him in the new world even after he changed occupations. He had left with his father, his mother and nine others, his brothers and sisters. Only Lisa, the youngest sister, remained in the village, as if to keep the house still open. To those who asked why she stayed back by herself she would answer—and still answers today—that she hadn't left because she had to feed the pigs, that she had to take care of the animals her parents had left there, in the fields.

I often meet Lisa in the streets of our village as I walk towards the main square. She is the only person I see, as she goes to buy bread, and we laugh about this solitude we share. She is now almost ninety years old and from time to time she acts as host to some brother or some sister from Toronto. She moves about with a cane and jokes often. She has always something to say about Giotto. Her brother, she tells me, has a great friend, *mastro* Emiliano, who is now also in Toronto, where he has moved with his wife, Emanuela, originally from Nicastro. The woman always reproached her husband, calling him a good-for-nothing, a loafer, and would say to him: "You certainly aren't a man of bread!"

In the past to say this to a man was the same as saying to him that he was a bungler, a tramp, an ineffectual person. Poor master Emiliano would go to Giotto and would complain. "My wife keeps telling me I'm not a man of bread!" and would almost feel like crying. One day after finishing his tour with the bread, Giotto realized that he hadn't sold much and that his van was still quite full. He hurried to the house of Emiliano. He knocked. The woman from Nicastro opened the door. "Good morning, signora Emanuela, this bread is being sent to you from your husband. Now you can have your fill of bread." The woman smiled, while, with a serious look about him, Giotto placed two large bags full of bread in front of the house of his friend.

It's a bit cold. The humidity of the fall months. The leaves of the maple trees have become reddish in colour. In front of a house a van has stopped. From the back a man takes out some loaves of bread and delivers them. "Here is Giotto," Ciccio tells me. I feel as if it's almost a joke. Giotto opens the van, takes a loaf of bread. "Please accept it," he says. "I remember your father."

Figs in Toronto

for Ciccio Bellissimo

T HE CLOUDS, WHITE, high up, touched the bell tower of the church. They seemed like a continuation of the façade. It was six in the morning, and this church, the main church, seemed as if suspended in the air, as if waiting to fly away. The sun had just risen on Mount Coppari and it lit up the hills to the northeast of the village with glares that almost matched the white from the shapes up in the sky. Franco had been up early, from before dawn, to go and pick up the fresh figs in the *rasule,* the small home-garden type of plots which, there, happened to be in the terraced land above Gianferrante. What a curious name, he always thought, when he tried to picture to himself the Spanish knight of some of the legends that were part of the history of the village. He was now sitting, looking at the landscape. He fixed his gaze on the bell tower, then moved it towards the Angitola, the big bridge built after he had left the village. In that direction he could make out the sea, which was blue and clear. As if he had a telephoto lens in his eyes, the gaze narrowed its scope, shortened the focus, and aimed towards the inhabited portion of the landscape. He looked for the house in which he had been born and raised, the one in which he had lived with his parents, his three brothers and his sister, up to the time when he, Vittorio and Giovanni had left for Canada. Two rooms: the ground floor, where in the evening they sat, ate or received visitors, and the floor above, where they slept, all six of them.

The view of the house—he still considered it as his, that house in which he hadn't lived for almost thirty-five years—was obscured by a series of constructions, three or four stories high. Unfinished buildings that seemed gutted, since they were without some of the walls, and the walls they had were without plaster, but sported double fixtures on the doors and the windows and pots of flowers and hot peppers on the balconies. The roofs were a mosaic of precariousness and improvisation: light-shaded asbestos, grey, red or terracotta brown; thin sheet metal plates, old red roof tiles burned by the sun, faded by the rain. The antennas found some space on the balconies or the roofs, scattered higgledy-piggledy, as may happen to herds of animals passing on the road.

He thought, with some sorrow, about the landscape, which appeared to him both familiar and foreign, then he concentrated on the clouds. He went over the different forms and the many colours of the sky above the church and the houses that, from there, he had seen as a child and as a young man. They seemed to him a good, recapitulating snapshot of the thousand stories about migrants, all similar and different. No sounds or voices came to him from the inhabited areas. They did come to him, instead, from the past, and he edited them on those images, as is done in film with no sound track.

"Greetings, *compare* Franco. You got up in good form, almost as if you had to issue the *meta,* the weighing scale for the fish." It was the friendly and playful voice of *compare* Vincenzo, whom he was to meet for the figs. He smiled, thinking about the allusion to the scale, which was released during the very first hours of the morning, in the village square, by the person responsible for the food administration, to the fish vendors coming from Pizzo. The expression *donare la meta,* to issue or hand out the scale, was used to depict anyone who got up early for no precise reason, without having anything to do.

"Good morning, *compare* Vincenzo," answered Franco, with a similarly friendly, playful tone. "I came early, given that I couldn't sleep in any case … You know how it is. The day before leaving one never manages to sleep. And then, to be honest about it, I was worried that you might gobble up all the figs."

"Don't joke about it," said, smiling, *compare* Vincenzo, the owner of those *rasule* that required constant watering. "If we were today as we were once, with hunger that spoke with the angels, I would really have eaten them all, like *compare* Peppe, who ate more than three hundred prickly pears, those that were *spatti*, overripe, and thus no good to save. What can I say, now we no longer need to do things like that, but there are also no longer any fig trees, If it weren't for you migrants, who, it seems, return only for the figs, those few plants that you see would have been surrounded by thorny bushes. And to think that fig trees are well-known for their strength. They can bore through stones or the walls of the houses people have abandoned to their fate in the countryside."

At the same time, as he talked, *compare* Vincenzo was gathering the figs. He did so with an ancient gracefulness, making sure not to break the stem, then placing them delicately, one by one, in the basket. He picked those that were ripe but not cracked by the sun: They had to be still hard, since they would be travelling a long way and had to keep.

Franco returned the leg-pulling. "You pick figs as if you're caressing a woman at your first love meeting with her."

"Those times have gone by, unfortunately, and, if truth be told, we weren't that delicate with women, whom we saw on the run and on the sly," answered his friend with a veiled sadness.

Franco thought about how he had binged on figs as a young man before leaving, late in the evening or at dawn, by himself or with friends, in the vegetable gardens nearby or, farther out, in the open countryside. Images of the past came to his mind, his father bringing the first crop of the fruit, the *fichi d'occhio*, the first figs the eye would discern when it wasn't yet summer, before the feast of the Madonna of Monserrato, and then the *posterari*, the figs that would still linger on the tree even up to the Day of the Dead, the second of November, when figs were free to anyone who wanted them.

He remembered *compare Cominciaru li ficu*, *compare* The-Figs-Have-Begun. Franco's group of buddies would roam the countryside caravan-style in search of figs or plums or cucumbers on a *Cinquecento*, the smallest of the Fiat cars, loading up to twelve people, on the inside or the outside of it. For the adolescents in their part of Calabria it was a pleasant, playful way of passing time, during the 1960s, before the beginning of the mass departures for work or study.

Often *compare* Franco and his friends would come upon a slender older man with a restless, mobile gaze, a hoarse voice, and his back bent from hard work. He walked always behind his donkey, which was weighed down with vegetables and fruit he had picked in his own vegetable garden, two kilometres away from our village.

A bit teasingly, almost as a kind of forewarning by which to justify the poaching they would commit on his land, when they would meet that amiable old man they would ask him: "Good evening *compare*, have the figs begun yet?" And he, visibly annoyed, without stopping and without looking at them, knowing full well what those sons of a gun were about to do, would continue walking repeating several times: "The figs have begun, the figs have begun." His rather irritated words would be submerged by the group's laughter, until then held back with some difficulty, as all of them proceeded towards the fig trees, now unattended.

Compare Vincenzo had deposited in the basket the last of the fruits he had picked. Then he covered them with leaves from the tree, in a way that made them look like some kind of embroidery, and with great skill had fitted in the basket four strips of wood so that the figs couldn't move and roll on the ground.

"Here we are," he said. "A nice basket, as full as can be, with the figs all assembled in a way that they can't be damaged, even if people were to put their feet on them. You can leave with your mind at ease. By now we've become experts at preparing packages of this sort."

"Thank you," said Franco, looking at the basket with some satisfaction. "You're always very gracious; you've done a great job. I don't know how to thank you."

"Let's say that you'll think of me when you eat them," answered *compare* Vincenzo touched by his words. "Or that when you return you'll bring one of your *soppressate,* since it seems that where you are now you make those large sausages better than where we are."

"Better probably not. But they do stimulate the appetite. We continue preparing them in the old style. If you have a hankering for things of days gone by—words, limericks, disputes—you should come where we are; here everything has changed."

"Yes," said *compare* Vincenzo, "to me too everything seems changed, and sometimes for the worse."

"Don't complain. How do they say? America is now here. It's not true that the village is to be found where we are. My children speak English and they don't eat goat meat, dried cod, or even spaghetti. You can imagine the kind of village you would find."

"Come back when you can; here now I don't know anybody. When I see you, it's as if I were seeing the good soul your father was, or my son, who now lives in Toronto."

Franco felt he had to go. He was almost on the verge of tears.

"Stay well," he said. Embracing *compare* Vincenzo, he added: "Give my best to all of your family; when I run into your son and your grand-children I'll say hello on your part." And he was already in the car, which his brother-in-law had lent to him for a month.

The streets and the main square in the village were empty, without a soul around. Only Gio's bar was open but inside there was no-one. Now, after the last feast day and the end of the holiday period as a whole, there was no-one; the roads, the back streets, the main square and the smaller square were like a desert.

In the past, when he still lived in the village and witnessed the departures and the emptying out, he would be caught by a sort of bewilderment. He felt lost. "What will I do? How will we pass the time?" he would ask, and would dream of leaving without even knowing where to go, or what his destination was to be. He didn't leave because of necessity but because the emptiness of the village and the flux of people going away saddened him.

Now he chose to return to the village a bit before the day of the feast, when the crowds were still there and the great throng of migrants had arrived from all parts of the world. He would linger more than a week so that, with all possible ease, he could pay his respects to the people he hadn't been able to meet and to understand what the village had really become. Summer plays tricks on people: It confuses them. Everyone acts as if they had something to be cheerful about, or to be mad, happy, nostalgic. They take on the role of the person who has left or of the person who has stayed behind, or of the person who returns because he or she has no choice or who remains because he or she has no choice.

The surroundings *svacantati,* vacated, which Franco found intolerable when he was a young man, he now caressed as you do with a woman lost and found again. It's not as if he relished being there when there was no-one, but to him the village seemed then to be more close to its true condition, more authentically mournful, more solitary. At times, when his parents were still alive, he had returned in winter but the emptiness of that time of the year appeared to him to be really excessive, really oppressive.

Without any taverns, tailor shops, stores, locales of clubs where members could meet, very few groceries and only two or three coffee-houses that opened in the morning and after lunch, during the hours in which the foresters would come in for their cup of coffee, the village seemed like a place people had abandoned because of some misfortune. The strange spherical street lamps on the side of deserted roads full of potholes sent off a yellowish, annoying light which gave the rare and solitary passers by a kind of spectral aspect, almost as if they were phantoms that had come to take possession of houses now in full disrepair.

The buildings that closed and became empty increased in number every time Franco returned. He couldn't stand the huge, ugly barrack-style houses that cropped up outside the village, in areas always disturbed by wind and fog, while the older houses were wasting away year by year. "Walls want to be talked to," Mico Tallarico used to say to him. "Otherwise they languish and deteriorate more quickly." The decision to build outside of the inhabited core of the village had been made in the name of convenience, so that the owners could have better looking, more hospitable abodes to show off, and because this is what everyone wanted.

Franco thought: "OK, got it … and yet there must have been a reason why our ancestors had chosen as the location for their houses that particular spot in the village, a location where the sun, the wind, the climate were benign. But what is it that I can or should reproach? And to whom should I direct my reproaches? I haven't remained in the village. My life now unfolds elsewhere and here I return as a guest. In the end, I'm a foreigner. I don't even know why I come back here now that the elders in my family are no longer here, and to find them I have to go to the cemetery. And there, too, it's not a pleasant sight: tombs never fully finished, spaces very scarce, chapels built any which way, flowers on the ground."

He wasn't one of those who loved things to be nice and precise, a world where everything had a predetermined, fixed place. Actually, as a matter of fact, the punctuality and the organization of the Canadian world bothered him somewhat. He felt nostalgia for some of the improvisations and whimsicality of the universe of his origins but, to be honest about it, the disorder he now saw wasn't a disorder that had a recognizable or perceivable order. He felt dispirited and ungrateful in making these considerations. He was one who had defended the village even when it wasn't defensible, continuing to speak well of it even when he wasn't convinced or felt distant from its reality. He found a good and pleasant side in everything. This is why he was able to traverse worlds of all kinds with delicateness, leaving a smile and a good memory in all people who knew him.

He was almost happy for not encountering anyone this day, the day before his departure. He wanted to leave in silence, unseen. He liked to imagine that if people didn't become aware that he was leaving he would in some sense still be staying in the village.

He leaned out from the balcony on the left side of the war memorial where as a child he had played a thousand games: riding the carriage, hide-and-seek, Indians and sheriffs, hitting a small length of wood with a stick for others to catch, or engaging others in word games that required answering in rhyming repartees. It was also where, as a young man, he had sung with other young men and women, who now could really be anywhere and some no longer of this world at all.

He looked in the direction of the sea. A train went by on the bridge with two tracks. "Perhaps it'll bring me luck," he thought, remembering the ancient belief that encouraged people to be under the bridge when a train went by.

He again saw the disarray of the roofs; with his gaze he surveyed all the houses, as if he wished to reacquaint himself with all the inhabitants once more. He went by his house. His sister hadn't yet returned from the fields in the countryside. He picked up the key behind the pot on the window sill. He opened the door, walked in the semi-darkness and reached the space underneath the staircase. It was humid. The area in which he lived was called *Li pontani*, a marshy area where water from natural springs would flow inside the houses and in the streets. The figs would keep for at least two days.

The road by which to get to Nicola's house was, as all the roads, full of surprises. As always, wherever he went, he found something to do, people with whom to talk. He soon retracted his resolution not to stop and say hello to anybody, to not delay, and knocked at the door of Rocco's Angela. The elderly woman, who was tended to by another woman from the village, didn't recognize him. She asked who he was, but her hearing was bad and couldn't make out the answer. Franco raised his voice while holding her hand and she, by some miracle, heard the word "Toronto." "My beautiful son," the woman started saying, "my beautiful son who died in Toronto. A pearl of a man, a generous man who each year would come and see me. Are you Marianna's Franco? Now I recognize you. You have to excuse me. I can't see and can't hear well. You were my son's friend. My beautiful son, it wasn't you who should have died but me, who am old, not you, still so young. You Christ on the cross, sometime you don't do things quite right."

She was crying and wouldn't let go of Franco's hands. He too had tears, thinking of his friend Raffaele, who had passed away less than a year before. He hugged her, stroking the nape of her neck and her face, not knowing what to say and not feeling up to speaking in a loud voice. She cheered up a bit, for a moment relinquishing a sorrow that would be with her for the rest of her days. Sitting down in a low chair by the small fireplace, she kept repeating: "Thank you. Thank you. My poor son, my poor son." The woman who looked after her when the family members weren't there signalled politely to Franco not to say that he was going: There was nothing further that could be done or that could be said.

In the street he heard two young women speaking in a foreign language. He made out some words in Polish that he had learned from one of the men with whom he worked. "Thank God they're here. At least they can tend to these few elders, now that we no longer return. We left to build cities and now if it weren't for these people who have improvised themselves as bricklayers it would be difficult to even have a roof repaired."

To see foreigners coming to work in a place from which thousands had left in search of employment seemed to him an irony of fate. It gave him a sense of the changes that had occurred in the world. He was getting old, he thought. Going back there, to the village, was impossible. And a mistake. It would be like returning to a foreign country.

"Everything looks as if it were the same: the streets, the vegetable gardens, the church. Nothing seems to happen, but everything has changed. Nothing is the same as before. Time stands still in a village, they say, and instead it's as if a thousand years have gone by."

Nicola had been waiting for him for almost two hours. Franco didn't make it. He would call his friend on the phone. Besides, they hadn't set a precise time for their rendez-vous. He had told his friend that later, perhaps, he would drop by. That "later, perhaps" made it almost certain that he wouldn't have been there. Nicola knew it quite well. He too was exactly like Franco. "We'll see each other" was a way of saying that seeing each other wouldn't have been easy. The desire was there, the nostalgia also but catching up with everyone he would have liked to meet was impossible.

As a young man Franco had dreamed of bringing together all the villagers scattered throughout the world, all the friends that had left, so he could be with everyone, have supper with them, do music, sing, go serenading with them. As the years went by he realized that the time wasn't enough. He was content enough to promise, postpone, regret, and ended up just assembling, once a year, in Toronto, all the relatives from both sides of the family, really all the relatives, about fifty people, old, adults and young, who didn't quite understand the whys and wherefores of that gathering.

He took part in all church processions, attended all the Friday meetings of the club of his fellow villagers, all the marriage ceremonies to which he was invited. He tried to be always available. Now and then he created confusion, mistaking the dates: Time was really a harsh master. "There always remains something to do and we die without really, exactly getting everything done," he thought.

At home his sister waited without too much hope. Indeed, she was surprised to see him arrive so early. As he entered, Franco smiled and greeted her. He looked at the tablecloth, at the table with the plates covered. He remembered that he hadn't eaten and also that he wasn't hungry. "You've lingered," said Rosaria, without reproach, "and friends and cousins have dropped by to say goodbye."

"There's time, I'll pay my respects later, they'll return or I'll go and visit," replied Franco and headed towards the telephone.

"Don't worry. There's no problem," answered from the other end Nicola. "I know you, however," he said, unable to avoid some pain as he involuntarily hit his head against the wood bearing the image of Christ on the cross he had tried to kiss at the Confraternity meeting where he had been, "I know that when you have to leave and have to say goodbye, you're never quite up to it."

Franco smiled at the quip of his friend, who at the right moment had always up his sleeve stories about the village by which to comment on events and the behaviour of people. He excused himself saying that yes, he really wished he could spend some time with him, but "You know how it is, how village life goes, it gets hold of you, you never do anything, never settle anything, and now I have to be at home, people are coming over, I want to stay a bit more with my sister, and must take care of the suitcases, the travelling bag."

He wasn't hungry but had a yearning to eat something. It was as if by doing this he would leave part of himself in that home. He also knew that tasting a slice of bread would please Rosaria, not to mention the fact that in Toronto he would never come across the flavour of the turnips grown in his sister's garden. Nor the aroma of the oregano on the crushed olives or that of the *soppressata* with the so-called tear, the cured salami which, if properly prepared, should emit just a trace of oil when the fingers squeeze it.

Brother and sister went on talking. Once in a while she would ask him not to leave half of his things there, as he had done other times. He started preparing his baggage, struggling with the thousand little packages people had left with him to bring to relatives or friends and that now he couldn't fit in the suitcases.

All the acquaintances who had relatives in Toronto knew when he was leaving and they all had forgotten something they now wanted to send: a thought, an object, some perfume, a sweater, all little things, in the end. Except that with these things he filled up one suitcase and two travelling bags.

After having sworn that this time he would leave everything at home, no matter who would be offended, Franco armed himself with all possible patience and slid everything, really everything, in the baggage. It wasn't easy to decide what to leave and for whom. Almost always he had put aside his things to bring those of the others. His cousins now came back to say goodbye; then a friend of his son showed up, asking if he needed a ride the day of the departure, and a neighbour who wanted to inquire if Franco could deliver his greetings to a family member. Greetings brought orally, in person, meant more than those sent via email or transmitted by phone. Individuals who travelled between one world and the other confirmed that everything was fine. They were direct witnesses, would connect together the various bits of village dispersed throughout the various continents.

It was already dark. He went out without saying anything to his sister. She was dabbling with bags, bottles and other gifts received by her brother, which no doubt would remain in the house to be found by him when, God willing, he returned. The heat of the preceding days had gone and the landscape appeared in all its brightness. The sea seemed to be just nearby, and so did the small hamlets that Franco had wandered in before leaving for Canada. Every corner of the village reminded him of some story, a thousand times over. He rehearsed in his mind the places of his childhood. "Here lived *compare* Ciccio, here the 'savage' woman, from that porch would lean out *donna* Vincenza." All closed doors now. There were no children in the streets. Only from the square came some indistinguishable words and sounds. He stopped at the house of the Tavigghia once more to give one last hug to his wife's parents. They lived alone, waiting for news or for visits from their four children strewn here and there in Canada, Rome and Verona.

"They're actually fortunate. Many die without seeing their children, who often return only for their parents' funeral and perhaps to argue over the inheritance of some small plot of land full of thorny shrubs which they hadn't even bothered to think about before."

He started out on Via Roma, then up the Belvedere. He saw the back street where Rita's parents lived. All the houses—ground floor, an outside staircase with a landing and a second floor, two rooms in total—were empty. The steps that she had seen full of noisy people were now silent, made granular by the debris the rainwater carried and by the summer heat, slivered by the time that had gone by. Franco remembered the account Rita had given of the only trip she had made to the village together with her parents when she was still a child, the phrases, half in English, half in dialect, she invented to describe that back street and the impression the small, narrow houses had left her with. He recalled their discussions and their smiles when they were so entangled on the bed and wouldn't let go for any reason, even if the world had been falling apart, without thinking about the past or stopping to imagine the future. He felt a lump in his throat. He became thirsty and made his way to the fountain nearby. Not much water was flowing through. He collected what he could cupping his hands, as peasants did in the countryside, and recognized the soft taste of the water as he slowly drank. He gently passed his wet hands across his face, which was now quite hot, and continued to walk.

He shouldn't have been thinking about what was happening to the woman with whom he had taken his first steps upon his arrival in Toronto. He focussed on the road. "There stopped the bus that would drive the students to school and from there would appear Don Nino in his red pyjamas, who when a couple would walk by would say to the young woman: 'Hey beautiful, do you really want to hang around with this turd you're with?' And the young man would swallow the insult and, without saying anything, would quicken his step, while the young woman smiled."

Franco wasn't just walking through those streets but also in time, in the past, in his childhood, his dreams. In Toronto, even if there was always something missing, he felt lighter. The places where he had lived on his arrival and for more than twenty years now seemed to him like another lost village, were part of the landscape of another life. The houses on College Street weren't just houses with the basement, a ground floor and a second floor. They too spoke to him and filled him with memories.

He had reached the end of the inhabited part of the village. There hadn't been a soul around, no-one for him to meet up with. In front of Gio's bar someone, whom he didn't recognize, was playing cards. He walked up towards the Fiumare section, passing by the house of the young woman who had been the beauty of the village, the object of desire and dream of two generations of youngsters. She had never married, remaining with her elderly father. Now she was sixty years old and, Franco said to himself, had still a fresh complexion, was still quite a looker.

The gate of the cemetery was open. Up to the end of September, for the migrants who returned and because of the heat, the hours during which entrance was permitted had been increased from five o'clock in the afternoon to eleven o'clock at night. Despite the disorganized order of the graves there was, this time, an air of cleanliness and care. The tomb of Franco's parents, of his paternal grandparents, to which the remains of some distant relative had also been added, was lit by a small electric lamp that had on its sides two pots with carnations of different colours. As if to test his memory, he read the dates of the birth and death of his father and mother. He thought of lives made of hard work, of countryside fields, of daily trips, of feasts that had their own predetermined rhythm and meaning. Of feelings and bonds that weren't always made explicit. That remained hidden.

One time he had decided to return with his brother at the end of the summer, and his father had waited with the hope that they would still find figs on the trees. Near the house he had a small plot of land where he kept chickens and a pig, grew vegetables and tended to some trees that bore fruit. One of the trees produced beautiful dark figs, egg-plant like, quite long, of the type that lasted all summer. *Compare* Annunziato didn't pick even a single one. He didn't open the low, wide basket where he kept the figs he had split with his knife so that he could dry them in the sun. He went there early in the morning to create some shadow for them with a wooden board or some sack cloth. He would count them and in the evening he would go to bed late to make sure that passers-by or some group of young men didn't touch them. He gladly offered figs and other fruit to everyone but that year he hoped to be able to have his children still find some directly on the branches. He was very happy when he saw his children under one of the trees, eating as they hadn't done for years. They all drank from the same jug, as they had done many years before, cleaning their mouths on the sleeves of their shirts, smiling as they thought of the comments they would have raised among those of their co-villagers in Toronto who had become more "civilized," more domesticated.

He felt enveloped by an unending emotion. His bones shuddered as when he was ill. He touched the photo of his parents, crossed himself and moved towards the exit. The Fellà river was sending out its voices, voices that seemed to him like a song, one of the tunes he heard as a child, something like a lullaby. Life and death, he said to himself. The air had become cooler. He saw some tombs, no more than two metres high, with name, surname, photo, date of birth and the space for the date of some death. Elderly people took care of things well before dying. Their children often couldn't manage to return from the places where they lived.

He noticed the grave which had the name, the surname, the photo, the date of birth and death of Raffaele, buried in Toronto. The name and the image perhaps made him present here too. After all, we're nothing but shadows, thought Franco, and surmised that this would have also been his place, with his own kind. He would leave the task of making a decision to his children, without leaving precise, binding, instructions in that regard. He couldn't make a decision on his own, never mind imposing a decision on others. To which place did he belong? To the place where his parents were buried or to the place where his children would bury him? To both or to neither of the two? "We belong to ourselves," said Franco to himself, "and we are the moments we've been. No single instant, no decade, no relation and no person can account for the life of anyone."

Nicola knocked on the door at six in the morning, half an hour before the time they had agreed upon. It was still dark, between starlight and sunlight, as the saying went. The boarding was at nine, but it didn't hurt to have some margin, time-wise, given the distance from the airport, one hour away by car, and given, too, that wasting time in goodbyes was their specialty when they were together. Franco was struggling with the suitcases, trying to close them once and for all and, as well, to move the basket of figs towards the door, so that he could put it right away in the car.

Coffee, with a bit of anisette, as was the custom with the first emigrants, for good luck, a final farewell to the neighbours, who had been up early, and to the sister, and he was in the car. Suitcase and travelling bags in the trunk, a handbag with the documents and the money together with the agenda and the figs on the back seat. Nicola started the car. Franco was waving to his sister, looking towards the second-floor window, as if to see his mother, who when she was old and ill would lean out to also wave and say good-bye.

They went past the street with the poplars, crossed the Abate river, arrived at the turns of Fascina. Silence. For them the moments of quietness were an important phase of their long, unending discussions. It wasn't easy to speak, to say something sensible, something they already didn't know, give a name to the emotions, comment on the departure.

Franco was sad; he felt a sort of emptiness and couldn't understand why he continued to be prey to a sort of confusion and of weariness right when he was returning home, his current home, to the place where his wife, his children, his grandchildren were waiting for him, where he had two brothers, uncles, cousins, friends, where there was the community Club, where he worked, where he had spent over forty years of his life now. Nicola realized that it was time to interrupt those thoughts, to bring some sprightliness in the silence. He decided to say something amusing that might serve to contain the flow of the emotions, the questioning, the affliction for which there is never any answer.

"And so, when it comes down to it, even when people stay for a long time, there's always the day of departure. The friends from the village with whom I feel I can talk, you're all elsewhere. In other words, you're no longer villagers."

"And who knows what we are. Perhaps not even you know, you who go and come back and never know where you are," said Franco, who from the one to be consoled had turned into the consoler.

"Yes, not even I know. The worst part is that I've always come back, thanks to the nearness of the place where I work and live, and in the end I've realized that I was considered a stranger both when I'm away and where I was born and grew up. Here I no longer know the young people and the occasions in which older people can meet up with the new generation are no longer there. I return but I no longer know why. For my mother. Out of laziness. For the land-scape. I don't know."

Franco followed his friend's thought.

"My children and your children hardly know each other. A long history of friendship, family relations, brotherhood is coming to an end."

Nicola answered, almost to reassure himself. "It doesn't necessarily mean that it has to be that way ... and at any rate it's a history that we know and that belongs to us. Belonging can't be transmitted. Who says that if we had stayed here our children would have hung out together. We can't decide for those who come after us. You've seen how many skeletons of houses have been erected imagining a future for the children? Children who then don't return, who go who knows where, with the houses remaining always unfinished."

They had gone past the artificial lake Montemarello, the bridge on the Angitola river. They decided not to take the highway but the *stradella.* It was the secondary road where as young men they would buy figs and *zibibbo* grapes, peaches and melons, from where people would make their way towards the beaches and the wooden shacks on the beaches. Today in those same stretches of sea there were the mega-villages put up by speculators and the destroyers of the landscape, all of them yearly welcoming German or Northern tourists not all that aware of which part of the world they find themselves in. Water, sea, sun, ice-cream is what counts; the place itself is really irrelevant.

"Where do memories come from? Who opens the door? Would I have remembered the road if I hadn't gone by it now?" thought Franco, while Nicola was languishing, almost as if he were the one leaving. The sprinkle from a pipe that irrigated the fields of flowers and strawberries reached the car, entering inside from the open windows, wetting both of them. They smiled and then looked towards the building, which was no longer in use, the failed dream of industrialization and of the damages suffered by the landscape. The roundabout that led to the region's administrative centre, the region's main train station, the region's airport, the under-passages that followed put Franco and Nicola in a state of anxiety. Separation was close by.

The parking lots were all full of cars and people that descended, pulled out the baggage, put on the ground purses and bags of all sorts. Nicola opened the door on Franco's side, helped him take out his suit-cases, delicately handed him the basket with the figs, pointed to a cart and drove on to find a spot in the parking lot. About three hundred people, each of them accompanied by two or three family members, sometimes by groups of friends or relatives, wandered about in the airport hall, waiting for the charter flight that would take them to Toronto.

The fig baskets brushed each other without any great bumping. "Let's hope they won't make a fuss when we board," somebody said. "Let's hope that they won't go bad, that they'll get there as they are, not squashed and not overripe and sour."

Franco went to do the check-in, left travelling bags and suitcases, keeping the basket with the figs firmly in his hands. Nicola caught up with him bringing newspapers. They proceeded towards the coffee-shop, had another coffee, greeted other emigrants from the village or people they knew from other villages near theirs. Nicola entered one of the shops, bought a herb liquor, some of the local biscuits called *mostaccioli,* and gave them to Franco saying: "The first night you're in Vito's basement have a glass in my health."

They were leaving with their baggage, the Calabrian emigrants that had built new worlds. They were leaving without outcries, speaking in a loud voice but with a courtesy they had learned as the years had gone by. They were bringing the land and the sun, their affections and their sorrows in the baskets of figs. They were leaving for a place that would never become really theirs and from a place that would no longer be entirely theirs again. They had constructed houses and bridges, metro tunnels and apartment buildings, gas ducts and factories, sent their children to school, who had become masons, painters, barmen, shopkeepers, entrepreneurs, lawyers, journalists, poets, musicians, bankers, politicians, had created clubs where often they argued and believed they could bring back to life the feasts and traditions of the villages where they came from, clubs and associations that united and divided them.

As if to complete these thoughts, Franco said: "Your politicians come to visit us, they talk on the radio, tell us how much they love us, how good we've been, we invite them into our houses, our churches, the parks in which we hold our feasts, and they speak and speak and don't know what they're saying. 'How well you speak the language of this country,' they keep repeating, and they eat and drink and don't realize that our children speak four languages and understand some of our dialects. 'How much you've remained faithful to your traditions,' and don't realize that the traditions they're referring to have changed or have disappeared even in our village and that our everyday habits are a mish-mash of memories, inventions, customs that we've learned in the new world, where we've mingled with all the other races, all the other cultures."

"Don't worry. All Calabria has moved on despite the tall tales and the tricks and frauds of the politicians. It's not that people are more advanced now, that they don't have their faults, their responsibilities but when they don't go under because of hunger or because of their desire for a life of riches they're wonderful people, and they manage to move this unstable and precarious boat forward, regardless of the thousands of currents that go in the other direction."

They were announcing the boarding of the plane. A quick hug and they separated as quickly, without lingering. They didn't want to find themselves with tears in their eyes. Franco entered the room where the boarding was to take place and started talking with some of the people. He held on tightly to the basket with the figs, careful not to be too long where the sunlight could fall on it.

He turned to look at Nicola, feeling his gaze. He saw him at the newspaper stand waving his hand. He knew that Nicola would have gone only when he saw the plane flying high above the gulf of Lamezia.

The clouds above Toronto were violet and glittering. A few seconds after the flight captain announced that the descent had begun, the plane entered a blanket of clouds that were light and dense, cut through it and let appear a landscape by now both familiar and dear to Franco. "Here they are," he said to himself, "the so-called little houses of Canada Italian singers sang about in the 1950s and early 1960s." He rested his forehead on the window and tried to pick out the big tower that he always chose as point of reference. While above, starting from the tower he was able to recognize the great arteries of the city. He could single out the various sections of the city and the streets he had hung around in during different periods of his life. He knew those streets one by one and so too those houses apparently all the same but which to him told something always different.

A flag, the statue of a saint in front, the image of the Madonna, the vegetables in the yard, the way the cars were parked were enough for him to determine whether a *Calabrese* or a *Friulano*, an Italian or a Portuguese, a Greek or a Canadian lived there. When he chanced to enter any of those houses for work he had to do or for other reasons he was able to say from which *calabrese* village originated the family that had welcomed him by a painting, the arrangement of the furniture, the votive images, the photos hanging on the wall or left in the china cabinet, the bed coverings in the bedrooms, the products in the cellar. Ceramics, carpets, pots, slippers at the door, wooden stairways and other details, identical in all homes, weren't enough to hide from him the other peculiarities, minute but distinctive.

He had refined here that sense of orientation which in Calabria enabled him to tell apart the different areas of the apparently same countryside, each of which had a different name, or to identify the fountains, the rivers, the groves, the cliffs, the pathways, and then the alleys, the back streets. A knack for detail that in Calabria, when he went around in the car seeking work, allowed him to single out from a distance each of the villages, which were always perched on some hilltop as if in a nativity scene and which to the untrained eye would blur into one, would be all the same.

At times the streets, the avenues, the roads in Canada appeared to him to be lines that continued the lanes, the back streets or the occasional widenings in the small village thoroughfares. The houses of his fellow villagers, now dispersed throughout the metropolitan area, were to him like an expansion of the spaces, narrow but open, of the place where he was born. At other times he thought that those houses were fragments, relics of a broken body and that, for incomprehensible reasons, some divinity prevented from reuniting. It was only for a brief moment. That labyrinth in which the emigrants, and even their children, remained forever trapped was familiar to him. He liked it. Loved it even, knew how to enter it and how to leave it. This is why he didn't know whether to stay or to go, why he had never excluded a return. But a return where?

Vittorio, Franco's younger brother, was a foreman at the Toronto airport, where for years now work to restore it and enlarge it had begun. He cut short his shift at 2 pm and ten minutes after was waiting for the plane. The landing occurred punctually at 3 o'clock, with the disembarking instead lasting some time. A festive throng was waiting or getting off the plane, smiling even if tired. With a shoulder bag on and the basket of figs in his hand, Franco walked towards Vittorio, who was talking with an acquaintance of his, also waiting for someone. The baggage didn't take long to arrive at the conveyor belt and the customs control was passed just as quickly. A policeman smiled at seeing all those baskets in line, exhibited one after the other as if they were a passport.

As Vittorio was driving, Franco updated him on the basic things, in the short version, about the village, their sister and the friends that sent greetings and were waiting for him back there. He saw the long arteries, Highway 7 and Highway 400, recognized the buildings and the overpasses, concentrated his gaze on the entrance to Scarlett Road that led to St. Clair Avenue. He took in without any comments the news about the family. All was going well. Battista, his eldest son, who was married to a Greek woman, had gone to work at the restaurant. Their son, Francesco Dante, a good-looking and quite lively two-year-old, already understood the dialect of their village, Italian, Greek and English.

Fabio, the youngest of Franco's sons, worked in a coffee-shop in the city centre. He wanted to make enough money to return to the village of the parents for Christmas. That village he had seen as a child, and he remembered the countryside, the beaches, a church with a round dome near a sanctuary with a grotto, the grandparents, the cousins and their friends but during adolescence he hadn't returned. On the insistence of his parents he returned when he was already twenty-five years old, in August, to see his grandparents. He was entranced by the rhythms of the village. He would get up when he felt like it and went to bed when he no longer could do otherwise. With his friends he made the rounds of the beaches and the discotheques, willingly participated in the nocturnal spaghetti sessions, and thus began fantasizing a "return" to the place where his parents came from and where they still owned the house they had left.

Not without reason, Franco suspected that something fishy was going on. In this case the fish had the dark hair and the green eyes of a young woman enrolled at the university of Cosenza. "It won't always be like this," Franco and Teresa would say to him. "What do you think? Sooner or later you'll have to start working. Do you think that here people eat and live really on nothing? And in any case what do you know of the village?" Teresa who would never ever re-establish herself back there insisted on making these arguments with her son.

Franco, on the other hand, wouldn't commit himself more than necessary. When it came down to it a marriage of the son back in the old country, if perhaps the couple could find ways to settle down in some center near the village, would keep open for him what was like a daydream. It came to him as something unexpected, as a pretext not to exclude for good his own return, once he retired.

Felicia, his third child, was on the point of receiving her degree in applied language studies, and was working part-time in a supermarket. "From all appearances," added Vittorio, "the relation with the Portuguese, who has a law degree, is serious. They've been seeing each other for some months now, and for her it's a record."

"Perfect," thought Franco, "Calabrians, Canadians, Greeks, Italian descendants of ancient Greeks, the family is becoming wider and wider. And, what's more, Greeks side with Italy in soccer. Too bad for the Portuguese. Great people, hard workers, friends of us, but they have one fault: They side with Brazil whenever Portugal is eliminated from the World Cup, or give their support to any other team but the Italian."

He understood that behind this attitude was a kind of reaction towards the Italians, who had become rich, entrepreneurs often conceited and arrogant. Even though they often had arrived with only some pieces of kitchenware or some seeds in their suitcases, they now looked down on the new immigrants, to whom they sold their houses in what used to be Little Italy. Franco thought of himself as being Italian, Calabrian from a village and yet fraternized with the newly arrived, and many Italians, some of whom from the same area of Italy he came from, brought to his mind a well-known saying from back in San Nicola: "God save you from the poor that have become rich and from the rich that have become poor."

He had entered St. Clair and then a street that went north and there they were, his wife and his grandson already in front of the house on Harteley Street. Franco smiled and walked towards the wife and Francesco Dante, showing them the basket with the figs. He hugged the boy first, stroking his head, while Vittorio unloaded the baggage.

It took Franco and Teresa only a few minutes to tell each other everything, at least the most urgent ones, the most practical things.

While they were talking, Franco took out of the suitcase the gifts for the child and the wife, and all that might break or go bad. He said that he would restart emptying the suitcase and the other baggage in the evening. He lifted the leaves off the top of the basket, opening it with great care. He was afraid that after nine hours of flight and eighteen after being picked the figs might have suffered. Instead there they were, nice and sparkling, a bit warm but whole and still as if asking "eat me, eat me." He took out more than half of them, peeled one and offered it to the grandson, who began tasting it with some hesitation and then said: "Good, grandpa. More, more." Franco was happy; he continued arranging the figs in a large glass bowl, and put them in the fridge. He then took some plastic and some paper bags and prepared four packages. Teresa understood.

"You just got here and already you're going out."

"What can I do? If I don't deliver the figs now, they'll spoil."

"But what's the point of giving seven, eight figs … It's no longer as it was once."

"I know, but it makes me feel good when I bring greetings to someone. I have to convey some messages and make arrangements for work. I'll go and see Battista and Felicia."

He thought about using the phone to say hello and to discuss work. But each call would have taken about a quarter of an hour. He opened the computer and saw that the mailbox was clogged up with messages. He didn't read any of them. Instead he sent messages about work to five or six people. "Hello. All is well. I'm back. Tomorrow we start again. Cheers to all." The little grandchild liked to play and kept grabbing his knees saying: "Grandpa where are you going?" And then he would start jumping.

"The stock keeps getting better and better," his grandfather thought somewhat amused. "He even likes figs. From Franco we've moved on to Francesco Dante, from Calabrians we've become also Greeks and Canadians. We also seem more high-spirited, thank heavens. Had I stayed in the village I would have been Ciccio, rather than Franco, all my life."

He was in Little Italy now, his other universe. He went up Ossington Street and turned on Montrose, stopping in front of the house of his aunt Maria, one of his father's sisters, who had arrived there in the 1970s together with her husband and seven children. When he knocked no-one answered. On Beatrice Street he entered a coffee-shop with a group of acquaintances, who were very happy to see him and asked questions. He managed to get away without even knowing how, crossed Grace Street, turned towards Clinton, then on Dundas and parked.

Between Dundas and College there was the church of Saint Francis, the church where Masses were celebrated, marriages and funerals held and where on Good Friday he dressed in the costume of the Confraternity to take in the procession that snailed through all of the old Little Italy. Right in front of the church, on Mansfield Street, lived the mother of Vince, the president of the club of those from his village. He knocked on the door. The woman was very happy to see him. She hugged him. Franco left one of the bags with the figs for her and another bag to, please, bring to Aunt Maria. Vincenzo hadn't still returned from California.

Vittoria from Schiaba left for Toronto in 1964. She had no fig trees, so she went to a neighbour, who boasted beautiful figs of all types, the early ones best for drying, the small white ones, those with the shape and colour of eggplants. *Compare* Peppe told her to pick as many as she wanted, and at her pleasure, adding only: "When you arrive in Toronto, call my son Antonio and give him a few." Antonio learned from his father, by phone, that some figs, picked by *comare* Vittoria on his father's trees would be arriving. "Did you see those figs?" Nothing happened, however; the *comare* hadn't called.

Antonio went to see her on Roxton Road, where she had settled. One of Vittoria's brothers opened the door, and said: "What figs, what figs! Don't even talk about those figs! When they got here they were all *spatti*, all rotten and we had to throw them away." *Compare* Peppe and

Antonio didn't appreciate this, not so much for the fact that the figs hadn't been given, but because it was an obvious lie and, in revenge, told the story about the gall, the ingratitude of *comare* Vittoria to all the people of the village they knew, both at home and in Toronto. In a world still based on principle and for which the word given counted, the episode became a sort of exemplary tale: It was told as a parable.

Franco got hold of that story from who knows where in his head, turned the car towards Woodbridge, the new residential development just outside Toronto where many of his fellow villagers that had arrived in the 1960s had moved as soon as they had gotten on in the world, thus putting some distance between them and their less fortunate compatriots. Except that now they realized that theirs hadn't been such a smart choice, since the old houses of Little Italy had become part of the downtown core, both a place where cultural events were held and a popular meeting spot for artists and entrepreneurs. Which meant that those houses were now more sought after than the new houses in the suburbs.

He rang at the house of Federico, the son of *compare* Vincenzo, who back in the village had picked and given him the figs. It was Federico who opened the door, and to Franco he seemed like a younger version of the father. Federico, caught by surprise, heard with pleasure the news about his elderly parent, and promised to himself that the following year he would go and visit him: the elders, it's better to see them before they die, and not to have to rush to their funeral.

In Woodbridge Franco drove in front of the church where there was the statue of the Madonna of the Rosary, put there by the co-villagers of the other confraternity. He stopped, entered inside and looked at all the statues revered by the many Calabrian communities. He went out, proceeded towards Martin Grove Road. He rang at the clinic where Rita had been admitted. He wanted to see her but was also somewhat wary about it. And she didn't want to have visitors. "It would give me great pleasure if you could come to see me and could stay here a bit without talking, without rehashing memories," she had said to him one day but then had added not to even think about surprises. He was to tell her in advance. She wanted to fix herself up, comb her hair, make herself look good, put on some perfume, dress with some elegance. An unforgiving disease was slowly wasting her away. Franco thought about this distant love, about this very beautiful woman who had led a very tormented life, with a lively, rebellious personality, in conflict with the parents she loved, a marriage behind her, an eighteen-year-old daughter, born five years after their relationship, fraught also with misunderstandings, had ended.

A nurse with a questioning look opened the door. Franco said hello, explained why he was there, took a card from the nurse and wrote: "I still care for you. I brought you figs from our village. Don't give up. I'd like to see you, to caress you, to understand why I wasn't able to stay with you. I came from the village, you were born there, I thought that sooner or later I would return back home; you were brought on a visit as a child and had even liked it, had made some friends with whom to play but when you grew up you never returned again. Don't let go now. Miracles do happen sometimes."

Now he regretted not having Nicola near. Only with him could he speak of the confusion in his head, of these apprehensions that didn't leave even now that he was approaching old age. In some respects, he was still like a child. He didn't think that relationships could end, that people at times disappear.

Quick, quick, move on, must rush, he was again in the direction of Dundas Street. He went by the Café Brasilero. It was closed. After Raffaele's death, a Portuguese had opened a new one with the same name, across the street. "Here too houses and shops close up," thought Franco. "Here too things, personal relations, lives come to an end." He turned towards Lisgar Street, looked at the house where in the 1960s Nicola's father had lived. Near Clinton Street lived Ricciarello, who too had arrived in Toronto in the 1950s. In his suitcase he had put plants and seeds of all kinds. Then he had toyed with the idea of growing a fig tree in his back yard. He had someone send him a small plant from the village. The ice, the winter, the snow, the thirty degrees below zero killed it.

Ricciarello didn't resign himself. He informed himself, studied the problem. He had someone else send him a plant of another kind of figs. During the winter he bent it, covered it in cellophane, buried it in the ground, freeing it when Spring came. In August there were two *scattagnoli*, two little burgeoning figs, still quite unripe, which as they grew in size began to look like figs but never acquired the consistency or the taste of real figs. Ricciarello viewed the outcome as a kind of triumph. In the years that followed he achieved better results, becoming a founding hero.

Antonio had lived here, with his wife and two kids, since ten years back. He too had left from one of the back streets near Franco's. And he too had initially settled on Grace Street and then moved on towards the northern part of the city in a pricey, lavish house, the sign of a well-being reached at the cost of many sacrifices, that well-being which for one reason or another escaped Franco and individuals like him. Not resolved enough, too caught up in relationships, affections, memories and such other self-questionings to be blessed by the fortune unthinking or hard-headed people enjoyed. He wasn't touched by envy, living, instead, the success of others as if it were one of his own achievements.

Antonio was a rigid person, one by all appearances without doubts and hesitations, but at the same time a good, generous person, always ready to help. Only in discussions he never made concessions. Franco didn't spend much time with him but liked and respected him, even if in arguments they ended up on opposite sides. The last occasion was at a supper at Vito's house on Lander Street. About thirty friends, male and female, the yarns, the jokes, the wrangles, the gossip: Why doesn't the club take care of the two feasts? Why don't we move beyond divisions that make no sense? Why even here the *Calabresi* don't have a cultural centre like the *Friulani* do?

Franco, as usual wanted to see everyone on the same side, hoped there would be harmony. What do you think it means, here, to belong to this or that confraternity? In the processions, why don't we march together and continue instead to go in separate ways, as we did in the village? Why don't we organize events that may be of interest to young people? Do we realize that in the club, ever since its rise in the 1970s, we're still the same people? That at Midland, to the pilgrimage of Christ on the Cross it's always us adults, those of us here who come from the village that go each year become fewer and fewer?

A drink here, a drink there. Whisky, wine. Pino that tells the stories of the village; Saverio those of fellow villagers in Toronto; somebody strums a mandolin, or perhaps begins to sing a song. Franco is happy but wrapped in thought, by himself, and whispers that these are nice stories but have meaning only for them; for the children they don't make sense, to the daughters-in-law or the sons-in-law who are Greek, Polish, Spanish, to the grandchildren even less. It's at this point that Antonio said to Franco:

"You're always the same. This is how traditions are destroyed. Do you realize? With your desire to change things you would change even the colour of the mozettas in the procession, just so you could include your friends from the other confraternity. You would bring to an end that little bit of the village we built here."

"Sure," answered Franco, somewhat bitter but composed, "to listen to you I would destroy traditions. You're all on the wrong track if you don't understand that everything changes, that the village is no longer the same and that there's nothing to preserve if not the memories and the stories and that, here, in this country, whatever we do becomes different from what we had imagined. You see that figs here don't grow as in the village where we came from and yet ..."

He wanted to develop the issues he had in mind but didn't know where he would end up and jammed as when a tape-recorder is suddenly without electricity. He was inundated with questions, what do you mean, you're right, I don't understand you, you have no idea, you haven't changed a bit. The tone of the evening was becoming heated and when, almost at dawn, Franco and Antonio said good-bye to each other they did so in rather cold fashion, even though they were tipsy, or perhaps because they were tipsy.

When Franco rang the bell, it was Antonio who opened the door. They embraced. They had forgotten the words they had exchanged. From the kitchen arrived Francesca, who was also from the village, and they made themselves comfortable in the spacious living room. A large canvas, on which someone had depicted the village, occupied half of the wall. It seemed almost as if it was looking at them. A large image of Christ on the cross, the arms sagging, the eyes sorrowful, included in its frame a photo of Antonio's father and it also stood out on the wall, against which lay an Italian-made sofa with at its sides plants that had arrived from Italy.

"How is it going? I came to say hello and to bring some figs," said Franco smiling. They started talking. At the beginning the discussion was charged with allusions and spiced with some bantering. "Well, what are people saying in the village?" said Antonio.

"In our village," explained Franco, "everything seems to be going well. Nothing ever happens, but nothing is the same. Places are as we left them but one doesn't recognize them. People come and go. The young leave but what's new is that they don't want to leave. What's also new is that they don't know anything about us. That we don't know each other. Is it enough for you? Everything seems still but everything is in flux. And you know what, even if I seem a stranger, if I have to ask who's this person, who's that other person, I feel good in the village. I get up well, I have fun, my hearing gets back to being what it was. I listen to the sound of the river, and think as I'm not able to do here."

"You don't work," added ironically Antonio, "you get up when you feel like it, you have a glass without thinking about tomorrow, you don't have the wife that keeps checking on you, the children aren't a problem, the machinery at the printing shop doesn't break, friends don't shoot their mouth off, you see everyone … and, especially, you know it won't last, you know that you can get back here, otherwise you would go crazy …"

Francesca had brought orangeades, juices, whisky, chips.

"No, no, here your husband is right," said Franco. "We have to defend traditions. Let's not mix figs with hard liquor and juices; bring some wine with, perhaps, a *soppressata*."

Franco remembered that he hadn't eaten and added:

"You know it's difficult to recognize the village. And that it's not worthwhile arguing here about things that no longer exist even there. Never mind quarrels about who has to stand in front of the statue of the saint, in the village feasts have changed. People argue about other things."

He alluded to stories of hostilities about the borders of plots of land left to the elements, untilled, which became objects of dispute as soon as someone thought of constructing on them some sort of building. He stopped. "And we add to this something of our own," he thought. "Many properties remain unsold and undivided, many houses are closed and run-down because we can't come to some sort of agreement, we, the many inheritors, brothers and grandchildren who have received as inheritance what we once deemed to be worthless and didn't care about and then becomes part of a well-being we don't want to give up. Our interest in village matters often has to do with self-interest and rhetoric."

He fell silent. He didn't want to start another debate. With bitterness and irony Antonio said: "The village is finished? It's become worse? It doesn't seem so to me. They're all well off, even those who don't work. There's the old age pension. When we return they feast us; if we don't return they don't give a damn. What could be better than this? It's us who always keep thinking about them. And, at any rate, the changes in the village are your own affair. I don't plan to return any more." Antonio concluded, knowing that he was lying, that perhaps between the two of them the one thinking about returning, and returning once for all, the one really wishing his departure had never taken place was really him.

"The problem," added Franco, thoughtfully, "is that even the village here in Canada has come to an end. Now we argue, talk and talk, we've spread out, our children do other things, they don't know each other. When this generation will disappear, no more pilgrimages and processions, no more village cuisine and music playing at the club. This too is finished. We should open up, attract the young, speak of another Italy, that we too don't know. We would be doing a favour to our children, who will never be like us but who will never be altogether Canadian."

The conversation was becoming serious, painful, almost without a way out. Antonio was revealing his fragility. He wasn't the grumpy person that he sometimes appeared to be. It was time to lighten things up.

"What can we do? Not everything depends on us," said Franco. "We can't change our past and can't predetermine the future, neither ours or that of others. We can barely decide what to do with our own time each day. Between the before we remember and the after we don't know about, there is us and what's important is what we're able to build without lamenting and without dreaming."

Antonio replied: "You know what I say? Do you remember *mastro* Colantone in the village? When he rang the church bells for a funeral people came out on the doorstep of their houses. Who died? So and so, poor guy, he was still young, and he died now that he was beginning to see some good in his life. 'Ah *mastro* Colantone. It's *compare* Mico that has died.' With a disenchanted and surly mien he would say: 'Too bad for those who die.' Time went by and *mastro* Colantone grew old. When he rang the death knell, someone, to tease him, would now say: 'Ah *mastro* Colantone, it won't be long before it's your turn.' And he would answer: 'Too bad for those who remain.'"

They smiled, with tears in their eyes. Even Antonio's father, on the wall, seemed to be smiling. And from the same wall, the houses that in the picture were leaned against the side of the hill also appeared pleased to see that those offspring of theirs were self-fashioning themselves. So it looked to Antonio, who felt reconciled with himself, and who thought he had done something painful but good and right when he left the village at night, without saying anything to anyone.

Franco understood that his friend had been moved from the exchange and that he was no longer in the mood to engage in the usual teasing, to continue with the usual disputes. He started eating a slice of bread, set his eyes on the olives, the cheese, the wine. The figs he left for his two friends. Now and then he looked at the fruit he had brought, that Antonio and his wife were eating religiously, slowly, as if to absorb the taste, and he felt the craving to join them, but didn't take any of the figs. He would have eaten some that evening at home, he said to himself, provided that he would find some left.

Two figs remained on the plate. Antonio said: "Eat at least one." "But no," Franco said, justifying himself somewhat artfully, "I've no desire for them now. I've eaten so many back in the village and will eat some more this evening at home." He actually hadn't eaten that many in the village because when the object of nostalgia is readily available the urge slackens, and he probably wouldn't try any here in Canada, now that he had come back. What did it matter? With the figs he had re-seen and re-visited all his worlds.

The figs, however, seemed almost as if they were inviting him. One was small and appealing; the other nice and large and almost ready to split open, with the honey beginning to surface on the skin.

At that point Franco said: "You know the story of the two ravenous friends who had managed to scrape together a pound of anchovies, which they devour, finally finding themselves in front of the last two? One was rather small, more like a little sardine, the other quite big and tempting. None of the two friends would make the first move. It seemed to them impolite, offensive, they wanted and didn't want to reach out. Finally one of them picked up the larger one. This caused the other friend to say: 'But *compare* that was wrong. I should be offended. I would have left you the large one and taken the small one.' His friend replied: 'So why are you complaining? It's the small one I left, just as you wanted.'" Without further ado, quickly, the hands reached for the larger of the two figs.

Interlude

Napuli, mu ti viju arzu de focu!
Ca a zzoccu passa 'nci fai la majia.
Salutami 'su giovani ch'è jocu
Salutamilu assai da parti mia.
Dinci si si 'nde vene o stade jocu
O puramente si scordau de mia.
Dinci ca si dimura 'n'atru pocu
L'ossa arriverà ma non a mia.

Giudici, chi si' giudici di amore
Cundannami sta causa manifesta.
Tu dimmi de cu' è lu cchiù doluri:
L'omu chi parte o la donna chi resta?
L'omu zzoduve va fade l'amuri
L'afflitta donna sconsolata resta.
Criju ch'è de la donna lu doluri
L'omu zzoduve va fa giochi e festa.

Naples, may I see you burn all to the ground
Those who visit you by your magic are bound
My greetings give to that young man you see around
Your hellos to him say they're all from me
Ask him if he'll come back or if he plans to stay
And if he has gone and all but forgotten me

Tell him that if much longer still is his delay
My bones he'll find when back but not me.

You judge who deem yourself a judge of love
Adjudicate if you can this question I do propose
Tell me who it is that suffers most in love
The men who leave or the women who stay
Men wherever they go they're free to love
The women who stay are always so morose
For me it's women who suffer the greater sorrow
Men where they go they feast from night to morrow.

(*Song of migration and separation from the end of the 19th century*)

The Shadow and
the Sewing Machine

PINO RECALLS THAT when he first arrived in Canada, his father, who had been living in Toronto for some time, told him: "I must buy you a *macchina*" [automobile, machine]. Pino was moved to tears. Back in his hometown he'd only had a little wooden kick scooter with ball bearings. He was still so young he didn't even have a driver's license. "This is the real America," he thought. A few days later someone knocked on the door and left a Singer sewing machine for Pino, who had apprenticed with the local tailor back in his hometown. This was his first encounter with the reality of life.

Home Land

At the wedding celebration, eight immigrants, all men, pose with obvious pleasure for a group photo. They are in Toronto in October of 1952. My father is the first one on the left. He is forty-three years old. Only a few months ago the ocean liner *Homeland* had brought him, together with many other people from his home town, from Naples to Halifax, Nova Scotia, Canada; from there he made his way, first to Portland, then to his final destination, the capital of Ontario, his potential new homeland. I was barely two years old. I hold on to this picture as something like the cornerstone in the building of my own life and memory, and, of course as part of my research.

I've never consciously chosen migration as the field of ethnographic research; rather, I've been chosen. In fact, the anthropological narrative is set up to unfold more or less like a slim autobiography that is more or less sure of its own certainty. In this case, autobiography is explicit, sought after and willed into being. I don't bend observed reality to fit my personal narrative; rather I offer my memories and my experience in order to account for an anthropological and historical phenomenon, migration, that has, at least since the end of 19th century, marked the lives, the culture, and the mindset of communities from the region of Calabria, to which I belong.

My maternal grandfather had moved to New York for many years at the turn of the 19th and 20th centuries. He returned during the Fascist era and used his savings to renovate our home, to buy some farmland and, together with other *mericani*, started projects of renewal in his hometown. My mother reminded me daily of my grandfather's success which helped to alleviate the grief of my father's absence. For me and for many other children, for almost all of my schoolmates, the boundaries of our world extended way beyond the streets, the alleyways, and the countryside that were our playground. There was a faraway world, an imaginary and fantastic world to which I also belonged: Canada, the place to which my father had emigrated when I was eighteen months old, and from which I received dollar bills in coloured envelopes.

In the early 1950s the village had expanded, become undone at the seams, migrated elsewhere. *Ontario, College Street, Subways,* had become parts of its invisible landscape. We grew up with words like *waiting, return, absence.* Our individual identity was built on absences, on the shadow of the father, on the overwhelming presence of female figures, mothers and grandmothers who were of necessity fiercely protective. The village had become the shadow of its own projection abroad. Its identity was swept away by the legends, the dreams, the images that came from far away, and on which a new identity was being forged.

All of us children grew up with our mothers, our grandparents, our cousins, and our relatives. Our father was but a name and a face that came to us in our dreams. One day, when I was four years old, my mother opened an envelope, looked at me, and handed me a picture that my father had sent as confirmation of his recovery from some illness. I was looking at his face for the first time. When the itinerant photographer came to town, my mother would ask me to pose on the street, underneath a *pergola*. The pictures were meant for my father. It was through photography that we got to know and recognize each other; photography built relationships and connections, but it also marked our separation. The village had become uncoupled and attempted to recapture, through images, the shadow that had left it.

I gazed on my father's face, looking for likenesses and contrasts. It was like meeting a stranger whom I would eventually allow to become a family member. Some photographic collages from the period captured in a single frame the full meaning of emigration. Brothers and sisters, who had never met, found each other together as members of a new extended and fragmented family, in a single image hanging on the walls of homes on either side of the ocean. Photography and its many allusions gave rise to dreams and longings for reunification. Photographs were everywhere in the home: in frames, wedged in the doors of china cabinets, hanging on the walls, in black notebooks with red lines, scattered among souvenirs, resting next to the pictures of the dead and the figurines of the saints. Emigration had become the newly minted form of death of peasant communities already in disarray, but also the element of a new sacramental faith in new forms of community.

The meta-historical peasant family was composed of the living and the dead, and of the saints who protected it. Emigrants were the new dead. The rituals of the community redefined themselves as rituals of exorcism of emigration, the sudden death that had struck the community. During Sunday rituals dating from the 15th century, the congregation of the SS *Crocefisso* (*Most Sacred Crucifix*) prayed for its "absent brothers." The ritual remembrance of the dead is a cornerstone in the founding of confraternities and the guiding principle of its rituals. When, as a child, I overheard members of the congregation mention the absent brothers, I thought of my father, and of my friends at school and my playmates who, day in day out, departed, on invisible streets in the village, for Toronto. I remember the leave-takings, like wakes for the dead, remember the tears and embraces, the people and the things they carried squeezing into the car. And the houses that had sheltered dozens and dozens of people and children, now locked up, empty: forever and ever.

One evening at the beginning of October in 1962, I had gone to take my leave from Vincenzo, my best friend, my schoolmate and play-mate. The following day he would leave with his mother and his brothers. They were on their way to join their father, who had left with my own. I brought him a small bottle of perfume, a hair gel popular at the time, and my mother brought "parting presents" to his mother. A small crowd had gathered in sadness, as though at a funeral. We embraced, and made a promise not to lose track of one another. We didn't lose each other, but in a way we did. His house, with its plant-laden balcony, has remained locked since they left.

I wept that night, feeling that I had lost part of myself, of my body and soul. My mother, her hands on my boyish shoulders, guided me back home. It was her way of expressing her condolences. I must say, though, that I wasn't fully aware of the risk I was running. My life too could change drastically at any given moment. Almost everyone had left, but my situation wasn't the safest: Sooner or later, my father might come to take us away to Toronto.

He came back on an autumn morning. He was carrying a trench coat in his hands and he looked lost. My mother pushed us into each other's arms. I was eight years old and was meeting my father for the first time. I felt as if a father had been born to the child. We ended up not leaving. My mother came up with a thousand reasons, invented a thousand excuses, dusted off many arguments to convince him that now it was better for us to stay put. I got to know my father on his many return visits to our village. Together we would make the rounds, delivering packages and cigarettes that his friends in Toronto had sent as gifts to their relatives. The wife of my godfather Franco, Angela, received an American trunk, green with metallic borders, filled with clothes, candies, cigarettes, and *gingomme* (*chewing gum*). To this day I can still see my father's cartons of Camels on display in my parents' bedroom; cigarettes to be gifted to friends and relatives. When I was older and started to smoke, Camels were the measuring stick of my life. I examined the package, and drowned my memories in it.

Canada made its entry into our villages with these small things: dollar bills, photographs brought over by returning emigrants. In the summer, the houses that had remained locked up during the long winter opened their doors once again. Feast days became livelier and more beautiful. Autumn celebrations were moved back into the summer months. From the early 1960s ancient agricultural fairs had metamorphosed into festivals celebrating the return of emigrants. The names of those who had returned for the summer months as well as of those who had sent offerings were called out from the stage: Emigrants had become the protagonists of the many processions. Canada came to visit with the returning emigrants who, armed with their cameras and 8mm movie cameras, captured what was left of their villages: the rubble, the faces and rituals that they would carry back to Toronto.

One day, after many years, Vincenzo made a return visit. We'd kept in touch by letter throughout this time. He'd sent money, dollars, so that I could buy him a movie camera. I'd imagined him in his high school in Toronto, and later as a young French teacher in Manitoba. He had come to the village after a short stay in Dijon and in Siena. He could hardly wait to get back. It was an evening of the mid-1970s. He couldn't recognize anything; everything appeared smaller, every-thing had changed. From time to time he disappeared, and I would find him in front of his house, staring silently in deep thought, as though he expected some answer from the stones. Could this be the house in which he had lived, the house that he had, in effect, never left? He roamed through the countryside near the old family farm-house calling out loudly after his dog, Guerriero. He waited in vain for a barking reply. The dog had not waited for him. He took many pictures, as though he might reconstruct, once back in Toronto, what had happened to the village. He left after only two days. His world was elsewhere. He felt like a man who had lost his shadow.

The Double

The airplane made its slow descent over the houses of Toronto. It was necessary to have heard about them as a child to be overcome with deep emotion, even *pietas,* after imagining, for the longest time, the life of one's father and his friends in one of these houses. You feel immediately at home in these places that you thought were different, only to discover their familiarity. I have finally landed in the place of my village's expansion across the ocean, the place of a thousand imaginings. It's the 18th of January 1981. The official reason for my visit—a fictional pact I made with myself—is to produce a documentary on the life of Calabrian immigrants in Canada. But in reality I'm here on a personal journey of research into my own self and my roots; the emptiness that has been my companion since infancy has never been filled. My father is sick in my village but, aware of my departure, he asks me: "If you can find the time, please pay a visit to my landlord." I can't confess to him that this is the real reason for my journey, that, in essence, I'm undertaking a kind of reverse pilgrimage, that I'll be visiting the places that have deeply changed the life of the village, and my own life.

Vincenzo is waiting for me at the airport. Maybe he's already imagined my disorientation, my disappointment. Outside it's snowing, just as it did in the letters and stories of the immigrants. The small houses in Canada are just as I imagined them: low standing, coloured, each with its own garden, all lined up as though in waiting. Ciccio Bellissimo, a friend from long ago and from his many return visits, welcomes me into one of them. He'll be my guide in all my visits to Toronto, will take me on an exploration of the hidden city across the ocean, where I'll meet people I only know by name, and others I've never even heard of. Ciccio had come to Toronto to find and meet with all of the immigrants from our village. He failed to accomplish this task and remained in Canada. I meander about in places marked by the shards scattered by the catastrophic event that hit my village; they struggle against dispersion, in the vain hope to come together again, to form a new body.

I didn't live through the birth of this "second" village, but learned about it from the "first": heard about it in my father's stories, from friends who failed to return, from people I met for the first time in the village. For the pioneers, true heroic founding fathers, those first years in a world hostile to them had been especially hard. I know thousands of stories on the suffering, the hard struggles of immigrants from San Nicola. The new home was founded on sacred deeds and acts borrowed from the culture of origin.

In Toronto, during the 1960s and 1970s, immigrants from San Nicola established many community associations: the Association of the Most Sacred Crucifix, and of the Madonna of the Holy Rosary, the Committee for the feast of the patron saint, Saint Nicholas, and the San Nicola Club. After twenty years of immigrant life the *paesani*, the villagers of San Nicola, take stock of their new reality and begin to integrate in the new world. Their strong sense of belonging to their home town extends to embrace their Calabrian roots, their Italian background and their new Canadian identity.

They finally accept that their decision to emigrate was irreversible. A return to the homeland wasn't only impractical and disadvantageous, but also deep down not even hoped for or desirable. Women, who had discovered new freedoms and comforts denied to them back home, were the most reluctant to return; here they raise children who speak English and who have adopted a Canadian approach to life. Returning back home was tantamount to turning their back on the future, to wipe out the dreams and hopes that had accompanied them on their journey. Nostalgia for a lost world was more of a concern for the men, who had enjoyed some privileges in their hometown—entertainments, transgressions, merrymaking—while the women were mostly homebound.

The strong ties to the village begin to weaken, to fog up, to change. With the passing of time the immigrants begin to realize that their feast must be celebrated where they live, that it's futile to keep sending donations of money back to support rituals in which they can't participate, celebrated in a place from which they have been missing for years, and where they are frequently no longer recognized. In time they come to the conclusion, with a clarity tinged with regret, that their past is elsewhere, but their present is in Toronto. Their lives are balanced between the past and the future. Faith, worship, tradition, and religion, embody the places of memories, a landmark, a call to integrate into the new world, not to return to the past.

Their meeting place is the heart of Little Italy. The back-to-back occurrence of the feast of the Crucifix and the *Madonna del Rosario* is celebrated with a Mass at the church of Saint Agnes, corner of Grace and Dundas: the gathering centre and mythical founding place for the community of immigrants of that generation. In 1967, when the Church of Saint Agnes is reassigned to the Portuguese community, the Italian community moves from their old Little Italy to a new place of worship: the church of Saint Francis, on Grace Street, between Dundas and College, only one hundred metres north of Saint Agnes.

As the 1960s come to a close there is talk of founding a *Club San Nicola*. The club opens its doors on College Street in the early 1970s, but soon relocates in a newer area of the growing metropolis: first on Eglinton Avenue and eventually in Woodbridge. The Club has the full participation of several members of the two confraternities and organizes get-togethers of the *paesani*: dances, celebrations for the feasts of *San Martino, San Nicola*, the Carnival and the *ferragosto* (or mid-August) picnic. But it fails to become the sole organizer for the two principal festivities.

The *paesani* of Toronto have merely copied their hometown, with all its contrasts and duplicities. Their arguments will reveal, sooner or later, the existence of an ongoing conflict in the village, dating back to the end of the 18th century and springing from different religious affiliations that has marked for centuries all aspects of the life of the community: deep wounds, internal divisions, and irreconcilable conflicts in the political and administrative spheres. Political elections in the hometown are followed with interest, participation, and an intense involvement, as though their lives in the new world depended on them; or perhaps, imagining a return home, they were concerned about the joy and suffering of families left behind. The competition to organize the most lavish feast, with the largest fund raising efforts, was reproduced and renewed even in Toronto.

The Shadow

The "double" nature of the homeland is exported to the "double" of the hometown. Infighting, game playing on issues of closeness and distance, on separations and reconciliations, are amplified, redefined, and reorganized. Tradition, exported to different social contexts, becomes a new tradition, giving rise to paradoxical results. My impression, formed in the course of many trips, is that the ancient conflicts have made possible a new cohesion in the community, thus delaying its fragmentation. Infighting and competition, in the end, need a place in which to meet. In their meetings, often forced by their need to express their conflicts, they come together and forge a new city in Ontario: a new place that is an expansion, and a territorial dispersion of their hometown.

Toronto looks the same, spread out, extensive, elusive, with identical houses lining streets that look alike. Yet, slowly, each ethnic group has placed its seal, its mark. A Calabrian home is immediately recognizable, and with a more focussed and attentive glance so are the homes of my *paesani*. They stand out among the many houses belonging to immigrants from Friuli and Abruzzi, or the Greeks and the Portuguese. On the outside, the house of Vincenzo Sisi's parents is decorated with pictures of the saints from the hometown; on the inside it's a little altar on which images of the saints, of dead relatives, and living family members are strategically grouped together. The arrangement of the images tells us a great deal about how they perceive the link with the past, with the hometown, and with the new world. The attempt is to keep everything together, to lose nothing from the past, even though there is no wish to return, or from the present, of which they have grown fond.

Cicerello arrived here in the 1960s. He was a peasant and loved the open country. Before leaving he had the ends of the sleeves of his jacket sewn together creating a sort of nest in which he placed two small sparrows. On the ocean one of the birds found an opening and flew away, creating a pandemonium among the travellers. These days he travels from Toronto to the open sweep of country extending to the lakes and forest in the North. His destination is an Indian Reservation where he's made a great friend. Cicerello always brings him some wine, and in exchange he returns to his home with stuffed birds that he places in some form of display in the cellar. In a few months he'll remove the plastic that protects the fig tree from freezing, and will wait to see if once again this year there will be a recurrence of the miracle of figs. A son, born in his hometown, is a Member of Parliament for the Conservative Party.

People, stories, faces, glances. Everyone has a story to tell, and all stories point to a lost world. Their memories are tinged with nostalgia, with disappointment. I confine myself to stark images, brief flashes, abandoning myself to the care of photographic impressions. Saro Marchese, Vincenzo's brother, is a minister in the government of Ontario. He is a member of party of the left and was elected by the Calabrian community with strong support from the *paesani*. In his parents' house we watch him on television in a repeat broadcast of an interview. His father and mother are incredulous, moved, their gaze shifting constantly between the image of Saro on television and Saro sitting next to them.

Sara and Teresa left their hometown when they were very young, in the 1960s, together with their godmother Maddalena, a close friend of my mother's. Their father had been living in Toronto for some years and was waiting for them. Teresa didn't leave the house for months, and wept for two years dreaming of a return to the village. She's currently employed in a textile factory, along with a sister and many friends, and is unsure if she'll ever go back. Her mother welcomes me as she would her own son. I have a slight headache. *Comare* Maddalena asks for a bowl of water, pours a few drops of oil and performs an exorcism. "You had a bad case of the evil eye, my son," she says, with some concern, and adds: "Do you feel better now?" "I feel well, *comare* Maddalena. Don't worry about me," I answer.

The figurines of the Crucifix, of the Madonna, and other saints seem to stare at me from the furniture on which they have been placed. A kind and devout woman, the *comare* repeatedly reminds me to bring blessings and gratitude to my mother and grandmother for their generosity. Why don't I stay with them? It's an invitation that is proffered by all the *paesani*, even the ones I hardly know, who can't understand why I'm staying in a hotel.

Vincenzo Iozzo, a hairdresser, guitar player, and songwriter, has travelled with me from Italy. He helps the Canadian crew with the organization of the filming sequences. He had migrated to Canada when he was sixteen and in the 1970s he started on a series of return journeys to the village, which he found to be vibrant, alive, and filled with joy. He kept thinking of a permanent return. Initially he travelled back and forth from Toronto to the village, now he goes back and forth from the village.

Raffaele Iori lived across the street from me in San Nicola. He left the village in the 1950s. He owns the Café Brasilero, a favourite of people who want an excellent *panino* and a refined Italian *espresso* made with Brazilian coffee. His goatee gives him a look of wisdom. Streetcar drivers are fond of making a quick stop smack in the middle of College Street, while they rush in to calmly sip their coffee before returning to the vehicle waiting for them. As he goes about making coffee, Raffaele pokes fun at the Portuguese who have taken over Little Italy. The argument never changes: Italy has won the World Cup. Everyone talks about the victory of the Italian national team. Half a million people descended in downtown Toronto, in Little Italy, but also in the wealthier neighbourhoods to where many Italians have moved. After many years attempting to blend in while still feeling ghettoized, they re-discover the pride of belonging, thanks to the triumphs of Rossi and Cabrini.

Sooner or later, in each of the homes into which I'm invited, a photographic album of memories is opened up. Look at us in the village. Look at us here. Look at us celebrating the World Cup. Children and youngsters, who know nothing of Italy or the village, proudly show off their t-shirts featuring the colours of the Italian national team. The three colours of the Italian flag flap in the wind in front of every household. All of this makes me realize how large and dispersed the community of Italians is in this city. Often when I point my camera to take a picture, I have the impression that I am capturing images of San Nicola.

If the communities of Italian immigrants in Toronto can be thought of as the *doubles* of their hometowns, the backyard dedicated to the cultivation of cabbage, rapini, green beans, tomatoes, peppers, and eggplants resembles the vegetable garden back in the village. The cellar, a storehouse for salami, prosciuttos, cheese, olives, sauces, wine, assorted herbs, chilli peppers, and pickled vegetables, is the *double* of the *cantina* (perhaps never owned, but only dreamed of). The refrigerators and freezers overflowing with meats and fish, cheese, milk and eggs, are the contemporary *doubles* of antique marriage chests, and *credenzas* stocked with foodstuff, fruit and produce that you could only find in the homes of the wealthy.

All this can be read as a nostalgic reproduction of the world of origin, but that would be a mistake. Planting a fig tree in this country has another meaning. Meals cooked in the traditional style are a dream come true, something that was only a fantasy back in San Nicola. The availability of resources is very different, not to mention substantial contributions from other traditions. The attempt to re-introduce a tradition gives birth to a new tradition. Everything resembles the village, yet everything is different. In their efforts to preserve, immigrants become innovators; the more they try to safeguard their past, the more they leave it behind, as they integrate into the new world.

At the San Nicola Club they've prepared a welcome *festa* for me, as they do for every *paesano* of note, going as far as preparing *pasta e fagioli*. Bonserrato plays the mandolin, Mico and Lele sing. Pino Marchese tells stories from the village and of the *paesani* who live in Toronto. If Ciccio embodies the sad, nostalgic memory that leads to the future, Pino embodies the joyous memory that is nurtured by the past. Together they represent the soul of the community.

A growing angst has been snaking its way into the community of immigrants from San Nicola. The young, especially those born and raised in Canada, participate less and less in the life of the Club and the rituals and ceremonies of their fathers. This is the leitmotif of all the conversations I listened to in those years. Fioravanti, who makes frequent visits to the village, shows me his son's room: it's filled with recordings of rock music. One of these days he'll throw them in the garbage.

Writers and poets of Italian and Calabrian origin have been expressing the discomfort of the young, voicing their hatred and their love for their fathers, their feelings of being suspended between two worlds with no landmark in sight. Saro D'Agostino, who was born in San Nicola, has written beautiful poems in English on his difficult relationship with his father. I meet with Calabrian Canadian poets such as Antonino Mazza and Joseph Maviglia. I become their friend.

I photograph everything, not wishing to miss anything: gardens, trees, cars, skyscrapers, the tower, stores, picnics, festivals, funerals, weddings, faces, glances, characters. I had already photographed, with Salvatore Piermarini, faces and places of Calabria. Together with him I'll photograph Toronto again in 1990. My *paesani* want their stories told and made visible also through my lens and on television. They want to be seen in the village. It's their way of thinking they still belong even though they are aware that they'll never go back.

The few, mostly older, who have made the decision to return have already sent a photo of themselves to be set on the unfinished headstone of the tomb that's waiting for them in the cemetery. Their date and place of birth have already been engraved. Their date of death, to come as far into the future as possible, will complete it. Here, in the local cemetery, I find the names and photos of dead family members who are buried in the village. It's their way to move them here, to feel close to them, to banish the sense of separation. Joseph Roth once wrote that we belong in the place where our parents are buried. I take a photograph of my shadow as I walk to the house on Lisgar.

De Junca recenter inventis

It's the 3rd of July, 1994. The alarm rings, but it's still dark outside. We're to meet at dawn. In the large mall a noisy crowd in festive mode is gathered in the plaza. Ten buses, their drivers ready to go, are waiting for the passengers. Many people continue to arrive carrying luggage of various sizes filled with provisions and changes of clothing. The skyscrapers, the billboards, the licence plates, and a greeting here and there in English, remind me that I'm in Toronto, where half a million citizens of Italian origin make their home, as do fifty thousand Calabrians and, it seems, about eight thousand from San Nicola, if you count those born in the village and those born here. We're on our way to Midland, an hour away on the highway.

The low hanging luminous clouds, the trees in the large forests, the long and straight highways that accompany us on our journey into the lakes and forests of Northern Ontario, rise and fall, creating the illusion that we're entering an unchanging landscape. The monotonous repetitiveness of the landscape is broken by the appearance of two characteristic church steeples welcoming us into one of the most emblematic sites of the new world, the shrine commemorating the Holy Martyrs, better known as *Sainte-Marie-among-the-Hurons*.

The shrine, built in the 1920s by the English Province of the Jesuit fathers in Toronto, sits on the site of the Jesuit mission built by their French brethren in 1639, in the heart of lands belonging to the Wendat indigenous people, whom the French had called the Hurons, because of their unique hairstyle. At the beginning of the 17th century the Hurons numbered around thirty thousand and lived in some twenty villages. They enjoyed a reputation as fierce and able warriors, and dedicated themselves to the cultivation of corn, fishing and trade. The Jesuit Fathers and French colonialists chose the Hurons precisely because of their settled way of life and their commercial contacts with other indigenous nations.

The Hurons were in strong conflict with the Iroquois, a confederation of five nations, which included the Mohawks, who lived in what today is New York State. Between 1641 and 1650 the Hurons and the missionaries came under repeated attacks. Nine missionaries were tortured and killed; the Hurons, already suffering from epidemic ailments, were practically exterminated. The mission of Sainte-Marie was evacuated. The missionaries and the Christianized Hurons took refuge on Christian Island and founded a village that they called Sainte Marie II; later abandoning it when they relocated to Quebec.

A long and complex mental leap across space and time: from the woods of the region of Vibo to the prairies and forests of Ontario. At the time of the killing of the missionaries, San Nicola at Junca, a village resembling a Christmas nativity scene near the town of Vallelonga, reclines on a hillside from which the villagers look out to the Tyrrhenian and its coastline still ravaged by Turkish invaders. It's home to a noteworthy religious and cultural fervour for a small community of seven or eight hundred. In 1635 Gian Giacomo Martini, the abbot in charge of that community, and general vicar to the bishop of Mileto, publishes (thanks to two itinerant printers, Battista Russo and Domenico Iezzo) the volume *Consiliorum sive responsorum juris* ... the first book to be printed in what today we know as the provinces of Vibo Valentia and Catanzaro. It's a volume of *consilia,* legal arguments, and verdicts, containing a wealth of names, events, and anecdotes, which are fundamental for an understanding of the history and anthropology of the village and its neighbouring communities.

It's a sort of cultural "announcement" for a religious event that was to mark in a decisive way the life of the village down to our own day. On the first of June 1669, the confraternity of *the Most Holy Crucifix* is founded and canonically erected. The *Statutes,* a well-preserved manuscript dated 1680 consisting of 296 cards (24 chapters of rules, with a preface of 41 cards), was written by an anonymous author, a very erudite priest. It refers to visits to the two dioceses by the missionary fathers D. Orazio Rocca, canon of the cathedral of Miletus, and Fr. Pasquale Martirano, member of the Order of Minors.

The establishment of this and other confraternities falls within the on-going work of evangelization of peoples as promoted then by many dioceses in accordance with the dictates of the council of Trent and the Counter Reformation. At the time the village bore the denomination *Junca,* with probable reference to the reeds growing in swamps and marshlands; almost a metaphor for the inhabitants of the forests that the Jesuits, in the 16th century, propose to evangelize. They had found a primitive wilderness within their own world, and had no need for the newly discovered New World.

What brings together events and stories so distant and different from one another? In both places, in the "Indies over there" and "Indies over here"—Calabria and other communities in the south, as the Jesuit fathers have written and Ernesto de Martino reminds us—we witness a similar process of evangelization of people living in forests, who were thought to be primitive and savage. Mostly, though, it's my own memory that brings these separate places together as, on my way to Midland, I witness once again the feast of my infancy …

Although it was expected, the sudden sharp loud blast that would come at dawn and shake the air, my sleep, the cot and the heavens, would never cease to surprise me. I would get up and run to the window, just in time to see the black and white smoke that accompanied the large bang, followed by the discharge of firecrackers. From old Papa's house, I would watch the fireworks shoot up into the sky and explode with a deafening noise. It was September 1st: The fireworks, the large bell and the smaller bell rang out in the morning, announcing the feast of the Crucifix which was to take place on the fourth Sunday of the month. The shaking of the windows and the walls caused me some fear, but it was the announcement of the feast. I preferred to watch the fireworks up close, and for a few years my cousins and I would get up early to go to the chestnut groves—vegetable gardens with fruit trees—and hide behind the trees a few meters from the stoker, to see the flash of fire followed by the loud explosion of the firecrackers.

The anticipation of the feast lasted at least twenty days. September was very beautiful, tender, and sunny. The holidays never ended. The hours extended into days, and in the fields we could still find figs, sweet grapes, and red dates that we would eat in the square as we watched cowboys and Indians, sheriffs and bandits fight it out on a sheet stretched between two walls.

Waiting for the feast was the best: We started to gather information on the band, the singers, on the fireworks, and launched skirmishes with our friends in the confraternity of the Holy Rosary. The playful insults between the "red sheep" and the "white sheep" were part of our childhood games, our worldview and our sense of belonging.

The truck with the illuminations, the arches and the stage usually arrived at the start of the holiday week. Strong men with foreign accents unloaded boards of all shapes and colours with holes and joints, poles, strings, wires and bulbs which they transformed, with skill and patience, flying up the stairs and on the balconies or along the poles, into magical, beautiful constructions and fascinating scenery in which to perform shows and rituals. We counted the bulbs, watched the shape and colour of the arches. For the Feast of the Crucifix the arches stretched out to the curve at the house of the Papa and at times even further down. This was the area with a larger presence of *crocifissanti*.

For me and my cousins, the sense of belonging was demanding, requiring attention and devotion even in our games and entertainments. There was always someone lying in wait to remind us that we were the grandchildren of Vito Teti, one of the legendary figures of the confraternity, whose songs, prayers, stories, he had committed to memory and which he could recite in Latin.

The day of the procession finally arrived. The white cassock with the *mozzetta*, the red cape and white *cimbolo*, to wrap around the cassock, were waiting on the bed, washed and ironed by mom. I left the house with my cousins; we would dress up in the church.

As the procession made its rounds, with fast or slow paced turns, stops, and U-turns, the "young" led the way followed by the "old." I should also make a list of the orders "stop" and "proceed" shouted by older brothers bearing a staff in their hands, of the smells of sauces and frying that accompanied us all the way, the stops and "sprints," the jokes, the sweat and fatigue, the proud passage in front of houses, and the *cimbolo* with which we played by twisting it into knots to unravel: almost a preparation for our future life, that would be woven from twists and turns.

I remember the arrangement of the brothers, the processional order with the brothers closest to the crucifix and statues of the Madonna Addolorata, the double passage of the processional march in the Papa area, the money pinned to a large cloth, the dollars sent by the "Canadians," prayers and songs, and the ancient hymns sung by the women. The procession lasted not less than three hours and sometimes we marched with the anxiety that the weather could turn, as the brothers of the Rosario jokingly wished on us.

The long clouds hang low over Midland where the ritual benediction of the statues of the Crucifix and the *Addolorata* will take place. They've come in droves, on this hot and humid July morning, from different neighbourhoods in Toronto. They've also arrived in small groups and delegations from other Ontario locations, from Montreal, the United States, and Argentina. Many have come from their home towns in Calabria: a sort of pilgrimage into the future, a returning exodus with no scheduled return, to confirm a link between those who had left and their country of origin, and to attest that the identity of the village could be reconstituted elsewhere. The mayor of the village came, accompanied by the municipal secretary, the prior and the deputy-prior of the confraternity, a member of the village council in Rome, also a native of the village, and many others who had family in Toronto. I also arrived, together with my wife. I can't say if my presence here is as an expert in village history, as an ordinary member of the community of San Nicola, as the son of an immigrant, as an ethnographer, or out of simple curiosity as a *"crucifissante."*

The new foundation ritual, the search for a new centre, and the building of a sacred place were conceived and organized, patiently, over time. In the 1980s the *crocefissanti* founded the *Crucifix Association of Toronto*. In 1983 they made their first visit to Midland, where they organized a procession of brothers and sisters dressed as congregants, as in the village. The association gained growing visibility within the Calabrian and Italian communities. Following a proposal by a member of the congregation, it was decided that brothers from different Calabrian and Italian communities would take turns carrying the coffin of the Dead Christ, provided that they wore vestments, gown and cape, of the confraternity of the Crucifix of San Nicola.

This rite of passion becomes a sort of rite of sacralisation of Canadian places, assuming a function of expiation, where feelings of guilt and disappointment, of gratitude and hope, and communal strategies of suffering and rebirth can find expression. The Good Friday procession, attended by communities from many parts of Italy and other European and Catholic countries, brings together, through folkloric and traditional elements which have disappeared in the country of origin, many disparate processions.

This gathering assembles many cults belonging to disparate communities and fosters a communal sense of belonging to one group, of not coming from this or that place but from a place with a common history sharing similar stories of failures and successes and problems with adaptation and integration. The procession connects together the places of departure and arrival, of displacement and rebirth, of rebuilding and new fragmentations: a thousand small homelands, a thousand Little Italies, into a new homeland that is no longer their village or Italy nor the Canada they found on arrival. It's easy to understand the *crocefissanti*'s vaunting of their pride about the decisive and central presence of their association for the purpose of the organization, the development and the morphology of the ritual.

Wanting to enhance their visibility, in the early 1990s they developed a new project and commissioned a copy of the statue of the

Crucifix for permanent placement in Midland. The chosen artist created, in bronze, a larger reproduction of the wooden original (190 cm compared to the original 136 cm). A statue of the *Addolorata*, resembling as closely as possible that in their village, was also purchased. They began the process of placement.

On seeing this place, passengers emerge from the bus in a state of frenetic excitement. Those who are here for the first time wander about with curiosity among the green meadows, and the unmistakably Canadian vegetation, looking for the shrine, the statues, and the starting point of the *via crucis*. From the *Made in Italy* handbags and carrying cases they retrieve the *mozzetta*, the gown and *cimbolo*, and after donning their robes outdoors they start the procession, making the required stops along the stations of the *via crucis*, which has been meticulously prepared.

Brothers and sisters of the confraternity of the *Addolorata*, which is affiliated with that of the *Crocifisso*, wearing the blue cape and white gown, are lined up in two rows at the head of the procession and carry a reproduction of the banner of their brotherhood. Right behind them, led by the banner of their own confraternity, a faithful copy of the banner in the village, are about sixty brothers and sisters of the *Crocifisso*, men and women in their forties or older, with some young people and children who most certainly have never been to the village.

The procession ends with those in charge of the association, the Prior and the Vice-Prior who have come from the village, the mayor wearing his tricolour sash, and two parish priests. About five hundred faithful, moved and in deep thought, follow. Many of them are members of the confraternity of the *Rosario*. During the march, between stops, they chant the litany and traditional hymns in dialect and in Latin, which are part of the rich liturgical heritage of the congregation and the village. Some of them I hadn't heard in a very long time.

The band, one of many in Toronto formed by Italian-Canadian musicians, blasts out cheerful and familiar marches reminiscent of village feasts in the 1950s. As I gaze at the contrite and pained faces I'm reminded of the history of the foundation and establishment, in the 16th century, of the Confraternity, as told by the anonymous author of the Statutes. The Statutes of memory, of rules and regulations as remembered by the elders and by my grandfather.

"In the year of our good health 1669, in many places of this diocese, the reverend *Signor* Orazio Rocca D., Doctor of Canon Law in the cathedral of Miletus, and Rev. P. f. Pasquale Martorano from Tropea, of the reformed Order of Friars Minor, preached on penitence as the route for many to reach paradise. Like evangelizing prophets they carried out God's Will, who, pleased with their efforts, shortened the way to paradise for many souls. By means of Holy warnings, they reawakened and empowered the minds of people immersed in the deep slumber of Sin, and granted them, with the authority bestowed on then by the Supreme Pontiff, plenary Indulgence and Remission of all Sins. *San Nicola della Junca*, in the territory of Vallelonga, was part of this Divine Visit, though it distinguished itself from the latter by eternal testimonials of the cruel war waged in times gone by against Roggiero Guiscardo Count of Sicily. This had come to an end after many months with the destruction of that land, which had been an almost impregnable fortress, and with the terrible excommunication of the count, launched against him by Callisto II, supreme Pontiff, in action he undertook with his *camauro* and armed forces to defend the rights of Guglielmo of Calabria who, while he was in Constantinople at the court of Alessio Commeno Emperor of the East, had placed them under the protection of the Pope."

A war, a curse, repentance and the creation of a partnership in an atmosphere of religious renewal: The author is reporting live from the scene, as he is a participating witness to the birth of this partnership. In the presence of "Reverend Priests," who are engaged in the correction of the sins of "about eight hundred or more people who have turned up wearing penitential robes, each of whom presses forward with prayers, discipline, fasts, and tears of true contrition imploring the Divine Majesty for forgiveness of their sins, which they confess to these messengers of God, and from whom they receive the sacrament of the Eucharist, making a true and firm resolution in their minds to never sin again."

This resolution brings together tearful adults and children "who, crowned with Thorns taken from their Mothers' heads, marched along all the pathways, shouting out calls for Mercy, and sobbing and beating their breast with stones they carried in their hands." Don Orazio "wished not only to keep alive the fervour that had flared up in these people in the service of the Divine and the Virtue of Penance, but to increase it. On Saturday June 1st, after Compline, he gathered together the majority of people from the village in the Parish Church, distributed commemorative figurines of the saints to all, and founded with them this pious Congregation, so that they could continue to practice their devotional exercises even after his departure, and to ensure that the flame of their fervour could continue to grow in their hearts […]."

At the same time "he appointed, in the same place, appropriate officers for the maintenance of this practice and handed them a sheet of paper on which the Divine Statutes were written down, and read out loud to the eighty brothers who had signed up as members, and who unanimously and in *viva voce* accepted them spontaneously singing out the *Te Deum Laudamus*, as a sign joy at the founding of such a holy institution. Spiritual exercises began on the evening of the following Sunday and were presided over, to the consolation of the members of the congregation, by the Founder himself. The following day he was called back to his business in Miletus, but he left in the heart of each one an affectionate memory of his person and a sacred envy of his devotion."

Everything has already happened

The authors of the Statutes could hardly imagine that centuries after they drafted them, they would be remembered in a new ritual of foundation in another world, and that the *Te Deum Laudamus* would rise in the forests of Ontario, and that the Sunday ritual of the congregation, which had been taking place from that day onwards every Sunday in the village, would find a new itinerary in a faraway place.

In the village, the procession with its stops and turns had the effect of sacralising a place, identifying a centre, and ultimately uniting separate territories.

What is the meaning of this walk along foreign trails that have no connection with our personal history? What kind of centre can be established far away from our own places, not only from those of origin, but also from those in which we have landed—Little Italy—and those in which today people live and work, far from the areas where most of the *paesani* live? Perhaps, this itinerary, rather than affirming a setting of roots, points to a displacement, to a need for a new "settlement," once we have reached the conclusion that the village is far away, a shadow. Perhaps it's a way of pointing to and affirming a presence in the new world, informed by all that could be learned from the old, with an eye on what our fathers have given us and what they left behind.

The new itinerary unravels slowly and with restraint in front of the altar and the platform of the statues of the Crucifix and Our Lady of Sorrows, the first wrapped in and covered by a large red cloth, and the second by a purple mantle, the colours of the two brotherhoods. The brothers gather around the altar, which is presided over by two priests, and on the edges of the platform. The faithful fan out into the wide-open space. The mood becomes more sombre and solemn. Some members of the congregation deliver a wicker basket wrapped in a cloth to the vice-president of the association. When he lifts the cloth, two doves fly up into the sky, just as it has been taking place in the place of origin. The band starts to play. The faithful sing the *Te Deum* and other solemn hymns of the confraternity. These Latin voices, rising up to fly over the crowns of the maple trees of Ontario, are most beautiful. Someone pulls on the strings attached to the mantles covering the statues of the Crucifix with the Angels, and the statues of the Crucified with the Angels and of Our Lady of Sorrows finally rise in this Canadian sky.

Everything has already happened, Corrado Alvaro writes. Everything had probably happened by the time of departure. But for everything to be truly fulfilled, many years were still needed. It was necessary for the older generation to make room for the young as they came to maturity. Everything happened slowly. And, on a summer evening in the late 1980s, I and Ciccio Bellissimo—he had returned from Toronto, and I from Rome—had the feeling that the our village was closing down, disappearing. During the day we had gone to see the ruins of Rocca Angitola, where many of our ancestors would have come from in the second half of the 18th century. In the evening we set out on a tour of the village, as we did when we were young. We walked along the narrow streets and alleyways only to remember that "Giamba lived here, and our godmother Nuzza here, and our good friend Nicola here …" as we looked at those uninhabited houses. They had been closed forever, no one would come back to open them.

In the 1960s and 1970s the two localities, ours and the one in Ontario, across the ocean, had lived through an intense exchange of visits, and from time to time weddings: Canadians returned and many villagers left for Toronto. The identity of *first* village was marked by the rhythm of messages, images and money that came from its *double*. It was a period of mobility, of growth and expansion, and nothing seemed to foreshadow its end. Then, over time, the summer return visits, which filled the streets, the empty houses and piazzas and swelled the religious celebrations, became fewer and fewer. On their first visits, the children of immigrants, roamed about happy and free in the streets and the beach, but as they grew older they had no desire to come back, had no reason to revisit the same four small rooms, which had become more and more uncomfortable, and held no more memories.

As the older generation slowly disappeared, the faces of familiar migrants were seen less and less: The village, like many other villages in the interior, went through a period of depopulation and dispersal. The nearly five thousand inhabitants in 1951 had diminished to fifteen hundred in recent years, in contrast to the presence of over six thousand *sannicolesi* in Toronto. The impulse to change that emigration had given the *first* village had in some way vanished. When one of our elders dies, we no longer say: "Another one has left us" but: "Another house has been closed up."

This bitter and painful realization is now repeated as a refrain, a lament for a world that is vanishing. When an old person dies, it's not just the end of a story, but the extinction of a family, and often of the family name. Often, with the death of a person and the closing down of the house, a whole neighbourhood also dies, as streets are abandoned. The life and culture of the neighbourhood are over, for decades. The winter months deepen the feeling that the spaces in which traditions thrived are being wiped out, that the village is at risk of closing down. The birth of the *non-place*, in a village which in the past had been the ideal place, distinct in all its hidden corners and inhabited even in its lowest depths, is another paradoxical outcome of today's abandonment. The place that is closing down doesn't announce its closure, and its inhabitants don't always realize it. We're now in the "post-migration" era. The departures may not have ended, but the need to build a "double" has. The two villages are extinguished simultaneously.

We felt these feelings, Ciccio Bellissimo and I, on a summer evening.

Footnote

In June 2004 I returned to Toronto, wanting to see what had happened in the *double* of the village, and to satisfy my need to be there after so many years. Immigrants of a certain age are often overtaken by a desire to see the village one more time before they become too old. I had the same feeling when I thought of the village overseas. My old friends were waiting for me: the same old friends, only a few years older. But someone was missing: Raffaele, the owner of the Café Brasilero has passed on. And Pino Marchese, too, and with him his jokes and pranks. The immigration story of arrivals in Halifax carrying cardboard suitcases belongs to the past. Only the bonds remain.

Interlude

Sugnu de Santu Nicola e lu sapiti
De soprannomu Colacchiu su' chiamatu
Vorria mu' sacciu de chi paesi siti.
Vorria 'nu pocu mu su' rispettatu.
Iji mi rispundiru tutti uniti:
—Vu' 'nd'aviti sajimi e suppressati?
Ed io 'nci dissi: Fati chi boliti
La cascia è aperta mu vi 'nde pigghiati.
Mugghierama chi stava cota cota
E singa mi facia de 'na ripata.
—Citta, mugghjere mia, no' mu si vota
No' ni la jetta sciocca la trempata.
Poi nc'era unu cu' 'na scimitarra
Paria lu Cummissariu de la guerra
—Citta, Nunzia mia, ca si 'nci sgarra
Ni fa cadire cu' la faccia 'nterra.

I'm from San Nicola and you know it
And Colamacchiu is my nickname
I'd like to know your hometown's name
To know you show me some respect.
They all answered in a single voice
Do you have sausages and *soppressate*?

And I to them: do as you please
The chest is open as you see
From the corner where she sat quietly
My wife was signalling to me.
Oh my dear wife, don't let him see you
Keep still, or he'll beat you black and blue!
That one wielding his scimitar
Strutting like a wartime commissar
Quiet, my dear Nunzia, for if he looses it
He'll make sure our faces hit the dirt.

(*Chant from San Nicola when it was under French occupation, written by Colacchiu, Nicola Martino, peasant and improviser*)

Murat's Nets

In memory of Sandro Onofri

I CAN'T GET to sleep. This night is worse than the others. Damn bloodsucking flies! Extermination project. This is all made worse by the stifling heat of late summer, and wine drunk to excess with the few friends left in the village. The night time sounds rising from the open fields, from the nearby stream, from the streets, where someone is still loitering about, bring with them, in no specific order, memories of a lifetime. No matter how I rearrange events, or reorganize the past, I can't find valid reasons for staying awake, or for sleeping peacefully.

I lean over the balcony, listening to the sound of the fountain at the end of the road, and I wonder once again why I find myself in my parents' house, in an empty village, a ghost, increasingly different from the dynamic and confident village I knew in my youth that had somehow managed to entrap me into remaining. I think, smiling to myself, that my ancestors keep me awake to remind me that I have to stay here to guard and protect the house, to take care of my old and sick parents, and the village itself with all its empty houses.

I walk into the kitchen for a drink. From the small terrace overlooking the open country the familiar night landscape greets me: the lights of the villages of the Gulf of Santa Eufemia; the railway overpass on the Angitola valley; a bright stretch of sea; the yellow street lights at the Sant'Onofrio entrance to the highway; the satellite dish and the castle of Vibo Valentia; the villages of the Mesima valley and the plain, peacefully asleep with their lights on; the waters of the strait of Messina with the Ganzirri lighthouse.

I shift my focus to a landscape closer to me and, trying to orient myself, look to my right for the village cathedral and its bell tower. Far away, in the stillness of the night, I see the Big Dipper. I'm reminded of an episode from my childhood. It is night. I'm in my maternal grandparent's house, which is in the highest point in the village. My father is in Canada, but for me he is only a photograph and many letters with coloured edges. Suddenly, I wake up. I call my mother and grandmother, but I get no response. I think they may have gone to the nearby fields to water the vegetable garden at dawn before the arrival of the heat.

I'm not afraid, but I'm seized by a sense of loneliness and sadness. I open the front door, the morning breeze is pleasant. I look up in the direction of the vegetable gardens close to the houses, and I see the bright intense purplish light of a cluster of stars. A feeling of enchantment washes over me. I'm happy and return to bed to sleep but I can't wait to tell my grandmother and my mother of my night vision. I never tried to find the name of that constellation, preferring to remember those bright and magical stars, with no name or explanation. My grandmother then told me that they were the souls of our deceased, who had come to keep me company, to keep me from being afraid. Such visions were only granted to children who had been good.

It's seven o'clock and the church bell has called the faithful to morning Mass. It occurs to me that Bruce Springsteen's *The Promised Land* is a good tune to startle awake the children of my neighbours who, during the afternoon, when the heat and flies are raging, let loose with wild and noisy games, revelling, finally, in their month-long freedom after a year of imprisonment in the village school rooms.

I play the CD at a low volume, in full knowledge, of course, that in September, when the village will once again return to its sleepy emptiness and sadness and silence will take over, those who had complained that migrants returned to the village in the summer only to collect the pensions of their aging relatives, to eat our figs and *soppressate* and to cause our water to be rationed, will return to their familiar rants: "There's no one in this village, there's nothing to do, let's hope that the summer will come soon." And the migrants, who had complained that there is no water in the village, that there is no parking, that fruit is too expensive, and they can't find what they need, take their leave with tears on their faces, all the while thinking about their next trip.

When the nostalgia of those who have left and of those who have stayed will give rise to a sense of dread, I'll start to move away thinking of the village, or keep still, thinking of what is far away, unable to find a footing in any place, like people who have been caught up in witnessing the end of a world. I hear a knock on the door. "Just as I was ready to fall asleep," I tell myself. I look at my watch: It's already eight o'clock.

The airplane glides down gently over the Sila Mountains towards the Gulf of Lamezia, and makes a sort of pirouette out to sea before landing. Nunzio looks out to the still familiar landscape, even after so many departures and returns, although when he left the first time for Toronto, in the mid-1960s, the place where the airport is located was a vast swampy field. He steps down onto the tarmac with only a carry-on bag; his wife will send his suitcase in a few days. This time he decided to travel light, to avoid long line-ups at customs. He looks over at the crowd of welcoming migrants, and the families who have come with them, waiting to board the airplane from which he has just disembarked. Many of them are holding on, religiously, to a basket full of figs.

He walks by a row of yellow chairs towards the exit, buys a local newspaper, drinks a coffee at the bar next and makes his exit. He walks along the long stretch of road that leads from the airport to the train station, and soon finds himself in front of a large hotel and a car rental garage, where he rents a vehicle for a month. He can already hear the reprimands of his family and friends: "A rental car? Why, when mine was available?" He thinks back, with amusement, that in the past, with all his friends offering him a car, he had often remained without one. He takes the road towards the Serre. He drives by the artificial lake that had been built to irrigate the Lamezia plains, but had never been used for this purpose. Peasants and farmers had dug out wells in their own fields and found water in abundance, like everywhere else in Calabria. For Nunzio the lake has become a part of the natural landscape of his memory.

He had left for Canada, wanting to see the great exhibition in Montreal, intending to stay a few days before returning. He stopped in Toronto to visit with friends and family, wanting to get to know them all. He never made it to Montreal, and by the time he returned home five years had gone by. In the village he had been a driver with a trucking company, and soon found himself doing the same work abroad. When he first returned to the village, he had the feeling that he had never left, but soon he became aware that everything had changed, including himself. He felt displaced in the place of his birth. The young girl who had been his neighbour had matured into a beautiful young woman, with black hair and large wide-set, deep eyes, like the ones he had seen on a *madonna* in his elementary school textbook. He fell in love at first sight. He proposed marriage. They would go to Toronto for a few months to settle everything and then they would return to the village.

Nunzio and Teresa have lived in Toronto for thirty years and have three grown children who return from time to time to visit with their grandparents and to go to the beach, but would never consider leaving Canada. Nunzio retraces the course of his life, all the false starts. Maybe someone else had chosen for him—chance or fate, as the elders in the village might say. He had already come to a stretch in the road surrounded by small oak trees, a series of hairpin turns uphill known as the *votate di fascina*, due to a vague reference to the fascination that these twists and turns exerted on those who were born here. The sun, making its way from the nearby Ionian Sea had already reached Mount Pizzolo. Nunzio, who had reverted to look at nature, at the landscape and the passage of time with the eyes of his peasant past, guessed that it must be eight o'clock.

When he reached the top of the hill he nodded a greeting in the direction of the *Mater Domini* church, rising in the midst of ancient olive groves and trees a few hundred meters as the crow flies from the village nestled on the hills, its houses looking, as in his friend Vincenzo's song, very much like the dumplings in a plate of *pignolata*. How could such a small village expand and move all over the world? There's no city or place in the world where you can't find a native of this place, Nunzio thinks as he passes by the fountain that marks the entry into the village.

The few passers-by don't recognize him. The cemetery is already open. Nunzio, in a state of commotion, climbs down slowly the steps that lead down to the family tomb, where only a few months before his father had found his resting place. He reads his name and family name, the dates of birth and death, gently glides his hand over the cement and rests his gaze on the photograph. It's a picture from long ago, when his father was still young. Nunzio sees his own image in it. He wipes away a tear.

He's thirsty. He turns to Carlo, asking for a glass of water. The caretaker walks towards a small fountain at the entrance of the cemetery. Nunzio walks behind him past all the gravestones that flank the walkway; he recognizes most of the names and faces. On some there is a picture, with name and date of birth, but no date of death. The old villagers settle everything before they die; they're no longer certain that someone will do it for them, and don't wish to burden their busy faraway children and families. I knew them all when I was a child, Nunzio thinks, and many of them had already emigrated before they died.

He hadn't returned for his father's funeral; he wouldn't have made it in time. His father would live in his memory, his shoulders hunched by hard labour and illness, and with the good-natured smile from last summer. He is reminded that we all belong to the place where our parents are buried. And I'll be buried in some cemetery in Toronto, Nunzio thinks, and my children will belong even more strongly to Toronto. And I'll be a bridge between generations, between worlds far away from each other.

He reminds Carlo to please make sure that there will always be flowers and candles on his father's grave, walks out of the cemetery, gets into his car and drives into the village. The door into his house is ajar. He pushes it open slowly to make sure there's enough time to be seen. His sister, as though she was expecting him, rushes towards him with arms wide open. Nunzio caresses Maria's head and hair; she looks more and more like his mother. "Mother is upstairs," says Maria, anticipating her brother's question.

Overcome with emotion, he climbs the stairs. Sitting on a chair, holding a cup of coffee with milk, his mother looks at him, and seems to see a familiar face whose name she doesn't remember. "Hello, ma'! I'm back, you see. How are you?" The woman is startled. "How are you? You've come from far away? Have you seen my son, Nunzio? The poor boy is in Toronto, for work. He didn't come back when his father died. He must have suffered so much."

Nunzio and Maria look at each other, unsure whether to laugh or cry. They smile, as only two siblings complicit in the knowledge of lives broken and reunited can. Nunzio caresses his mother's face, who, if only for a moment, seems to recognize him and so she begins to tell him, in an ancient chant, about her past, listing facts and names, and events. Within minutes Nunzio and Maria have told each other the bare essentials. They'll need days to go over other matters, not so close to their own lives: village stories and stories from Canada, stories of relatives from there and from here, of who came to pay their respects for their bereavement and who is still to come, of who died and who's ill, who'll be getting married at the end of the summer, where to find a gift.

"I'll go to visit Stefano," Nunzio says.

"You don't have time! It's too early!" Maria replies, unconvinced.

"I'd rather see him before I meet so many other people. Otherwise it'll be more difficult to have time just for us, with a thousand other persons asking how I am, and how's work."

And he is out the door. On the road he walks at a brisk pace, so he won't be recognized. He isn't accustomed to hurrying, and his quick step reminds him of the story of a *paesano* who worked in the North, and who returned every summer to the village only to be asked the same questions over and over again, to which he replied with increasing tiredness. One year he returned early in the morning, said hello to his parents, left his luggage, went out and marched up and down the street leading from his house to the church, yelling out over and over again, without stopping: "I've arrived this morning; I'm well; I am leaving in a month's time right after the festivities." Nunzio smiles to himself, and climbs the stairs to his friend's house.

I ask: "Who is it?" as I open the door. Nunzio smiles at me saying: "*Ciao*," like we had just seen each other the evening before. "There you are?" I say with a smile as though we were playing a game of hide and seek and I just found him. We embrace, after two years. I look into the eyes of my *double* in Toronto, in an attempt to measure the passage of time on his face.

"You're looking good. How are things?" I say.

"It's all good, like always, this time a little sadder ... and you?" he asks me, looking for my eyes.

"I knew you were coming. Your sister had told me, but I wasn't sure of the date. Now that I think of it, just a while ago your arrival was announced by the Big Dipper."

He tells me: "I wanted to give you a head's up, but I didn't know if you'd be here. I didn't want you to change your plans for me, make you rush to the airport, and this time around I really wanted to come into the village on my own, say hello to my father ..." I keep quiet, not wanting to swell the emotion that has engulfed us. "Let's go for a walk, before I start losing, or maybe earning, time in the village," with the air of someone whose mind is made up as to where to go and what to do. "Let's go to Pizzo, so we can make up for lost some time in the Piazza."

"Ok," I reply. "Just give me time to take a shower while you look over recently published books on our region. I know you like them, but I have to read them as part of my work, and it's not always a pleasant exercise. The more isolated the villages become, the more we invent and write stories about their past. As more and more houses become vacant, the more we long after the good times of long ago, without doing anything to make sure that the houses, the streets and the village return to being lived in as they once were. We write books that no one reads and we feel good about our history."

The sun is high and burns our faces. Nunzio drives with the ease and calm of someone who knows these roads by memory. I've seen him drive his red truck with the same confidence, loaded with concrete, on the long roads of Canada, every time I've been for a visit to the places where my father had lived and in which I didn't grow up.

We exchange information on the two places to which we belong in different ways. I'm reminded of that time in Toronto when it took us five hours to cover the few kilometers from College Street to St. Clair. Every fifty meters or so Nunzio would stop: "Let's say hello to this person." "So-and-so is waiting for us." "That shopkeeper over there is the son of *paesani*." "That man wants to say hello, he was a friend of your father, he would be offended if he were to find out that you'd been here and hadn't gone to pay your respects."

I receive embraces from people I didn't know, inquiries from people I'd never seen, invitations from people I'd just met, kisses from people who remembered me as a child. "The village was born again, but different, from itself," I thought, while attempting to tell Nunzio that we should hurry on. It was eleven o'clock when we arrived at the dinner reception, where many *paesani* were waiting for us. We waited in front of the door, facing a metre of snow, chilled to the bone, but not worried. They were familiar with Nunzio's rhythms and were beginning to know mine as well. With Nunzio we'll always be late, but the places and people who know us, know how to wait for us.

We've reached the area known as Montemarello. I say to Nunzio: "Do you remember what we used to say about this place?"

"Sure. I heard those stories ten years before you did. Whoever could cross that stream bare foot, and reach that little hill with dry feet, would find a splendid treasure chest. I can't tell you how many have tried."

"And you?" I joke with him.

"I've made a thousand crossings over water for as many kilometers and I never got my feet wet, but I never found a treasure chest.

Something went wrong, other *paesani* made a fortune," he replies, a big smile on his face.

We're now under the Angitola bridge, driving underneath the railway with double tracks. Nunzio blows his horn to listen to it echo, as we did in the past, when we returned drunk from some nocturnal excursion on the beach. We take the *stradella*. The traffic is heavy with tourists and migrants on their way to the beach. The piazza in Pizzo, with its bars, chairs, and tables al fresco, is almost empty on summer mornings, tired from the rowdy crowds of the evening before. Here and there someone is browsing the morning papers, sipping a laced coffee or lemon *granita*. We sit at the Bar Ercole and order coffee and croissants. Wenders said he couldn't have lived without rock music; I certainly would have lived very badly without the piazza in Pizzo. Nunzio points to the castle, which overlooks the sea.

"Why don't you tell me the story of Murat's capture?" he asks, out of the blue, reminding me of a story I wrote long ago.

"I can tell you what I've read about it even though I don't even remember where. The king was well liked by people of the Kingdom, although the French were hated in these parts and were violently opposed by the people, who considered them, not without reason, as invaders. It was the early 19th century, the time of the terrible exploits of the brigand Vincenzo Moscato of Vazzano—known as Vizzarro—who lived for a long time in a cave and in the woods near our village, as we've heard thousands of times from our grandparents. The fortunes of Napoleon and his family were coming to an end—everything comes to an end, you see, even kings and their kingdoms—and Murat tried to regain the Kingdom, which was now in the hands of the Bourbons. He landed here with a group of supporters. He headed towards Monteleone, now Vibo, where he hoped to find additional support from the local garrison; instead he was violently attacked by his former enemies and old friends, who had switched sides, as often happens when the wheel of fortune turns. He was captured by a captain Trentacapilli while trying to swim to safety to the boat that was waiting for him offshore. He was trapped in fishing nets he had failed to see while fleeing to save his life. He was executed by a firing squad on October 13, 1815 and now the Castle bears his name."

Nunzio looks away and remarks, in a compassionate voice: "Maybe that was his destiny. Now I'll tell you a story, which has as a king as its protagonist. But let's order something first. What do you call that cocktail that was the favourite of our friend the film director who believed that time spent in a bar is never wasted?" I smile, and order two Negroni, of which Buñuel was so fond.

"So?" I remind Nunzio.

"When I lived in the village, I was one of the first young people to get a driver's license, and I was often offered driving jobs, something I ended up doing forever, under the illusion that I had managed to turn my life around. The town clerk at that time, a very good man in his forties, would call every week on Saturday afternoons asking me to drive him to Pizzo in his '600, which he couldn't handle so well. Everything was simpler then, more intimate, and people came from nearby villages only to shop or trade. We would arrive here in the piazza at sundown, and park right over there. 'Wait for me wherever you like,' he always said.

"I would go down to the balcony, from where you can gaze on the beautiful sea, the bay, the port of Vibo Marina and the coast that leads to Tropea. But I kept an eye on the comings and goings of the clerk: He would go to a newsstand at the entrance to the piazza, buy a newspaper he couldn't find in our village and then he would sit down at a café to read it while sipping his coffee. When he was done, he would leave his table and come towards me, lean on the balcony railing, look out to sea in a pensive mood, and ask me if I had anything I needed to do. I would shake my head. 'Now we can go back,' he would say.

"That trip has always remained a mystery for me. I thought that the clerk came here because he had an unrequited love, that he waited for someone who never came, that he wanted to see a secret son. I imagined all sorts of things. Now I know that he came here just to feel alive, just to put some distance between himself and the village. On the way back, up the hill full of twists and turns we would always end up behind a big truck. Even though we couldn't see the road ahead, I always pretended to overtake the truck, and he would take a firm grip of my wrist to make me slow down. 'Secretary: should we pass him?' 'Fuck! Don't you see what beasts we have in front of us?' he would reply. 'Should we stay back, then?' I'd say. 'Why not? What's the hurry?' I would smile to myself, but I sensed that he too was smiling."

"Nunzio, are you telling me of your slowness in school?"

"No," he answers. "I thought perhaps that if poor Murat had taken his time, he wouldn't have ended up trapped in fishing nets."

Clouds and Back Streets

"HOW CAN YOU still stand to stay in the village?" Mara asked Vittorino in full voice, in the middle of a long speech, full of pleasantries and half lies, of skirmishes and carefully chosen words, as happens to people after the end of a love affair who continue to be on good terms and even see each other from time to time. In villages like this one, relationships, good or bad, never really end.

He looked at her carefully, but without any surprise. Sooner or later, the inevitable questions arrive, punctual like a summer storms, or the feasts of the saints: "When did you come?" "How are you?" "When will you leave?" He was lying down on the bed in his room. The sun's rays flooded that side of the house with great intensity. The village—thought Vittorio—always questions about the village—how can I continue living in this village, what's happening in the village, nothing but the village seems to exist for her, and every time she returns it's the same ball-breaking routine, what are people talking about, why did you do this or that, who died, how can you live here, the town is emptying out more and more.

"You should have stayed here if you didn't wish the village to become an empty shell, and instead of talking to us about the world, the places in which you live, you come back to talk only about the village." Vittorio had wanted to offer this reply, but he simply said: "The village doesn't exist."

Mara fixed her black, fleeting eyes on him: She saw right through him. She was still beautiful, the woman with whom he had had an intense and long romance. He'd forgotten how and when their story had started and still couldn't understand when or how it ended.

"You're right," she said, after a long silence in which she searched for something intelligent to say, "the village isn't the same. Everything has changed, everything is different, I can't say in what way; maybe it's due to the fact that we've changed, we've gone away, nothing is the same as before, but I can't seem to stay away ..."

Vittorio cut short this ancient, monotonous litany that had become part of their ritualized summer meetings and which, after so many years since their story had ended, for no reason or many reasons, they still couldn't avoid. He had remained in the village, not sure whether through conscious choice or need, and this litany rang out to him like a declaration of war from which he could defend himself with all the artillery in his possession: irony, sarcasm, silence, indifference. He feigned an excessive sense of belonging to the village in order to put into difficulty, with such an unpredictable attack, all who thought they'd left the village behind them, simply because they'd moved to faraway places.

He was aware that he was making himself wretched, but it was the only way to create discomfort in all who had come looking for confirmation of their choices, and perhaps even of their failures. In the end, though, it felt like he was the one who'd gone away. Many who returned, though not all, seemed to be in the throes of torment, of being in prison.

"No," she replied, looking a bit distant but with some affection, "that's not what I meant to say ... I'm sorry, I don't think I can make myself understood today."

Mara stood up from the chair where she was sitting, approached the foot of the bed on which Vittorio had settled comfortably, and waited for him to continue the conversation. She urged him on with her gaze.

"It's not that the village isn't the same as before. I mean something different: It no longer exists for me and I no longer exist for the village. Don't worry, I understand very well your desire to find the village wherever you are, whatever you do, however, always. It's a drawback for all who have left. Those who've stayed have lost their village; those who left can never be free of it."

As he listened to himself talk in this way, he felt he was bringing to the surface forgotten heartaches, ancient resentments, traces of old battles in a war that they'd both lost. He detected aggressiveness in Mara's questions, in her gaze, perhaps the distance that she had never accepted. Full of sadness and detachment he said pointedly: "The village doesn't exist, it has never existed."

Mara smiled, moved closer to the bed, stroked his hair; she hadn't forgotten Vittorio's weakness for burying himself in the present, and resorted to her ancient ways to bring him back to the surface. Vittorio sat quietly, looked out towards the sun caressing the crowns of villages in the distance: in a short while he would dive into the sea. He realized that he'd exceeded the limits of Mara's tolerance. He sensed that the woman from his past was about to lose her patience, to put an end to the conversation with some banality, and he forestalled her.

"Come closer," he said, sitting down on the bed, resting one foot on the floor. "I'll make room for you." He felt the nearness of her, of the body that he loved so much.

He smiled, thinking: "Even Mara doesn't exist."

"Are you having fun playing the mysterious type or are you simply joking?" she asked.

Yeah, Vittorio thought to himself, when she doesn't understand I have no escape: I'm either playing at being mysterious or I'm simply a dumb ass.

"No," he said complacent, but with a hint of the sweetness of the good times, "I don't want to give you the run around. Do you see the great show out there, with the setting sun? Soon it'll cut across the clouds, hide in them for a while; then it'll cross over the mountains on the horizon and fall into the sea."

Mara listened, silent, tense. Vittorio went on: "See the dense and blond clouds that surround it, that hide it and reveal it? I feel like I'm their driver. I'm on top of the clouds; I leave and return. When I'm in the village I hide in the clouds. The village is no longer there because I'm not there anymore; I know how to become invisible, and appear whenever I want."

Mara looked at him, somewhat annoyed, which is what Vittorio had wanted. She became serious; she couldn't speak, as though she was remembering something or looking to be forgiven. Mara asked Vittorio to put on a record.

"Our first record," she said, almost chanting the words.

He didn't reply, and turned his gaze towards the church steeple. He looked on the rooftops and the narrow streets, and thought for a moment about the blue and gray clouds in winter. Many afternoons, when he rose from his desk, he stared at them with intensity and anxiety as we do when we're waiting for the return of a loved one. They hung so low and were so close that he wanted to caress them with his hand, to gather them and put them in his pocket. Sometimes he wanted to secure them to the ground as when, as a boy, he played with the cards of soccer players. He was tempted to fill the empty, dark streets, the deserted alleys and the abandoned houses with clouds. Other times he would hold on to them, lift them onto the rooftops, and raise them up high as if intending to build tall skyscrapers like those in Manhattan.

The notes of Springsteen's "New York City Serenade" reminded him of times gone by. He had first listened to it when he was a student in Rome, when only a handful of music lovers from overseas knew *The Boss*. He remembered, as though it had happened only yesterday, an evening at the home of his friend Salvatore, in the company of two girls he had met at the *Alessandrina* library where he studied in the afternoon.

That summer he returned to the village and brought back the LP, and he made everyone who came to visit listen to it, especially Mara, and just at the time when their story was coming to an end. Their lives were out of sync: He was in Rome, and she was still in the village. Now she would move to Bologna to study at the Faculty of Arts, Theatre and Music, while he would return to the village from where he would commute to Messina, where he'd been offered a term appointment to teach comparative literature at the University.

Vittorio listened in a daze to that sweet serenade of love to New York, to the stories that spoke of the innocence of youth, of their running wildly and aimlessly in the nights along Robert De Niro's and Martin Scorsese's *mean streets*. The "Serenade to New York" turned into a sorrowful serenade of love to the village, a tale of the sadness and longing of the young, of their desire to escape. It had become the soundtrack of frayed landscapes coming apart at the seams, of empty and abandoned houses, of closed and desolate neighbourhoods; a longing for life, just like the songs of leaving and separation had been for a generation of emigrants, who left dreaming to return only to end up building a new life far away from these lost and abandoned places.

Sometimes he thought that the world was becoming all the same, that, truly, the world had finally become a village, and the village, in spite of it all, a kind of world. That song accompanied the loneliness and the flights into the night of the youth in the Big Apple, but also the dreams of young people in a place whose inhabitants were fewer than those who lived in a single skyscraper of the American metropolis. When he travelled to New York or other cities, however, it became apparent to him that both those who stay and those who leave need to tell each other fables, and that the world isn't at all the same. The soul of the places where we live forms a part of our own soul. In the streets of New York he felt comfortable, serene, without a past and imagined that it was a place where he might be able to live. He stared at the faces of passers-by as if seeking his own happy double.

Mara walked over to Vittorio and fumbled for his hair. She rested her head on his shoulder, as if to say: "Something remains, it's not all over." They embraced as if to confirm that they hadn't disappeared, as had happened to the old village. Vittorio got up and went to the balcony, looking for the sun that had already set.

"Never mind, I beg you," he said with the tone of someone who is returning from a mysterious world. "It doesn't make much sense now.

Don't let me stay in the village, don't imagine me in a place outside of time where nothing happens. We're no longer who we once were, and even they didn't fare so well together. I don't want to think any more, I want to go far away, to fly up, like a child on his wooden horse, over that tuft of white and purple clouds, chasing after the sun to catch up to it near the sea just before it hides in the water and darkness falls."

The Stones of My Cousin Giò

*A stone that gathers no moss
Is washed away by the river*

—Proverb from San Nicola da Crissa

The village was behind us. Once past the last curve, the one known as *Pietra di Sale* (*Salt Rock*) Junca would disappear from his view, unless he turned back to look and risk crashing on the asphalt. As he negotiated all the curves Giò liked to play the game "now you see me now you don't" with the village as it came into view only to disappear again. At the crossroads, the turnoff to the left led to Vibo Valentia on the provincial road, while on the right the Via Regia (*The Royal Road*), so called in memory of a journey made on it by a Bourbon king, led to the Angitola, to Pizzo and the entrance to the highway. On one side the road would take him to the shop where he worked as an apprentice mechanic, while on the other side the road led to the sea, the beach and the summer.

Giò was torn between duty and pleasure, between work that would teach him a trade, and his friends who were waiting for him, beer in hand, at the beach. He was caught in a bind and juggled as best he could to choose the road that led to pleasure without feeling too much guilt. He'd already told his parents, in no uncertain terms, that school was his own fucking business, and he had no use for it. His mother and father knew very well that this child of theirs would find it difficult to graduate from school. In order not to add to their disappointment Giò promised that he would become the best in whatever field he chose to work.

He was still a teenager when he began to help his mother in the *cantina*, after his father could no longer manage, having lost one of his legs as a result of an infection that wasn't treated properly. It was a tragedy for the whole family. His father recovered but he refused to leave the house, not even to go to the *cantina* where he had practically spent his whole life. He was ashamed to be seen hobbling along with a stump.

He spent the rest of his life looking from the balcony onto the main street of the village. From there he could keep an eye on everything and learned all about the goings-on in the village. He was ironic, and couldn't refrain from scolding everyone, much to his wife's chagrin. The prime targets of his jokes were members of the *confraternita* and members of the opposition party, but he was so funny and polite that everyone loved him all the same.

His wife and children rolled up their sleeves and shouldered the burden of running the family business. In the morning Lina, the first-born daughter, set off on the mail bus service to the nearby town where she studied at the local Teacher's Training School, and after lunch she went to the *cantina* where she worked alongside her mother till late evening. Giò negotiated his way among the glasses, the drunks and the blasphemers. But the times were changing and the *cantina* was fast becoming a meeting place for students, and occasionally even women might show up. Giò looked and served, talked and served, and it was here that one day he noticed a girl, and from that day on he couldn't stop dreaming or talking about her. Even Vito, a few years younger than Giò, made himself useful by helping his mother and siblings in the *cantina*, always busy with two or three groups of card players, who would end each game with many rounds of wine, sodas and beers. Things were going quite well. Customers were plenty, and sales were good and dependable. Wine in winter, beer in summer.

Giò was pleased and found the whole thing amusing, and occasionally even played the wingman to the card players; but he wanted to travel, to see the world. He felt wasted in that place and, in any case, what would it mean to make it to the top here? He had a passion for cars. He could recognize engines even from a mile away. As soon as Vito managed to handle glasses, barrels and patrons on his own, Giò announced to his family that he was setting out to become the best mechanic in the world.

No sooner said than done. A mechanic who owned a shop in Vibo, where Vito often hung out with friends who were skipping school, took a liking to him. So began an apprenticeship that kept him always busy. His skills improved by the day and customers often returned to him. "At this rate," his friends would tell him, "you'll steal your master's craft and send him packing; he'll have no choice but to fire you." In the summer, however, he'd end up in crisis: He couldn't bring himself to be away from friends who had come from far away to be with him.

He managed to find a way to not feel guilty, to make his friends happy and to satisfy his desire for idleness, sun and sea. On a patch of straight road downhill near the junction, he would let go the handle bars of his *cinquanta*, and raise his hands smiling as if to say: "I trust in fate." His beloved motorcycle, which he had named *signorina*, just as the peasants called their cows "Bettina," gained speed down a pre-determined path that led straight to the sea. Giò laughed all the way on his wild, hands-free ride towards Santa Maria, then took the handlebars and negotiated with elegance the twists and turns, the double curves of the *Fascina* on his way to the sea.

One morning, an unforeseen event he had failed to take into account put a spanner in the works of his "trust in fate" gimmick. Just as he had let go of the handlebars and raised his hands to the sky, the front wheel of his *cinquanta* gained speed, went straight over a *petruja*, a tiny rock that had fallen from who knows where, sending the bike lurching and wobbling. To avoid a crash, Giò lowered his hands and gripped the handlebar, but in order to keep his balance he had to steer in the direction of Vibo.

And so he found himself dispatched, unaware of how or by whom, to the mechanic's shop. Giò, not wanting to go back on the deal he'd made with himself, didn't lose his composure, and accepted his fate. The master mechanic, who couldn't believe his eyes, greeted him with a puzzled smile, as if to say, why, what fair wind blows you this way, what an honour. Giò, with a wide and spontaneous laughter, greeted him: "Good morning *maestro* ... I came to work." But he thought to himself: "That shitty little rock."

The master mechanic gave him a grim look, but was happy to see him. "It's a miracle. Go figure! There's an engine of a Mercedes belonging to a migrant that needs be redone ... get to it!"

And so it came to pass that for a week Giò abandoned his friends and the sea, the beach and the *mortadella* sandwiches so he could give renewed life to that jalopy, a veritable wreck that would never run again were it not for him. Iozzo, Giò loved to refer to himself by his surname, had the skill to make new again cars that seemed destined for the scrap yard or the sheet metal and chassis cemetery just outside the village. Within a few days the owner of the Mercedes returned to the workshop and asked for Giò.

"Well done," he said, and handed him a ten thousand lire note, adding: "*Maestro*, you're wasted here. You belong in a big factory away from here. You'd make a lot of money."

Giò flashed a big smile and thanked him, and although in his heart he was thinking of his friends by the sea, for the first time began to weigh the possibility of emigrating.

Giò was only eighteen when, with *mastro* Pino, a close friend and relative who was older and had more experience, they opened a small garage together in the village. Customers who were in a hurry to have their car fixed would be told to take it easy. Almost to allay his own anxiety, he repeated to himself: "*Rigettati nu pocu*, take a rest, will you! There is always a *petruja* waiting to change your chosen path or your plans."

One day Giò, just for fun, told the story of the *petruja* to his good neighbour Peppe, a master mason, who knew stories, facts and anecdotes from all over the village and of all generations.

At the end of the story *mastro* Peppe said: "Excuse me for saying so, but you were just a dickhead. I forgot for a while that you are called Peppe, like me, and all who share this name are said to be dickheads. With real dicks! Don't you remember what the ancients used to say? There are three certified dickheads: those who smoke while going up-hill, because they tire quickly; those who urge their wife to eat, for she is already full from tasting and cooking; those who have a pebble in their shoe and don't remove it because they wish to avoid needless suffering."

Giò laughed. He liked to listen to *mastro* Peppe, who came from a family of storytellers and improvisers, and knew more stories than you can imagine. He turned to the *mastro*: "But the pebble wasn't in my shoe" and waited for the answer with that look of enchantment that his friends found so amusing and attractive.

"So? You should have been careful. You should have kept your eyes on the road so you could see the pebble, dismount and remove it," *mastro* Peppe said, in a tone halfway between comforting and mocking.

"If I have to move all the stones that are put in front of me … I'm done for," said Giò.

"Of course you must be careful. Why do you think our Lord turned stones into bread? Because he loved the stones; he never missed a single one; he gathered them all and turned them into small loaves of bread for poor people of good heart."

"I can never win one with you," Giò said. "The bike's ready; let's ride into town for another beer."

Giò had the gift of simplicity, or perhaps I should say, he was essential, concise. He couldn't speak well. He was tongue-tied, he stammered, and stuttered. He took forever to make himself under-stood, to come to the end of a complete sentence. He would break into a happy smile and wonder why, and seemingly take pleasure in the fact that his listeners had such a hard time grasping what he said. What for others might have been a real handicap he was able to turn into good fortune, into joyful laughter. In the village people are still talking about him.

One day he was talking about his fishing exploits at the river Fellà. "So, I threw the hook and caught a trout …" *Compare* Nicola was amused and listened attentively. "I threw the hook and caught a trout …" continued Giò.

Compare Nicola didn't miss a single word and waited for the ending, certain that the river couldn't yield more than one or two trout at best.

"I threw the hook and I caught a trout," Giò repeated, much like a broken record.

After a while, *compare* Nicola asked: "But in the end how many trout did you catch?"

Giò smiled, raised one finger in the air, and said in perfect Italian: "One trout." And broke into a loud laugh catching *compare* Nicola off balance, who was unsure whether to join in laughter or be angry.

Giò's simple nature became an art when he was face to face with car engines. He disassembled and re-assembled them with the same speed he resorted to when consuming a *mortadella* sandwich. At the end of each job he always said: "All done. This car won't break down any more."

One morning, a customer who came to pick up his repaired vehicle noticed that about a dozen pieces, including screws and bolts of different sizes, were left on the ground. The owner of the car took the keys that Giò handed over to him with a seraphic smile, but he managed to say: "Excuse me *maestro,* what about all those left over pieces? Did you not put them back?"

"Those," Giò said, looking in the direction of the pieces left on the ground, "are factory errors. The more pieces they put in, the more quickly the cars break down, and the more they are able to sell. That's how the big car factories make their money."

The owner of the car shifted his gaze from Giò's face to the pieces lying on the ground that seemed to say: "And what are we doing here?"

Giò knew he was in danger of losing a customer. "Look," he said, "you see that grocery shop at end of the road … How far do you make it? One hundred metres max? How long would it take you to go get a *mortadella* sandwich? Thirty seconds? Maximum, one minute. Well, if instead of walking straight to it, you step down this alley and then turn right and take other alleys that you come across until you come to the shop, do you know how long you'll take? At least an hour. And how long will you have walked? About a kilometer. Listen, we need to watch out for those who want to complicate our life, take us away from the straight and narrow, to get us to buy unnecessary things."

It took him ten minutes to make himself understood, but when the man, more confused than persuaded, sat behind the steering wheel and fired the engine, it eased into a beautiful spin.

"You see," Giò said, waving to his customer. "The car sounds so factory-new that you'll have to break it in." He waved proudly, while master mechanic Pino, who could hardly hold back his laughter, finally burst into a laugh so loud and long that he had to keep his sides and stomach muscles from hurting.

Master mechanic Pino's and Giò's shop quickly became a meeting place in the village, just as in the past barber salons and the shops of tailors and shoemakers had been for the poor people, while pharmacies catered to the social needs of the wealthy. Friends came and went. "Giò, will you take a look at my car's engine, change the oil, come and have a beer, tonight we'll go for a pizza." Over time Giò noticed that between customers who greeted saying: "I'll see you later," "I'll be back soon" and never paid, friends and family from whom he never took a single cent, the pizzas, beers or sandwiches that went around and which he shared with his uncle Graziano and his young apprentice several times a day, at the end of the month he couldn't even manage to pay the rent for his workshop.

If it weren't for the money made by his father's *cantina*, Giò could hardly scrape together enough money to pay for matches and cigarettes. He took it all calmly, but was working himself to death, and although he wasn't a slave to time, he would work at night and even on Sundays in the summer when it was necessary, even though, "*due di queste facevano mezza canna*" (two of these amount to a half-barrel) joining his thumb to his index finger, as if to say "*cca spachija*": You won't see a penny here, even if you shoot yourself.

One day he took his leave of everyone. He was moving to France, to Saint-Jean-De-Maurienne, to join a colony of fellow villagers, many of whom had been childhood friends. Those who believed they knew him well thought he would be back in a few months. Those who barely knew him wondered what someone who could hardly speak his own dialect could possibly do in France. Sure, he was a hard worker, a good person, an honest man, but how would he be able to manage in a foreign land, where he would have difficulty just buying his own groceries? His father, his mother and his sister took the news of his leaving as a joke.

If I remember correctly, it was 1973. After a period of hopes and returns, Junca was hit by a new wave of departures and flights, almost like in the 1950s. Emigrants and students would return for the summer and at Christmas, but the village was beginning to empty: a levelling out due to death and emigration.

Giò returned on time every summer. He embraced his relatives, arranged as quickly and as best he could his suitcase and duffel bag, and off to the *cantina*, to the bar in the *piazza* and then the sea. He never failed to pay a visit to my mother, his father's sister. He would hug me, smiling and with feeling, and always call me "cousin Vito." The degree of kinship was inseparable from the baptismal name, confirming a brotherly bond. He had a real sense of kinship and knew all horizontal and vertical ramifications. He'd learned from his father's family the art of recognizing and respecting all relations of kinship. He was a little younger than me, and we lived in neighbourhoods far away from each other. We were different and had embarked on different paths. But we loved each other, as happens between first cousins, who know that their parents love each other deeply. I still remember my mother's despair when Giò's father's leg was amputated, and her daily reminders to my sister and me to go visit our uncle.

I went willingly. I walked along streets familiar to me from my childhood. Uncle Michele's *cantina* was first opened for business by one of my great-grandfathers and had been inherited from my grandfather, "*the American*," the first of the family to be called Giò and who had made a fortune and bought some land and small farms. In the *cantina* I'd had a sort of initiation into life. My grandfather, who lived with us, would take me with him, and I stood by him, enraptured by the card games, and by patrons who drank up to five litres of wine. Even after I stopped going to the *cantina* I felt a sense of belonging to it, and was happy to know that the place of memories and life lived on, thanks to the efforts of my aunt and cousins. I've always had a poor tolerance for the closure of places, houses, relationships and friendships. Maybe that's why I'm never the one to bring closure, but all of this has no bearing on the story of my cousin Giò.

Even without knowledge of Italian, or a word of French, Giò had made his fortune, thanks to his way of being and doing things that made him an agreable figure.

After many work experiences, he'd found a steady job in a mechanics shop far away from Saint-Jean-de-Maurienne, on the border between France and Italy, for the construction of the Fréjus tunnel. He earned respect for his work ethic and know-how and after a few years he was invited to work in a large shop at the Centre for Nuclear Energy in Geneva. "I move about like a gypsy, but wherever I go, they love and respect me." When he returned, to the village, every time I ran into him he would speak, without affectation, but almost amazed and intimidated, of homes he'd bought and savings he'd put away in the bank.

The *paesani* who knew him, and who came back for the summer, spoke of the wonders of Giò, who was able to move about in his new world with the effortlessness of someone who had been born in it. He could talk to businessmen and bank managers, workshop supervisors and salespeople, French women and people from his own country. He kept, as it happens, close ties with the large community of *paesani*. His smile and his skill to make engines sing, to give them new life, had made him relatively well off. My aunt and my uncle, Lina and Vito, thought it no less than a miracle. Giò had made it. In their hearts they had expected it, even though they had lived with fear and trembling Giò's life journey far away from home.

One summer about ten years later Giò returned with Annie, who came originally from Cameroon. Later, their child Michel, Michele for us, joined them. At first his aunt and uncle looked upon him with suspicion, but soon accepted Annie as their daughter and doted on their nephew who kept the name of his grandfather, and his grandfather's grandfather, alive. Michel was growing up to be slender and beautiful. His dark complexion wasn't a novelty. The Calabrian Giò was darker than his Cameroonian partner, who was the quiet type and always followed with a smile her husband's endless storytelling. When Giò was busy translating for his wife and son, he was so amusing that those who knew him thought they were watching an ancient farce from the village.

Many summers passed without my meeting him. Sometimes he came back in winter, at Christmas. On a cold rainy day in December, he returned for his father's death. Uncle Michele was felled by a heart attack at four in the morning. He went quietly. During the funeral, Giò accompanied his father with reverence, and held on to his son Michel as though to protect him or to seek consolation for the loss of the older Michele. I think that was the time when he remarked: "Cousin, time flies for us. I would hate to return one day and not even find mother."

When we saw each other in calmer times he would talk to me, not about his life, but his plans. "Dear cousin, a few more years, some more sacrifices and I'll be back for good. We'll use the little house in the Rizzi area of the countryside, the one that belonged to our grandparents, and we'll build a wonderful meeting place, a great pizzeria. It'll be beautiful by the river; it's always warm and breezy. Just wait and see all the singing and drinking! Then in winter we'll harvest the olives. Not us; we'll hire others to do it. How beautiful! We got along well, with never an issue, and our families always loved one another. We can't let such a paradise go fallow."

Smiling and happy he talked of his plans for workshops, an addition to the bar, a job for Michel, who instead of going from Saint-Jean to Turin to see his team, *Juventus*, play soccer, he would go from Junca to Turin; he would fly there, which is more comfortable.

I listened and nodded amused. "Of course," I would say, "come back and we'll open a business together."

I knew he was serious, though short on details: He didn't know what he would do. But he was sure of one thing: He wanted to return to the village. Not because he wasn't doing well where he lived; on the contrary, he had friends and acquaintances who loved him. He wanted to come back because of a decision he took when he left, because he couldn't let go of this idea, and because he missed his mother and his siblings. When someone asked him how Annie and Michel would fare, he shook his shoulders and flashed his big smile. He indulged in exorcisms, playing a role for which he wasn't cut out: the patriarchal father. He was as soft as a loaf of bread, and tried to compensate by playing at being tough. And his woman? She would follow him and would fit in. And his son? He would come with him even if his mother were to stay in France.

"If they won't follow me, I'll tell them: 'My bags are packed. Whoever wants to can join me, but I'm going back.'" His mother cautioned him: "Think about it, what would you do here?" The misgivings she had felt when he left had turned into a foreboding and concern for his return. In her heart, Aunt Nuzza had been praying for his return, but didn't really believe in it; she had seen so many people leave and never return. And what would his wife and son who were born in another country and spoke a different language do? And how could Giò even think of translating?

"This time I'm coming back for good, dear cousin. I'm coming back. Forever. With my wife it's over. We don't get along anymore. We don't understand each other. It's not a question of words, but one of languages: we no longer agree on values, our characters are different. I'll tell my son to come with me. He may not want to, but over time he'll understand. I don't know what he'll do. She'll always be his mother.

"I'll be back, cousin, I'll set up a mechanics shop. So many people ask me: 'When are you coming back?' At first I thought that I would work so many years in France, put aside some money and then come back to the village to open a large shop, with a car wash, and body shop and lubrication facilities. *Mastro* Pino and my apprentices would come to work with me. Twenty years later. As you can see they have good memories of me. I'm sorry to leave France. It's been good to me, giving me my daily bread and much more, friends, my life, and houses I was able to buy. No matter, my lawyer will look after my affairs.

"At first I didn't understand a word of French, but fortunately I ended up working with people I could trust. Now, the only person who no longer has my confidence is the mother of my son. She looks only after her own affairs; I don't even know what she's planning but I think she's after the bar we opened and the houses we bought. All that I built belongs to Michel.

"I'll return, cousin. I'll make my poor sick mother happy. She's had such a sad life. And I'll make my sister and my brother happy as well. I'll build a brand new modern bar, and will fill it with customers just like the times of grandfather Peppe and my father's wine cellar—do you remember, cousin? All those blaspheming drunks, all the students who started drinking in that *cantina*! At the time there was great shame in this, but eventually more students than tradesmen and labourers became regulars.

"I'm not so sure it was a good idea to turn the *cantina* into a bar, but the time has come to fix it. I'll join in, cousin, and will feast my eyes on the girl I once loved when she walks by, the beautiful Maria, who never gave a damn about me. She came with you and your group, and I looked on, with envy, sometimes after a drink or two, I wanted to come and give you a piece of my mind, but she was smiling, she was too beautiful, and never really paid any attention to me. Oh sure, she laughed at my jokes, found me amusing, but never took me seriously. When I left I did think for a while that if I came back with a lot of money, and wearing an elegant suit, she might notice me.

"Then my life has changed: mines, tunnels, mountains, Saint-Jean, Fréjus, more tunnels, workplace fatalities, Geneva, backbreaking work, scrapes, machines, engines, bosses, loans, banks, investments and when I returned to the village I saw that she was engaged. Now she's married, but I like to look at her all the same. She has children, but for me she's still the love of my youth. Did she ever know this? It's better this way. The best girlfriend is the one who doesn't know about it. In your thoughts you can love anyone you want, how you want and when you want, and she doesn't even have to know about it. You can even make love to her. Come on, cousin: tell me it's good for me to come back. How can I continue living in a place, maybe even in the same house, where I lived with a woman I loved as a grown-up, and who now has chosen another life? I'll be back sooner than you can imagine."

Giò didn't tell me in one fell swoop about his desire to return. But when I think, with affection and concern, about his jokes, his smiling and sarcastic gaze, his stammered words, I get a sense of the pleasure that comes when one tells a family member about his intention to return to the village.

And Giò did return. Sooner than he had imagined, and for reasons vastly different than he had planned, only a month after his latest departure from the village. Twenty years after his first departure. I was entering Junca following one of my trips. I remember the fog and darkness, unusual for the month of September. The main street was full of people, with many small groups gathered in quiet conversation. Surprisingly, they spoke in lively but subdued tones. It was the kind of crowd reserved for big events such as rallies or celebrations. But it was also the crowd of tragedies, when the village is under a pall. I rolled down the window of my Renault 5. I approached my cousin Franco, who was then the village mayor.

"You haven't heard?" he asked. I looked on in alarm, imagining the worst. "There was a terrible accident in Saint-Jean. It seems that your cousin Giò is gravely injured."

I understood immediately. There was no need for further questions. Giò was dead. That very afternoon, Giò, lost in thought, had crashed his vehicle into a car coming from the opposite direction.

Nothing could be done.

The fresh air in mid-September felt like frost. Words vaporized into thin air. I stepped down like a zombie. I noticed Giò's brother Vito across the road: a shadow in search of a body. He danced in pain, crying like a baby. Words were useless. He was getting ready to board the train. Who'll tell Aunt Nuzza? I made my way home on foot. I greeted my mother, pretending nothing had happened. Then, the painful and familiar game of small exploratory lies with my mother. There has been an accident. Where? In France. Is someone dead? No, but there are serious injuries. *Paesani* or relatives? No one died, but Giò is seriously injured. We hope it's not serious. We're waiting for news. My mother knew right away. Her sustained weeping and despair left no room for lies.

He would no longer come to visit her, her dear one, the unfortunate son of her brother. He would no longer call out: Aunt Caterina. He would no longer bring along his brother's nephew.

"My Michele, my own Michele," she called out to the dead brother. "You were unable to look after your own Giuseppe." And she wept. I would live again through this same scene with Aunt Nuzza: two days of tears, silences, lies, utterances, heartbreaking comments, of visits, of questions, of despair, of "we must go forward, we must think of those who remain."

Giò's body arrived on Sunday, a day on which funerals couldn't take place. It was placed in the church near the junction that led to Vibo or to the sea. Many friends, relatives, and apprentices came to the wake, making sure he was never alone. The longest funeral in my memory took place the following day. People came and went from Giò's house. Uncle Antonio, my mother's brother and also of Giò's father, was absorbed in his grief, thinking that this is life and that "blessed are those who have faith and believe in miracles."

He'd been living in Rome for almost fifty years, after many years in America and Africa. He'd worked in the post office and now, in retirement, remained in the village three or four months in summer and fall. He was the keeper of the flame of kinship. Every time he came back, he'd visit everyday with my mother and with his uncle Michele. But this wasn't enough for him. He would send his two children, and then his nephews, and then us, his sister's children, to visit his housebound brother. He accepted condolences in silence, occasionally standing up to take a break from the women's litany of bad dreams, of strange premonitions, the saints in heaven, and of the Lord who loves us and calls us to him.

Maternal cousins, who had been raised in the same home with Giò, alternated deep despair with pleasant memories. They embraced their aunt, who saw this as a wake-up call, and sat composed with the attitude of someone who is waiting for her own death, thinking that to live even a second longer than her dead son is an injustice and a form of needless suffering.

Santo, Giò's brother-in-law, answered the phone, took care of the documents, and summoned the masons for the burial. From time to time he stood up, walked over to the next room and, unseen by his sons, he would dry his tears.

Giò's friends came, and his buddies from the beach and from the *cantina*. They wept in silence. Someone murmured in a clipped phrase: "It's not fair … he was the best." Someone brought up his bad luck in recent times, the suffering caused by the break-up of his family, the shattering of the dreams of his childhood. Mothers and sisters of those who had died young came to weep and keen even as they thought of their own loss. Giò's mother and sister clung to them, looking for some explanation or comfort, or simply for some sign of what their future held, what would become of them or how they might survive. Giò's friends sent coffee and croissants, fruits and juices, from the local bar. Relatives prepared soup with mini meatballs. Aunt Nuzza wouldn't touch anything. "I have my own food … I'll eat what fate has provided for me."

The brothers of the congregation of the crucifix, wearing their red capes, came in large numbers. The funeral procession moved quickly and silently. I was a cousin and so I took my place in the receiving line for condolences, and extended my hand. It wasn't my first time: I'd lost another cousin and uncles and aunts. I shook hands firmly and replied with warmth to the embrace of those of those who knew me. I studied the faces of all who came seeing in them an older version of myself. I did a rough list of absentees and also of those who seemed strangers. A funeral always strikes a balance: It's a list of losses, an inventory and a roll call, but also a time of good intentions and well intentioned promises that will be forgotten in a few days.

Aunt Nuzza continued her lament: "I should have died in your place, I'm the old one, my son ... you were young and a hard worker ... you made so many sacrifices. What cruel fate! Did your father come to gather you when you were dying, to console you? What went though your mind before you died? Your fate lay waiting for you, my beautiful young son."

Mastro Mico, who was standing beside me, said: "*Lu malu passu è duve cadi* (one wrong step and we're done for). No one knows in advance his or her own destiny. Maybe we should have left too; maybe we would have made a fortune, or we'd be back in a closed coffin like poor Giò."

Lina, who'd married in a neighbouring village where she was a teacher in a nursery school, couldn't stop wailing. She looked with loving care at her two children, Marica and Giuseppe, and repeated that Our Lady of the Rosary, to whom she was particularly devoted, hadn't protected her brother, had failed to look after him. "You were distracted, my beautiful Lady, forgive me, but I don't know what to think."

Vito felt a sharp pain in his heart, and sobbed, pulling his shoulders tightly together as if to soften the devastating grief and to protect himself from some other misfortune. He understood that sad and hard days were waiting for him. This grief would never end, not for him, nor his family.

Annie came, silently, holding on to a friend's arm. She and Michel had presided over her husband's funeral service in France. A friend who came with her was supporting her by the arm. She made an appearance, like a ghost, and like a ghost she disappeared. Many thought she had been an apparition, while others said that it hadn't been her. The fifteen-year-old Michel did not come to the village.

Someone said: "Children belong to their mother." Another: "People belong to the places where they were born and raised."

Aunt Nuzza wailed: "My son, my son, how will your own Michele grow up? An orphan, my son, that is our misfortune. Had you come, Michele, I would have been able to see my son one more time. What bitter life! We're born, we suffer and die. And your father died young, while I have to live on, old and sick and of no use to anyone."

Someone whispered: "The son will be all right; he'll grow up like everyone else. We all managed to grow up when there was no bread, without mother and father. Surely they won't have any difficulty growing up now. The worst is when someone dies."

"Sometimes it's worse for those who go on living," said someone who was holding on to some personal suffering.

"Only one second, one moment," repeated Lina, looking intently into space as though she could still change the turn of events. "He could have stopped for coffee with friends he had gone to see? He could've stopped at the bar as he'd done so often? A second, only one second. An instant."

"It was his fate," many replied.

"His hour had come," a woman in tears said. "No one knows when his hour will come. But that was his hour."

Giò was well known through the many stories, anecdotes and "legends" that were told about him. When a person disappears, especially one that embodies the spirit of a place, a kind of granite-strong collective memory forms around his absence to ensure that he won't be forgotten, that his memory will live on. We make a clear and tacit pact with the dead that what has happened won't be forgotten. In this way we manage to soften the sense of guilt that inevitably comes over us when a young person dies. We resolve the meaninglessness of the loss by committing to forms of social obligation. As time marches on, inevitably, we rightfully tend to forget. Once a couple of decades have gone by, only a few older people will still remember. Suffering will remain for only a few people, mostly in the family.

My cousin Giò hadn't had the time to go to school, and there was no way he could even be made to hold a book in his hand. And, as we all know, you can't get blood from a stone. Once, someone explained to him that one day he would need a piece of paper and that he should consider getting a high school diploma, as many were doing. No one would deny him a piece of paper. Mazzé, a teacher who was married to one of Giò's cousins, took on the huge responsibility of trying to convince him to take the exams for a high school diploma. He was extremely patient in explaining principles of geography and history. Italian was a lost cause from the start, though he did assign some exercises to him.

On a hot summer day, the teacher asked Giò to write how he had spent the *ferragosto* holiday. You must write down everything, but everything that happened to you. My cousin Giò took it in stride and wrote for a long time. He filled many pages, describing almost in real time what had happened to him. His dialect became a kind anthology of jokes and stories of the village. He made a list of all the quarrels he had seen in his father's *cantina*, then of those in the neighbourhood, and gave an account of the festivities on the vigil, with all the drinks, the lording over the stew, and the all-nighters in the barracks while the women were praying and singing in church.

He lingered in particular, with a wealth of amusing details, on *Don* Lando Lupino who, in a fit of drunkenness, started slapping his lover Mela only to receive a thorough beating himself. He gave an account of a sultry summer evening when some daredevil street kids emptied, through a window that had been left open because of the heat, bags of cold water on two lovers who were in the throes of make-up sex after a quarrel.

He wrote about the interminable auction to win the right to carry the statue of the Madonna, of the procession through the olive groves, about the litanies performed by the faithful and by the band, and the singing and playing. Then he wrote of his return journey on foot from the church of Mater Domini to the village. He spoke of the never-ending sultry heat, in spite of the evening breeze, the coolness he felt near the *abate* bridge, and named all the people who were travelling in either direction by car. He had a joke for everyone, and he remembered everyone's stories, not forgetting to mention those who had greeted him, those who had pretended not to see him, and those who had, in reality, not seen him. He wrote more than ten pages, in an invented dialect that the teacher found befuddling.

At the end of his assignment Giò addressed the teacher saying that once he arrived at the *cona* (icon) of San Nicola, he felt tired: "Still hot it was, Oh mother of mine it still hot was, my master teacher. I stuck my head over the bridge to catch a bit of coolness. Nah! The crickets were singing and I laughed with happiness. Then a toad and a frog began their *cri, cri, cri, cri*. Look at that, I said! I found a rock on the ground, picked it up and threw it in the water. The water broke into circles making the sound of waves that got larger and larger until they stopped. Look at the fucking toad, I thought. Couldn't he find another fucking place. This will bring me bad luck.

"I thought of the stories of the ancients and broke into laughter. So, as I was on foot, I started hitching for a ride. Nah. Everyone was running about in a hurry like a bunch of crazies. A curse on all who hurry by! They went by straight as lightning. Then finally, I noticed your car, master teacher. The Fiat 600 that was going as fast as a donkey. I'm off the hook, I thought, the teacher will pick me up. I made a sign in your direction. Nah! You were marching along straight ahead and didn't even see me. You, master teacher—a stone! Unmovable. Stubborn as fate, that doesn't look anyone in the eye or take pity on anyone, you marched on straight ahead."

The Emperor's Funeral

*Farces didn't spare anyone. Gentlemen didn't
show any hostility to the masks and collaborated with
them even though they understood very well that the farce
was directed at them. In front of their round bellies and
ruddy faces, other emaciated faces, haggard and yellow in
complexion showed their hunger and misery.*

—Turi, 1994

Turi

Pardiu, no 'on' cchiù eu,
No 'Sugnu Turi,
Su' Mo General de l'Imperaturi.

By God, I am no longer myself
No longer Turi now
I am the general of the emperor.

TWO SMALL FADED and blurred photographs, taken by an "American" who'd returned to the village with a camera, show Turi on the highest step of the monument to the fallen. He's dressed up as a general, with a garland of flowers and sausages, getting ready to meet the Carnival King. A large crowd, some wearing masks, with many well-dressed women and children, celebrate and

157

beseech the general. "Once I took off my costume as Turi, I returned to my role as an important citizen who recited the funeral eulogy." This was the story told by Turi de Magurillu, aka Salvatore d'Eraclea, of his memory of the last great carnival in 1952.

The carnival procession of masked citizens and *farceurs* made their entrances in the piazzas and the streets with these words:

> *Largu, Largu de 'sta chiazza,*
> *Ni volimu accomodà,*
> *L'allegria e la cuntentizza*
> *La portamu a Carnevà.*

> *Away, away from this square*
> *Make place for joy and good cheer*
> *The Carnival is here.*

In a written statement, Turi emphasizes the practical and concrete reasons underlying the irrepressible passion for masquerade and celebrations at carnival time:

"I remember that when I was still a boy, tattered and eternally hungry, with the Carnival approaching, I felt within me an indescribable joy not only because I loved the masks so much, but mostly because during the festivities that took place on the four Sundays leading up to the Carnival, I could at last, thanks to good-hearted friends, gorge on meat, meatballs and lots of macaroni, drenched in pork meat sauce with lots of cheese on top.

"This manna from heaven lasted for the whole month of February, the time when pigs were slaughtered, which coincided with the carnival festivities. Farces started on the first Sunday in February. The first one was dedicated to friendship; the second to *cumpari* (good neighbours); the third to kinship; and the last one to him, the Supreme Carnival. As the first Sunday approached the people began to breathe an air of celebration. In fact, even before the crack of dawn, the first masks, to the sound of a fanfare, made their way through the village streets announcing the good news.

"A very close relationship existed between feasting and feeding. Although the wealthy families of the village had never in actual fact neglected the poorer families, especially the old and the children, at carnival time they lavished greater generosity on them. What the hell! They would go on and on saying. It's Carnival and it should be a feast for all! But, due to the never-ending unemployment that is a curse on the people of the South, the poor were many, and sadly, every morning you had to witness the humiliating spectacle of older villagers and children roaming around the houses of the wealthy to receive a penny or two and a loaf bread.

"The Carnival explodes like a bomb of enthusiasm and mad joy. The masks run about the roads and alleyways and in many homes women and men are invited to work on the slaughtered pigs, making sausages until evening when they leave to return to their own homes carrying with them God's bounty: a generous cut of fresh meat, pork rinds, *'polponi'* (parboiled bones with meat on them) and *'sanguinaccia'* (blood sausage) still hot and steaming."

Farceurs and Improvisers

In my youth, the village was known as a place of contrasts between the *crucifissanti* and the *rosarianti*, or as the village of the *farceurs*. The first "snapshot" went back at least to the end of the 18th century and referred to the contrasts and conflicts between brotherhoods that have marked the religious, economic, and social history of the community, thereby determining the mentality, the culture, and the sense of belonging of the people. In local parlance, the other image, *farsari di San Nicola* (*farceurs* of San Nicola), referred to a joyful, happy and clever people, with the gift of the gab in writing, improvising and inventing, but also in oral versification.

To foreigners *farsari* translated into a kind of insult denoting people lacking in seriousness, unconventional, unreliable people. Often the villagers of San Nicola assumed this negative stereotype, calling themselves *farsari* to refer to that lack of seriousness, or that kind of inability to take things seriously. Foreigners generally appreciated the cheerful and lively spirit of the villagers and made a point of coming to the village for the Carnival, to participate in the farces, to organize eating and drinking sprees, and serenades with my welcoming fellow villagers.

The second image, in short, denoted a well-established tradition of authors and performers of farces and of 'mprovvisaturi' (improvisers) of verses, that showcased their know-how, their art, and their creativity, on the occasion of parties, weddings, and above all during Carnival. 'Mprovvisaturi often had a negative connotation, referring to a teller of tall tales, someone given to playing tricks, someone who, in fact, "improvised" his way.

The two images, the true and the stereotyped, give the sense of a kind of double soul (in reference to an identity that is ambiguous and fluid, contradictory) of the inhabitants of the past. On the one hand there is a certain penchant for "conflict," a tendency to exasperate divisions; on the other hand a joyful and *carnivalesque* attitude that somehow balanced out the tragic and mournful aspects of the social and religious affairs of the community. The tradition of 'mprovvisaturi, of authors in rhymed or in free verse linked to the daily life of the community or to exceptional events, is documented and dates back to the second half of the 18th century, although many clues would justify moving the date further back. Verses, shards, fragments have been miraculously preserved thanks to the oral transmission of more than two centuries.

In the house in the Papa neighbourhood I grew up listening to the stories and verses of Pappu Colacchiu, Nicola Martino, my ancestor, who, at the time of the French invasion and the terrible repression carried out against bandits and civilians, became famous for the verses with which he attacked the invaders. To the French troops, who wanted to rape all the women and pillage the village, stealing all the food from small and large owners alike, Colacchiu responds with great courage and calls for respect and proper treatment: a proud and dignified claim of belonging—"*Sugnu de Santu Nicola*" (I am from San Nicola)—but also a strategy of entrapment of the invaders.

In fact he had hidden his wife's very fine charcuterie in a secret place in the garden, and the urgent request of *soppressate* by French soldiers is met with an invitation to serve themselves in the trunk that's in front of them, while giving his wife a warning sign not to give herself away. In the 1960s a local folk band, "I Crissi," took up his verses, set them to music and turned them into a kind of anthem, a song of protest and rebellion. The song became part of the local neo-folkloric scene and finds a new life in political-administrative skirmishes, but also in serenades, on ceremonial occasions such as weddings, christenings, birthdays: a universe open to the circulation of ideas and goals, to the dialogue between high culture and the culture of "the people," to the transference, translation, and shift from the oral tradition to writing, to singing, to the stage.

A remarkable flowering of oral texts (songs, proverbs, "stories") occurred as the 19th gives way to the 20th century, during the great emigration. It's a time that gave rise to songs devoted to cursing Christopher Columbus, who was held responsible for the "ruin" of villages, and in which a malediction is invoked on Naples, the port from which emigrants boarded ships that took them away. With a touch of irony, the songs point out the many changes introduced by emigrants, the dissolution of families, but also the many innovations introduced by the Americans.

Farsari and *'mprovvisaturi* were, after all, held up as, and considered themselves to be, the guardians of social order and traditional values. They were feared because they could speak truth to power; often resorting to metaphors to unmask hidden facts, to censor the "immoral" behaviour of the people, and issue troubling judgments. Even in the 1950s and until the 1970s, the last *farsari*, as was true in grandfather Colacchiu's time, warned those who teased or bullied them: "Be careful and try to be good; otherwise I'll put you in a story."

Improvisers (*'mprovvisaturi*) enjoyed respect, freedom and the power to reveal in song all that was usually hidden or said in secret; and they had the authority that came with being part of the dispossessed, of enjoying little "economic fortune." They led decorous, though not miserable lives: Versifying didn't yield much in the manner of bread.

My friend Mico Tallarico recalls the proverb: "*Poeti, 'mprosaturi e pittasanti / Sempe moriru poveri pezzenti.*" (Poets, improvisers and church painters, always died as ragged tramps.) The poets, the authors of stories and verses, the painters, the sculptors, the local artists who built or painted the statues of the saints for the churches would all end up beggars. *Mastro* Mico, weaving stories within stories, recalls that when he repeated this proverb to Michele de Gore, mason, who was kneading the clay to make statues of shepherds, he, Michele, would look up with a puzzled look, reflect for a moment and reply: "Fuck what they say!"

Peasants, agricultural workers, small owners, artisans, municipal employees, tailors, shoemakers, carpenters, and barbers participated in the various stages of the Carnival celebrations. Notables, professionals, and migrants who had made their fortune in America, collaborated by donating suitable clothing and various objects deemed useful and original for the masquerade. A white robe of the brotherhoods, an old jacket with upturned sleeves, a piece of coal to use as make-up for the face, and the mask was ready.

The rich and ancient tradition of farces, stories, songs, tales of 'mprovvisaturi and poets who sang in dialect should not be thought as separate from an elite tradition familiar with writing. Turi created dialogues and exchanges that forged links between the oral tradition and writing, and between the popular and the elite classes. He was an "interpreter" and "translator," as well as inventor. He often spoke of the ancient *farsari*, and was proud to be the heir of Domenico Pileggi, Mico de Don Nino, the head of the municipal guards of the village and main protagonist of the Carnival between the wars. He spoke of them with admiration and smiled whenever he was told of their creative resourcefulness.

For the farce of a Carnival of the 1920s, Mico had constructed an enormous mechanical hen with two very wide wings that he could operate from the inside, followed by twenty-one chicks. One year, just in the final days of the Carnival, Mico fell seriously ill with a bout of pneumonia. The village doctor had gone to his home, late at night, to visit him. "He finds," writes Turi, "a sick man lying on the bed, his face made up in a blotch of colours, not between the blankets but on top of them and wearing the costume that he would have worn on the day of the Carnival. There was a general embarrassment, but the sly Mico kept his composure and turning to the bewildered doctor said in a weak voice: 'It's Carnival, I did it only out of devotion. I'm sure you understand.'"

This story, like a legend, points to the sacred, almost religious aspects of the ritual. Tradition implied an obligation to respect and honour it in all circumstances, even the painful ones.

How Turi became the Emperor's General

Turi welcomes tradition but introduces innovative changes, elements of a high culture he had learned in Africa. In prison camps he had an opportunity to show all his imagination, his organizational skills, and his love for the theatre and culture. Working with students from that time he becomes a performer of comedies, dramas, and farces. He becomes the enthusiastic protagonist and the creator, of the Carnival and the popular theater after World War II and into to the mid-1950s. He took elements of popular culture and subjected them to the magic of the written word.

He became a great storyteller. He enchanted his audience with words, gestures, and with his eyes, but he had also read a lot of literature, history, and theatre. He did his best to get hold of books and visited with the children of the well-to-do in the village only to gain access to knowledge that he couldn't afford. His mother worked as a maid for a family of notables and, thanks to her, as a young man he had access to magazines and books. I remember the seriousness, the passion, and the knowledge with which he spoke of books he had read. He devoured whatever he could put his hands on: Balzac and

Tolstoy, Pirandello and Brancati, the serials and "erotic" romances of the early 20th century. Often he regretted not having had the opportunity to study, and complained about not knowing how to write, though his passion for writing came second only to his passion for women. He was a seducer and women liked him. Always gallant and polite, he cheered up groups of friends with his jokes.

The first great exodus had expelled peasants, artisans, dialect poets, artists, musicians, thus helping to add to the sadness of villages already at the mercy of poverty and disease. Late in the 19th century, Apollo Lupini, in his famous book on the Carnival farces in Calabria, noted how the "joy" of the carnival period had become "forced" among the peasants and craftsmen of Calabria: "The Pulcinella that provokes laughter with his monkeying around among the passers-by is getting ready to leave for America tomorrow, seeking bread and new sufferings." In the post-war climate of hunger and misery, Turi remembers: "For many, the idea of leaving the village became real" and the Carnival often staged the fear and anxiety of leaving.

The gathering of costumes and "masks," the "writing" of the texts of farces, the parades, the representations in the streets demanded meticulous organization, careful study of the "parts" and gestures, as well as the ability to invent and improvise. The procession that carried in triumph the fat Carnival started in the *Citateja* neighbourhood, led by the brass band of the village, and followed by knights, donkeys, Carnival himself, "brothers" masked as village "princelings," parish priests, obese bishops with protruding bellies and opulent nuns. The poor and the beggars came next, and invoked "father" Carnival with complaints, cries, and curses.

On the Sunday of Carnival, masks poking fun at gentlemen, priests, the wealthy, but also migrants and women who had been left behind, cheating merchants and untrustworthy foreigners were staged in the village streets and piazzas. Elegantly dressed in female costumes, masks performed dances to the rhythm of music and dances of the time. On Monday, Carnival, who had drunk way too much and had eaten more then his fill, took ill. He died on Tuesday at the end of a long procession. The bishop intoned the eulogy to the accompaniment of the wailings and mockery of the masked villagers, the poor, and Carnival's wife as they tore away at their clothes and scratched their faces: Carnival as a great exorcism of death itself and as a parody of those who wield power and of the penitential and funereal rites of the confraternities. And, in the end, the band played Chopin's funeral march.

The Carnival of 1952

The police sergeant called Turi, who, worried to death, rushed to him. The sergeant asked Turi to oversee the exit at the end of the Mass, where his wife and daughters had gone before the celebrations got underway. Turi, dressed up as the General, promptly replied: "Aye, Aye sir!"

Once the Mass was over, the festivities began. Turi entered the piazza astride a donkey, welcomed by the band playing *Aida*. A man in a Carnival costume was being transported on a truck. "General" Turi dismounted, approached the "Emperor" Carnival and placed the imperial crown of flowers, intertwined with sausages, on his head. The band played Radetzky's anthem: a twenty-one-gun salute marked the coronation.

There was nothing special about the carnival of 1952. It had been just like the others. What made it unique is the fact that it was the last Carnival. We never know when something happens for the last time.

Within a decade about a thousand people left the village. Even Turi tried his hand at emigration. He moved to Salerno, where he had some relatives, and started to work as a tailor. From here he sent a letter in verse to his master—a very good tailor and trumpet player in the village band—inviting him to set aside village feuds and travel to a land of marvels and freedom.

Chi bellezza, o Cavalere'
Ntra la spiaggia de Salernu
Ca partivi a currifuju
Non mu staju 'ntra lu 'mpernu.
Pe' mu dassu su paisi
No' mu viju si facciazzi
Ca parrandu cu' rispettu
Mi 'nchianavanu li cazzi.
Venitinde, venitinde
Dassa futtere li 'mbrogghjie
Ca li cazi e li juppuni
Li fai quandu ti ricogghji.
Senza cricca e propaganda
Né partiti e né funzione
Trove a Turi stabbanatu
Cu la lente e la retina
Chi passija 'ntra la spiaggia
Certe cose capisciti
Ti li cernenu davanti
È lu mundu chi boliti.
Trigghji, alici e capituni
E sardeja no' vi dicu
'Ncuna vota vi succede
Ca si scassa lu vijicu.

What beauty, my dear Sir
On this beach here in Salerno
I had to leave in hurry, Sir
To escape from that inferno
To depart from that village
With people of such ugly visage
Although I mean no disrespect
Their mere mention makes me erect.
Come away, come away, Sir

Leave your troubles there to burn
Jackets and pantaloons
You can mend on your return.
No gossip or gangs here, Sir
No politics or rallies
Just Turi in his casuals
Keen eyed and on the look out
On the beach he walks about.
Many things, if you get my drift,
Are danced right in your face, Sir
In the world as you see it.
With mullets, anchovies, large eels
And sardines, I must say, Sir
At times, if you're not careful,
You'll just burst your bellyful.

The return of Turi

Turi, donning his "Emperor's General" costume with two cheese graters for epaulets and an alarm clock for a wristwatch, struts majestically, with aristocratic seriousness. He smirks at people who have turned out to glance at him from their windows and balconies. "Brothers," who recite a litany backwards, lead the Carnival procession in front of Turi. They don't resemble, except in their imitation of words and gestures, the masks of the 1950s. They're young people who've won the elections, who dream of a job, a different country. They would've been disappointed, but that's another story.

In the procession, behind Turi, there's a puppet of the dead Carnival, followed by young manager types and girls in peasant dress who weep in a parody of the older women. The masking of women is completely new, as are the dances and masks worn by the children.

It wasn't a movie, not a dream or an apparition. Turi was really back in 1979, twenty-five years after his departure. He thought he could pick up—or so he imagined—the Carnival where he had left it.

After having wandered all over Northern Italy, he had landed with his wife in Morbegno, where he had worked as a tailor and where his son, Mariano, was born and raised.

He looked at the windows where people greeted him like an emperor. He felt that the time had passed, but then he saw himself again like in the old times. He thought about this unexpected return. After such a long absence, in the mid-1970s, he had decided to return to the village on vacation with his wife and son. The village had changed; he found it alive, full of young people. He discovered that many who were engaged in the organization of festivities, of the Carnival, of political rallies, of evenings devoted to eating and drinking, knew him and were waiting for him.

When I met him in the village piazza he was entertaining the crowds. Everyone marvelled at the magic of his theatrics and storytelling; some broke into laughter while others were moved to see young people respond with such joy. We hit it off immediately, like long lost brothers. Those who leave are remembered as legends, shadows, and "masks." Turi had told me this, but his image of *farsaro* was reductive, stereotyped. Turi was also many other things.

I'd invited him to return, with the help of some RAI networks and the ARCI [Associazione Ricreativa Culturale Italiana], and he donned the costumes that he thought others wanted him to wear, tight as they were on him. He became what others had wanted him to be, even though he suffered because of it. At the time—just as the dream of returning and remaining in order to change the world that had been left behind—intellectuals, scholars interested in the meaning of place, and lovers of tradition, often invented new traditions, dusted off old rituals and constructed new identities.

Anthropology has destroyed and created identities, often only as a rhetorical exercise. Often unconsciously, by reference to the good old days: more often than not, claustrophobic and narrow-minded, closed, identities. The problem isn't invention—new cultures are always the result of continuous and problematic construction—but the how and why of invention: for what purpose, what project, with what passion, with what love for the world in which we live and work. The founding figures of the new folklore often didn't fully understand the old. They confused the old with the new by stoking the fires of regret, by imagining an authenticity and immutability that didn't exist. Tradition is transmission, invention, "betrayal," but to be able to betray it you have to have lived it. Nostalgia on behalf of third parties is unpleasant.

Turi looks out from the balcony where thirty years ago he had waited for the truck with the dead Carnival, but he is a different Turi. He has changed. The village has changed. The Carnival has changed. The masks have changed. The world has changed. Turi performs a new farce that follows traditional rules, that still speaks of food and hunger, but is linked to the political reality of today.

> *Certo fu la morte tua*
> *Chi mi deze l'occasione*
> *Pè mu tornu allu paisi*
> *Pè mu assistu alli funzione*
> *Mu ti lodu e mu ti ciangiu*
> *Mu ti assistu all'agonia*
> *Preparatimi mu mangiu*
> *Ca su chinu d'animia.*
> *Preparatimi 'nu porco*
> *Quattru sacchi de ruttami*
> *Trenta poste de satizzi*
> *Trenta poste de salami*
> *'Na frittata de cent'ova*
> *'N'ottantina de ricotte*
> *E 'n braccetto accantu a mia*
> *Berlinguer e Andreotti.*
> *Quandu 'nchiani 'n Paradisu*
> *Prega tu Carnelevari*
> *Pe' mu fannu na riforma*
> *Mu ni caccianu li corna*

Pe' mu vascianu li prezzi
Pe' mu 'nchiana la pensione
Domus mea, domus mea
Mu ni passa la diarrea.

Your death brought me back
To this village in the outback
To take part in this ritual
To sing your praises, mourn your loss
And assist you in your death throes.
Make me something to eat
For I'm consumed by frailty
Slaughter a pig for me
Feed me four sacks of macaroni
Thirty sausages in a string
An omelette with one hundred eggs
And at least eighty ricotte,
And let me walk arm in arm
With Berlinguer and Andreotti
And pray for me Carnival
That when I get to paradise
They'll start a movement to remove
All horns from our head
To lower prices, and pensions to increase
Domus mea, domus mea
Please cure me of my diarrhea.

His voice rises into the sky, his gaze hides his pain, laughter seems to collapse time and bring everything closer. Turi is overcome with deep feeling as he listens, laughs, and looks around. Carnival isn't dead, he thinks; the village isn't dead, he thinks. Perhaps I can return, he thinks.

As soon as he settled back in the village, Turi started dreaming up projects, theatre companies. He made a gift of his books to the ARCI association to encourage young people to read. Carnival is still celebrated. Vincenzo Iozzo, Vince de Lucia, born in 1947 and emigrated to Canada in the 1960s, returns in the 1970s and becomes, with the help of the young people from ARCI, the driving force behind the carnival. A hairdresser by trade, he composes words and music in a popular style that will become songs of protest, of emigration, of condemnation that young people perform in serenades and during the festival of emigration. The climate of renewal and confidence, however, begins to lose steam. People, once again, start to leave and the village begins to fade.

Turi dispenses advice, but the Carnival of the 1970s and 1980s, rather than helping to create "unity," in an increasingly gloomy Italy obsessed with modernization and concrete, forges and foments alienation. An air of spiteful vindictiveness permeates the public festivities. Turi grows sad. Gloom and doom rule the day, and infighting breaks out in the village. Turi finds it difficult to find anyone interested in talking about anything beyond local gossip and small talk about village events. Every time he sees me he repeats the same thing: "They don't even know how to lose gracefully when playing cards; they hit the roof over a badly played card because they'll have to buy a round of beers." He regrets having come back to the village.

In the past, the village was animated by conflicts, struggles and contrasts of a political nature. That's all gone now. The last great political thrill occurs during the meeting in which, following the historical split in Bologna, a new name had to be found for the Italian Communist Party. The party headquarters behind the church is full, just like in the old days, brimful with memories of struggles and passion, of isolation and hope. Everyone's passionate in expressing their reasoning; an air of defeat hangs over their gloomy looks, over the silence, and disappointment.

The meeting goes on for hours. Everyone wants to have their say, as if the new name for the party and the fate of Italy and the world depended on this meeting. Everyone's living through his or her own personal drama. Those who'd been members of the party immediately after the war, those who had participated in the occupation of agricultural lands, and had been looked upon as "people who ate children alive," those who ended up on police files, those who had been active in the events of 1968, those who had entered into dialogue with the Christian Democrats and the Socialists, those who were angry with the wealthy and the managers, those who were seeking help with an application or were looking for a job—they weren't sure why they had been communists but all knew they wanted a better world.

Turi looked troubled. He listened silently. He had to have dinner at about eight so he could take his medication. He stood up and said: "I was a communist in my youth. Now, I wouldn't know how to be anything else. I don't think I made a mistake. I can't stay to vote, so I leave it up to you. I must go and eat now."

He said it in his own way, without making a drama of it. He got up and walked out. I joined him. He was upset. "Professor," he said, "there's nothing left to do." I took him home. We drank a glass of wine.

"Give me something to eat, for I am taken over by anemia," I said, quoting a verse from one of his farces.

He smiled. I knew he was bothered by the repetition of the same verses speaking of food, especially since he had written about freedom and equality. We have a tendency to be reductive, to trivialize and to simplify things. I embraced him and returned to the party headquarters. I knew that this would be our last embrace. There was nothing left to do, we would have to reinvent ourselves. Once again there was only one choice: departure. And so I left, once again. Turi left, never to return. The village, he said, comparing it to the one he had left, had died, embittered, become wealthy, but populated by "jerks" and "snobs."

How sad! There was more respect and solidarity when we were poor, but he couldn't live on memories, and not even with the few people who understood him and loved him. There were good people and some friends, but they were all asleep. True, his choice was the result of long reflection: He thought that his son would never have a future in that place.

He left and returned to Morbegno. He gave me the books that he had kept with him. I went to see him twice. The first time was a surprise. When I called him to tell him that I was coming to Morbegno for a visit, he broke into tears. I remember the hugs and the copious tears when he came to get me at the station. I remember the care with which he served the delicious dishes prepared by his wife Teresa. He lived in a comfortable house. He was happy that Mariano had found employment with the local police; that he didn't have to bow to anyone. He was well liked and respected, but he wasn't happy. He missed the fucking village: the fucking village that you detest when you live in it only to miss it when you are away, that fucking village from which you can never be free. You leave it at your own peril, as you won't be happy anywhere else.

He was writing a story about four people who return to a dead village. He was writing a memoir about the Carnival. He wasn't fully convinced. He said he didn't know where to place commas, periods or uppercase letters. I told him I would do that for him; you just write it, and we'll fix it after. He wasn't convinced. He was a perfectionist who had great respect for himself, and for the art of writing. We spoke frequently on the telephone, and he always asked about the village from which he had fled, but wasn't able to leave behind. He asked about Calabria.

The news in the daily television broadcasts wasn't good, and he was called upon to provide explanations, though he had no knowledge, to mount a defense even though he didn't share their point of view. He had to make things clear to cold, stingy people who never even offered to pay for a coffee, who never even pretended to reach in their pockets for money. Murder, destruction, and crime, did nothing else happen in Calabria? Although he wasn't soft on his region, he couldn't bear to hear it vilified. There were good people and there were bad people. Had he not made that point in his farces for the Carnival?

The Lamp

He returned to the village in 1995. It was his final journey. Turi arrived in the morning, in a coffin, with his wife and son, and his dearest friends. True to his principles to the very end, he left word that he didn't want a church funeral. He had his own religiosity, and it didn't include phony homilies by greedy priests. The turn-out in the piazza was smaller than when he was performing his Carnival, or when political rallies and festivities took place. It was morning, the weather wasn't the best, and few people knew of Turi's death. I felt that he shouldn't leave us without being remembered to the few young people who accompanied him. I gathered my strength: I became Turi's general. I climbed onto the balcony from which he'd declaimed and performed. I managed to say that he was the masked image of a world that had hoped for the best.

Turi's funeral was the last funeral of Emperor Carnival. Carnival has become a festival for children who gather in the village piazza to throw confetti, streamers and lather each other with modern multi-coloured foam sprays. For many days leading up to the carnival, the search for costumes of Spiderman, the Incredible Hulk, Barbie, Princess Sissi, and the Winx is all consuming. Having no public stage, the children visit their grandparents, their relatives, friends and small groups, knocking on doors hoping to collect sweets and candy, but especially to be seen, to show off their beautiful costumes. It's their moment of greatest visibility, second only to the competition for the most beautiful costume, which always turns out to be the most precious and expensive.

For some years now young women have been writing and performing their own farces, in ancient words and gestures, poking ironic fun at the men of the village and on the drawbacks of village life. These are educated women with diplomas and university degrees, and they juxtapose the language of tradition against the culture of television, thus inventing a new folklore and a new culture, to which we should pay closer scholarly attention. They are the descendants of the *farsari* and speak and perform as if they had absorbed stories, gestures and mimicry. Women who have become the new protagonists are rescuing the tradition that kept them at bay and in the background.

Turi returns often at night, when time follows no order, and I hear my children, Stefano and Caterina, and my sister's children, Nicola and Angela, clattering about fumbling for confetti and costumes to disguise themselves, laughing at the idea of making jokes and surprises. As my *farsari* were fond of saying: We must always take care of the oil lamp of life and hope.

Interlude

Caterineja, χuri de lu linu
Ti manda salutandu don Luigi
Non vogghiu lu forgiaru ca mi tinge
Ca vogghiu a chiju chi pitta li porte
Pitta li porte e pitta lu visu
Pitta li mei porte de lu Paradisu.

Caterineja, no' jire alla missa
Ca la gatta si mangia la piscia
Gatti cca e gatti jà
Mu la fade mu si 'nde va.

Cateriné Cateriné
'Nde ave 'nu filu de basilicò
Si morirai o schiatterai
Basilicò meo no' 'nde addurerai.

Sweet Catherine, flower of linen
Don Luigi sends his greetings
Not for me the smith with his dyes
But the door painter with his paints
Who tints doors and colours my face,
And paints the gates to my paradise.

Little Catherine don't go to Mass
Or the cat will eat the fish
Here kitty cat, kitty cat there
Go away and don't come back.

Sweet little Catherine of mine
Of fragrant basil here is a thread
But if you leave or if you die
My basil's perfume you will not smell.

(*Nursery rhyme from San Nicola da Crissa*)

Quandu la Madonneja ja a la fera
Pe' ad accattare na pisa de linu
E San Giuseppe ja cu' la lumera
Mu vide pe' mu mpascia lu Bambinu
Bombi Bombineju
Chi sì duci e chi sì beju
pietre di pane
Chija notte chi nescisti
Chiju friddu chi patisti
E Sant'anna e Santa Maria
Janu cantandu la litanìa
Pe' li vivi e pe' li morte
Pe' li giusti pellegrini
E la seggia de diamanti
Chi sedianu tutti li santi
E li santi piccirilli
Chi jocavanu alli nucilli
Li nucilli si spezzaru
Rose e χiuri diventaru
Cogghimu cogghimu
Sti rose e χiuri
Ca nci li levamu
A nostro Signuri
Nostro Signuri è a Munti Carvariu
Cu' 'na grande Cruci 'ncoju
Chija Cruci chi non potìa
Era figlia de Maria
O Mamma chi siti a 'nu cantu
Aviti 'nu pocu de consulamentu
Quandu cala lu Calici Santu
Lu Patre Lu Figghiu e lu Spiritu Santu

When the Madonna went to the fair
To buy a ball of linen
Saint Joseph took his lantern
To see the swaddling of the child
Little child, oh little child
So beautiful and so sweet
On the night you were born
Oh the cold that you did bear
As Saint Anne and Saint Mary
Sang a litany for the living and the dead
For the good and just pilgrims
For the chair made of diamonds
On which sat all the saints
While the little saints at their feet
Played a game of hazelnuts
And the hazelnuts were broken
Flowers and roses they became
Let's pick the flowers and the roses
Let's bring them to our Lord
To mount Calvary where he stands
With a great cross on his shoulders
That heavy cross, daughter of Mary
Oh Mother who are on our side
Show us a little consolation
When the Holy chalice comes down
Father Son and Holy Ghost.

(*Prayer from San Nicola da Crissa*)

Village Mother

M Y MOTHER SPENDS most of her time sitting in a wicker chair from Soriano. An orthopaedic doctor advised her to stay that way, and so she sits, like a good girl, "as the little Madonna of the stone": It's been years now, since the fracture of her thigh bone from which she has never recovered. In the days when I'm in the village, in the house where I live on the second floor, I climb down the stairs to the ground floor where my sister, her husband, their children and my mother live.

My mother has reached the age of ninety-two, and I mention her age hoping to ward off bad luck. People look at me with the attitude of those who might think: "What more do you want?" But I can't tell them about the twenty or so years of stasis, of a long stretch spent between doctors and hospitals, the story of survival through illness and pain, thanks to my mother's will to live and to someone who for many years has put in the time and effort to care for her. My mother loves life and doesn't complain.

She can't walk by herself, and must use a cane. But her body is mobile and her mind in full flight into the past and the future. She's sure of herself and makes the best of every moment. And when she's able to, she doesn't shy away from imagining, organizing and following the lives of her loved ones.

Last August, as soon as I entered the room and greeted her, she said: "Fifty years ago today grandfather died." She speaks with the longing of someone who is telling me of a loss that's just occurred, a recent bereavement. I look at her and listen to her memories.

"So many years ago today, my grandmother Caterina died," she says another day, remembering the mother of her father.

Sometimes when I'm about to leave—restless from a sleepless night, lost in thought and impatient, "with a *poker* up my ass," as she says—and I look in to greet her in a hurry, I reply: "Oh, bless you, mother! You do remember everything, don't you: deaths, births, miracles. You're a library of never ending mourning." Almost immediately I regret my ironic outburst.

My mother doesn't want the past to be a dead weight; she wants to remember it and re-live it. She remembers names, last names and nicknames; remembers ancestors, the deceased, births, and deaths; remembers stories, and ceremonies, and weaves kinship tapestries, in the belief that something remains of what's happened, of what she lived through or simply heard. I follow her stories and try to fix dates and events. Like her, I think that stories, once they've occurred in life, will continue to have a life of their own so long as someone remembers to tell them. I'll certainly not be able to tell them as my mother can, to make them come alive the way she can; I don't have the listeners she had.

Places are a coagulation of different times and periods. And my places are also made of stories of people I never knew, events I haven't lived, questions on faces I've never seen, asking for some sort of hearing. I own all that is transmitted and delivered to me.

My grandparents, the mother and the father of my mother, a dead baby brother I've never seen, grandmothers and aunts, *chaste* aunts— unmarried through religious choice, cousins and relatives: they're all there, somewhere in a corner of my mother's mind, in her family tree, in her narrative of times gone by.

My mother isn't racked with melancholy. Melancholy doesn't spring from her. Her will to live is strong. Although she recalls, with infinite longing, and meticulously reconstructs origins, goals, friendships and ties from the past, she is convinced that she lives in the present. "What do you want to eat today?" "Why are you leaving today?" "When are you coming back?" With these questions she claims her place solidly at the centre of my daily life. Her "Call, when you get there," accompanies me like a refrain during my travels.

My mother has a sense of the other, and would like her children to do everything she can no longer do herself, such as keeping relationships going: "Did you go to the funeral of so and so?" Or: "You should go and visit such and such a relative, find out how they're doing."

Sometimes I lose my patience: "But we hardly have to time to visit with each other!" I reply. My mother's time was one of duty and respect, of friendships and visits. They belonged to a past that she knows very well is no longer with us.

I often sit and talk to my mother, even though she says: "You're never here," "Always in a hurry to leave." I listen, with mixed emotion, to her stories and memories, which, even though I've them heard before, are surprisingly new. My mother is surprised that I remember everything from my childhood, even when I was only two years old: my father in Toronto while we stayed in my mother's house; the move into my father's house when he came back from Canada; my childhood years and my youth. At times I'm not quite certain if I'm remembering life as I lived it or simply my mother's stories.

She questions me with her sweet, firm gaze. With her white hair and fresh and youthful skin. The memory of this strong, suffering and ailing, but always present woman will stay with me for a long time. I'll remember her many illnesses, nights in hospitals, scrambles to get a doctor or medications at the drugstore, for her and for my father.

"I'm exhausted," a friend at the University told me. "For three days I've done nothing but run around looking after my mother. I haven't been able to write anything."

I'm humbled: I've learned to keep silent on the issue of my parents' illnesses, on the many days and endless nights that I spent by their side. I would otherwise be looked on as an oddball, unproductive, not suited for our times of speed that don't allow for so many emotional ties and affections. My mother taught me that life is sacred and that we are the others. I leave aside the myths of productivity and speed. I'm content to see my mother's smile, to get angry with her, to listen to her.

My mother knows thousands of stories and anecdotes, songs about the names of people, songs of the saints, morning and evening prayers. *Let's go to bed with God, Mark and Matthew, who'll keep us safe through the night, and spare us from deathly plight, who'll keep us safe in the morning light and spare us from cruel fate …* My children, Stefano (named after my father), and Caterina (named after her), and my sister's children move back and forth with ease from their Barbie dolls to the traditional Christmas carols, from the exploits of wrestlers Eddie Guerrero and Rey Mysterio to the stories of the Ogre of folk tales who makes a refreshing snack out of an egg, or falls into despair when the hero hits him smack in the mouth with a rock.

I'm the one who is disoriented, suspended between two worlds; hovering, between a world that has ended and new ones that I don't know very well and in which I don't feel at home, even though I live in them. Children and old people find it easier to move back and forth between the past and the present. They share a sense of wonder and a lack of regrets, which for various reasons, brings them together. We are stuck in the middle, hanging on a wall.

The older Caterina, my mother, sings many stories on the name Caterina, to the young Caterina, my daughter: "Pretty Caterina don't go to Mass or else the cat will eat the fish …" And my child turns up her nose. My mother is full of irony, but when she realizes that the child has had enough, she changes her tune: "Caterina, my treasure of beauty …" And my child smiles happily.

At Christmas, the children's *Merry Christmas* carols are backed by my mother's traditional songs about Baby Jesus who, after a long wait, is welcomed into people's homes with a soulful:

Bombineju de jocu avanti
Venitinde alla casa mia
Mu ti consu 'stu letticeju
 Pe' sta povera anima mia
Anima mia no' stare confusa
Ca Gesù ti vo' pe' spusa
E ti vole e ti governa
E ti la duna la gloria eterna.

Little baby from far away
Please enter my humble home
I will prepare a cradle of hay
For my lost and poor soul.
Soul of mine do not despair
For Jesus wants you as a bride
He wants you and will guide you
And will give you eternal glory.

The children know "when Baby Jesus went to the fair ..." and "sweet Baby Jesus and nice little Baby" and my mother hides her pain with a smile. With much effort and joy, she joins in song with the children.

My mother isn't a bigot and didn't waste valuable time in church, didn't go for appearance's sake, but for the meaning. She doesn't like gossip but loves to speak well of people. She is neither gullible nor superstitious. From time to time she says: "Who knows what's next!" Then she pauses and adds with nostalgia for those whom she misses and hasn't seen again: "No one has ever returned to tell us." She never talks about magic spells but she believes in the evil eye, not out of conviction, but because "you never know." She doesn't believe in the force of envy or power of blasphemy. The magic spells she believes in are grounded in myth and religion.

Until a few years ago, when the Posterare sisters—Custodia, Caterina, Maria, Nella—were still alive, my mother would call me from her chair and send me, on the morning of the first day of the year, to wish them a Happy New Year. I had to get there early in the morning, before any woman crossed the threshold. The wishes for a "Happy New Year, bring me a gift or I'll wither away" had to be made by a male person. Now the neighbours' house is empty, like so many others in the neighbourhood and in the village. Now my mother sends me to visit my father in the cemetery.

This year on New Year's Eve, an ancient ritual took place once again. My mother says: "Tonight I am afraid, I wouldn't want to wait for midnight, the dead might drop the little stone when they pass by." At midnight the dead walk by, and it's important not to leave washed clothing hanging on the line, as they might be overcome by longing; or leave water outside the door, as they might be overcome by thirst. We must be careful not to hear the small stones they drop as they're harbingers of death. Once I asked her, smiling: "Mom, didn't you hear a pebble drop only a few years ago on New Year's Eve?"

Midnight has passed and my mother hasn't heard any stones drop. She is happy, as though she has made a narrow escape from certain death. You never know, she tells me; the dead let the living know about their death with a little stone. "Mom, haven't you heard the news?" I reply. If a war broke today, how many stones would the poor dead have to carry?"

"That's why there should not be war," she said. "It brings suffering even to the dead."

"You're pulling my leg," she tells me at other times. This year we threw a big party and the children launched fireworks, so it was difficult to hear the dead. When people stop believing that the dead pass by, the dead stop passing by. In villages that are almost dead, even the dead no longer pass by.

I went to the cemetery to visit my father and I brought a Christmas star. I visited many other deceased. "My parents are there," my mother says, and I'm reminded that many of my own dead are there as well. My mother prepared Christmas dinner and lunch, even though she doesn't eat anything herself. We must follow a strict order and eat small portions from a variety of different traditions. Thirteen things, plus sun dried cod, broccoli and goat meat, figs stuffed with walnuts: not liking something doesn't count. The table must be laden with all the traditional dishes, even if she doesn't eat anything. Of course nothing should be thrown out. "Don't you see how many children are dying of hunger?" So says my mother, who knows all the prayers that accompany the making of bread and all the signs to prevent its waste.

As my mother had taught me, on the day of the Epiphany, before going to bed, we removed Baby Jesus from the Nativity scene, kissed it, tucked it away, before Herod would come. Then I opened the computer, and I sent many e-mail greetings and best wishes around the world. I really don't know in which world I live. And it's not true that the Internet makes all worlds the same.

Every death and bereavement that occurs in the village wraps my mother in deep sorrow. Last summer, after an absence of fifty years, a cousin from Argentina came to visit. They embraced for an hour. When he left they wept uncontrollably. They caressed like children. They sobbed through their good-byes.

My mother follows the lives of her children and grandchildren, and although she isn't intrusive, she asks and worries but doesn't get involved. She is curious about what is going on in the village, keeps an eye on and listens to news of wars and collapsing towers, deaths in subways and tsunamis, violence and disease that remain a mystery to her.

The geography of the world appears to her like the geography of suffering. Far away from home, wherever I go, bad things happen. Wherever I go I must be more careful, of the heat, the cold, aircraft, and bombs. "So," I say, "it's the end of the world."

"You're pulling my leg again … the ancients used to say that the world lasts for many, many years, and many years have passed and now only a few are left."

The apocalypses and folk fears of ancient times join in marriage with those of our own time, and my mother seems to me more in tune with the times than I am. Her sense of piety towards herself and others, her suffering and joyful attitude towards life, her sense of being part of events involving saints and ancestors, her desire for life at the end of a long life, the power of memory and the capacity for oblivion, the desire to tell her story and the ability to be silent, all of these provoke in me a boundless longing for the mothers of old.

When my mother hears of a young person who has taken ill or of diseases and suffering, she exclaims, with deep longing: "Only those who were never born are blessed." This is a concept steeped in Western cultural tradition, with deep roots in ancient Greek thought, later layered with *pietas* of popular Catholicism and Greek-Byzantine expression complete with saints who walk among us, rites of welcoming and frugality, and an attitude according to which happiness isn't of this world and life is a journey of suffering during which everyone must carry a cross.

I walk downstairs early this morning to say goodbye to my mother. It's half past seven. She sits in her chair, as she always does; she has already had breakfast, sipped her milk, and she smiles as she plays with the stuffed doll of Snow White that little Angela has handed to her. She wakes up early, around five, but is unable to get up by herself. So she waits, quietly, like the little Madonna of the Stone; sometimes she gets impatient. She isn't mistress of her own body, and she suffers greatly at not being able to control her own movements, and to have to depend on others thereby limiting them.

You know from the look in her eyes when, according to her, something has gone wrong, is out of time or out of place. She has an obsession with cleanliness, order and with things being done at just the right moment. She suffers in silence when she isn't washed immediately, or changed into clean clothes, or if she sees any clothing on the floor.

"You're up early this morning," she tells me when I wish her a good morning.

"Yes, do you know why?" I say, resorting to my usual playful and teasing tone.

"Why? Has something happened?" she asks, with her usual fearfulness.

"Not at all, I got up to write about you." She gives me an intense look. It's her way of asking for some clarification. "Yes, a woman friend asked me to write a story about a young woman from Calabria, about how women are changing, and I thought of you."

"Oh sure … she must be joking. But I was young once! And I didn't sit motionless as I do now. I was constantly jumping from one place to the next. At five I had already put on the sauce. And then I ran to the river, to the vegetable garden, to the piazza. Then I waited for you and Costanza to get back from school. I did thousands of things." Now we're all tired. We're always in a hurry and often we accomplish nothing. "And I was beautiful, you know, beautiful, not as lame and toothless as now."

I remind her of the poems written about her by the famous and skilled *farsaro*, Bruno Galati, aka Brune de Betta, celebrating in verse her beauty and elegance at the time of her engagement to my father.

> E cummare Caterina
> Sincera camminava
> Ca 'ntra la ruga era pratica
> E non si vergognava
> E tantu ch'era bella
> Parìa la 'Ndolorata
> Era vestuta cu' n'abitu
> Nero orlato bianco filamentatu.
> Lu dottore Teti
> 'Nchianava tuttu arrussicatu
> Ca 'ntra la ruga non era praticu e si vergognava
> Ca alla prima dominica cuntata
> De furgola si vitte accumpagnatu.

> *And Cummare Caterina*
> *Walked along in candour*
> *On streets she knew so well*
> *Beautiful as Our Lady of Sorrows*

She showed no signs of shame
Splendid in her black dress
With borders of white filaments.
Doctor Teti walked towards her
Red-faced and embarassed
For he had lost his way,
But on this first Sunday of Carnival
A burst of fireworks lit his way.

"See how time passes. Everything fades away: beauty and suffering." Silence. "Look at my wretched life in rags, where has all the time gone, why won't it come back?" She speaks with quiet melancholy. My mother doesn't regret the past. She has a clear sense of the passing of time, the precariousness of things. "You're leaving again, aren't you?" She adds.

"Did you have a bad dream?" I ask, making light of the many dreams that she remembers and tells in every detail. Although she knows I must leave, she hates to see me go. I quote an old saying: *Lu jire e lu venire Deu lu fice,* Our comings and goings are in God's hands.

"Ah, Yes. *Cu 'conza e sconza no perde tempo mai.* He who makes and breaks things never runs out of time," she says, ironically. *Conzo* and *Sconzo:* We all build things and tear them down, we do and we undo, but we're no longer Penelope; we don't have a project of our own, and in our doing and undoing we run about wasting our time. We don't know how to stop; don't know how to find our point of stillness in the flow of time, as you say *mamma.* We rush about without any conviction. We run back and forth and only rarely stop to look and listen.

I don't feel guilty, at least not in this. Oh sure, I did my share of running, had my share of commotions and panics, but I knew when to stop and listen. I gave up on reading many books, *Mamma,* but the stories I heard from you are more valuable to me. I missed out on many boring faculty meetings, but I've accompanied many dear departed on their last journey, have shared suffering and illness, and taken part in festivities and rituals. Did I really waste a lot of time?

Do we gain time by giving up on our own humanity? In my journeys around the world, in my village and other villages, I've drunk and talked so much, have listened to our world and perhaps in the end, I found time. Everything passes, everything ends, *Mamma:* The only thing that remains are stories and with them the people who live to tell them.

I come and go, I do and undo, *conzo e sconzo,* across this world, across these worlds, our own and the ones we've never seen, *Mamma.* The world is a village. The village is a world. We're all in the same world, often without a clear aim, often at random. I feel that I won't get lost, and even when I'm at risk of losing my way, the kind and gentle face of *Papà* appears out of nowhere: a slow flowering of the *pietas* and strength that you have bequeathed to me.

Note on the Texts

"THERE IS NO fate more uncertain than that of books on travel. Among the literary products of men they're the most vulnerable. The writer of a book on travel puts himself in the hands of his enemies more than anyone else." Thus Joseph Conrad. And it would suffice to add the term "voyage," the verbs "to remain," "to return," "to leave again," "to wait," in order to have a sense of the extreme vulnerability of this book, a book that in its pages narrates stories both of going away and of staying back.

The villages and the places discussed here resemble quite a bit the villages and the places I have known but they aren't exactly those villages and those places. The people, the tales, the events about which I speak are the fruit of my imagination, of my writing, of my memory and of my forgetfulness, even when they seem to be real or are real events that really occurred. My way of seeing and living places, of living or seeing stories, events, persons, the dialogue I have had with them or imagined having with them, my complicity and my gaze, my being inside and outside them—this is what is at stake.

And even when the narrating "I" seems to be the same as the "I" that writes and resembles unequivocally my own, real "I", I'm doing nothing more than privileging, than choosing, than bringing into play one of my many "I"s, none of which accounts for the infinite multitude residing within me. Often, on the contrary, one of my most deeply-abiding "I"s lies hidden within other characters that appear in these minuscule tales in which nothing happens because everything has already happened, or because everything has occurred without clamour, and there is no need to invent events that are striking or stirring.

Nothing is more dramatic than ordinary life, everyday, common life. When it comes down to it, these stories aren't a figment of my imagination. They're "real" and "invented" in so far as they're filtered by my gaze, by my practice as an ethnographer, as a wanderer on foot, as a listener and an idler, by my way of narrating, my writing, by my selection (or the sudden emergence) of my recollection or my forgetfulness.

The chapters that make up the book are accompanied by interludes, bits of oral poetry that I've "stolen," mostly from my mother and other women rooted in the same cultural landscape to which I belong. They're only small slivers of the great trees of songs, fables, proverbs, oral texts that I've been gathering since my youth and which I've dealt with in other works, whether finished or imagined. Even if they're silent excerpts, they're the soundtrack of the book. I've transcribed them in a form that is conventional, approximative, accessible and legible, without dwelling on problems of phonetics, philology, glottology, of which I'm very well aware but that in the end, here on this occasion, would have given an altogether different colouring to the general approach and underlying intentions of this book.

I translate songs and at times terms originally in dialect quite directly and scrupulously but in accordance with my own literary sensibility and with the presumption that I have interpreted correctly the translation and the thoughts of the persons from whom I first heard them. The lullaby on pp. 45–46, the nursery rhymes and silent prayer on pp. 176–179 were told to me by my mother Caterina Iozzo, born in 1913, who, in turn, heard them from her mother Felicia Galati (San Nicola da Crissa 1878–1960). The song on page 184 I've heard since childhood in our family and from our neighbours, the Martino sisters, nicknamed Posterari. A version of them was published by Raffaele Lombardi Satriani in *Canti popolari calabresi* [*Calabrian Popular Songs*]. Vol III. Napoli: De Simone, 1932, pp. 281–282.

Before putting it on paper, I "lived" this book with all the people that figure in it and with the many others whose story remains still enclosed in bottles not consigned to the waves, in other pages of my memory, of notebooks, of computer files. To all of them, starting naturally with my father and my mother, go my grateful thoughts. Thanks are also due to those who, for various reasons, have felt touched by this book, enriched it or wished that it be written and published: Alfonsina Bellio, Tommaso Greco, Felicia Malfarà, Lavinia D'Errico, Ciro Tarantino.

The texts that compose this book—short stories, reflections, essays—have been published mostly in the last few years, and have been selected, revised, re-written for a work entirely new.

The prologue, "Del restare," is an amplification and a re-writing of "Restare," published in *AM—Rivista quadrimestrale di antropologia museale*, 22 (2009): XLIV-XLVI; "Il cammino di Vallelonga" re-elaborates almost entirely, the autobiographical piece "La mia Vallelonga, tutte le Vallelonga del mondo," in Vincenzo Barberi, ed., *Vallelonga. Immagini di una storia*, Grafica Enotria, 1996. 143–151; "L'ombra e la macchina da cucire" is a revision of "I percorsi dell'ombra. Immagini dei Calabresi di Toronto," *Voci*, July-Dec. (2004):129–154; "Le reti di Murat" picks up the short story "L'arte di perdere il tempo," *L'Unità*, Aug. 8 (1993):3; "Le pietre di mio cugino Giò" is the new version of a piece by the same title written for Marco Ambrosi ed. *Ad esempio a me piace ... Un viaggio in Calabria,* Rubbettino, 2009.29–46; "Madre di paese" reproposes a story by the same title first published in the volume edited by Ofelia M. Alati, Silvana Bilotto, Biagina De Giorgio, Marisa Gagliardi, Maria Teresa Stranieri and entitled *Il femminile nella realtà calabrese,*Tip. L'Alternativa, March 8 (2006): 11–16.

Passages, fragments, pages of this book at times revisit themes, issues on which I have lingered, during the last few years, also in reviews, magazines, daily newspapers (particularly *Il Quotidiano della Calabria*) and, above all, in essays that I have referred to only in part in the bibliographical notes that follow.

Bibliographical Note

T HE TOPICS DEALT with, or hinted at and briefly touched upon, would probably require a more wide-ranging and more complete bibliography. But that bibliography would be purely ritualistic in purpose here, and thus of little use, given the nature of the book. I've chosen, then, to furnish only the information that pertains to the works from which I've directly quoted, to the oral and historical sources of which I've availed myself and to texts that for me have been major signposts. In this sense I should add that the other works I've written have been prompted by my desire to interweave the themes and stories I've broached here with research that has involved me for "almost a lifetime," to borrow the expression of one of my favourite novelists. The bibliography I mention, then, has to do only with those footprints which suggest some of the trails leading to the immense forest of possible references.

Prologue: Of Remaining

The poem entitled "La città" by Constatine Cavafy which opens this text appears in his *Settantacinque poesie*, edited by Margherita Dalmati and Nelo Risi, Einaudi, 1992, p. 49. The English translation of the original version can be found in: *Collected Poems*. Edited by George Savidis, translated by Edmund Keeley and Philip Sherrard, Princeton UP, 1992, p. 28.

The quotation by Fortunato Seminara, which here serves as epigraph, is taken from the collection of his writings entitled *L'altro pianeta*, Pellegrini, 1967.

Claude Lévi-Strauss' words open what is probably the most celebrated work of the anthropological tradition, his *Tristes tropiques*. They're taken from the Italian translation of Bianca Garufi, Il Saggiatore, 1960. [English translation, *Tristes Tropiques*, Athaneum, 1973].

The quotation on Ulysses' wanderings can be found in Eugenio Scalfari's *Per l'alto mare aperto. La modernità e il pensiero danzante*, Einaudi, 2010, p. 40.

The literature on Ulysses—the person and the myth—is boundless and can be encountered even beyond the Western tradition. For some of the things that I say about it in this section of the book see Vladimir Jankélévitch, *L'irréversible et la nostalgie*, Flammarion, 1974, parts of which appear in *Nostalgia. Storia di un sentimento*, edited by Antonio Prete, Cortina, 1992, pp. 119–176. See also Piero Boitani, *L'ombra di Ulisse. Figure di un mito*, Il Mulino,1992, as well as, on the same topic, Giulio Giorello, *Prometeo, Ulisse, Gilgameš. Figure del mito*, Cortina, 2004, Laura Faranda, *Viaggi di ritorno. Itinerari antropologici nella Grecia antica*, Armando, 2009, pp. 100-121.

The expression "men without women" is an implicit reference to Robert Harney's *Uomini senza donne. Emigrati italiani in Canada. 1885–1930*, in *Canadiana. Storia e storiografia canadese*, 1979, pp. 67–95. On the demeanour of the "women without men," the women left behind in Italy by "americani," I have written in "Note sui comportamenti delle donne sole degli 'americani' durante la prima emigrazione in Calabria," *Studi Emigrazione*, 85, marzo 1987, pp. 13–46.

The allusions to the various types of "narrator-travellers" have to do with Adalberto von Chamisso, *Storia meravigliosa di Peter Schlemihl. 1814.* Trans. Giuliana Pozzi, Rizzoli, 1984 [English translation of original version: Adelbert von Chamisso, *Peter Schlemihl. 1814.* Camden House, c.1993]; Josef von Eichendorff, *Vita di un perdigiorno. 1826.* Trans. Lydia Magliano. Rizzoli, 1976 [English translation of original

version: Josef von Eichendorff, *Memoirs of a good-for-nothing*. 1826.
Trans. Bayard Quincy Morgan, Ungar, 1955]; Xavier de Maistre,
Viaggio intorno alla mia camera. 1794, Trans. Nicola Muschitiello,
Rizzoli, 1991. [English translation of original version: *Voyage Around
My Room.* 1794. Trans. Stephen Sartarelli, New Directions, 1994]. On
the "writers-wanderers" there now exists quite a significant bibliography, within which I would point out Ottavio Fatica ed. *I narrabondi.
Scrittori eccentrici nel cuore dell'Inghilterra,* Editori Riuniti, 1989. The
reference to James G. Frazer, who without moving a limb organizes
systematically in a vast anthropological narration the research and
the writings of ethnographers, explorers, folklorists, historians, pertains to his *Il ramo d'oro. Studi sulla magia e la religione.* 1922. Trans.
Lauro de Bosis, Boringhieri, 1965, the Italian version of *The Golden
Bough,* MacMillan, 1922.

On the *Unheimlich,* the German term generally translated in
Italian as *spaesamento* and in English as "the uncanny," see Graziella
Berto, *Freud, Heidegger. Lo spaesamento.* Bompiani, 1999. We would
need to recall how for Heidegger it is by going along the paths of the
countryside that we run into that which is there not to be counter to
us but to encounter us. How to be at home is our problem. In *Essere
e tempo,* 1927, translated by Pietro Chiodi, Longanesi, 2003, [English
version *Being and Time.*Translated by John Macquarrie and Edward
Robinson, Harper & Row, 1962], Heidegger presents in radical terms
the ontological priority of not-being-at-home, of dislocation as the
fundamental condition of being-in-the-world on the part of Dasein.
On these aspects and on their relation to the thought of Emmanuel
Lévinas see Caterina Resta, *Il luogo e le vie. Geografie del pensiero in
Martin Heidegger,* Franco Angeli, 1966, particularly pp. 41–97.

Of the rich bibliography on the double here I will mention only
Otto Rank's *Il doppio. Il significato del sosia nella letteratura e nel folk-
lore.* 1914. Trans. Maria Grazia Cocconi Poli, Sugarco, 1979, and his
Don Juan et le Double. Études psychanalytiques. 1932. Payot, 1973.
[English versions respectively *The Double: A Psychoanalytic Study.*
1914. Translated by Harry Tucker Jr, University of North Carolina
Press, 1971 and *The Don Juan Legend.* Translated by David G. Winter,

Princeton UP, 1975]. See also Enzo Funari ed. *Il doppio tra patologia e necessità*, Cortina, 1986.

On the motif of the shadow I would recall Mario Trevi's "Sul problema dell'ombra nella psicologia analitica" in Mario Trevi and Augusto Romano, *Studi sull'ombra*, Marsilio, 1990, pp. 17–71. The concept of the shadow figures prominently in the works of Carl G. Jung. See his "L'io e l'inconscio," 1916, and "Psicologia dell'inconscio," 1942, in *Opere*, Vol. 7, Boringhieri, 1970, as well as "Aion" in *Opere*, Vol. 9, Bollati Boringhieri, 1980, both volumes edited by Lisa Baruffi, and *Risposta a Giobbe*. 1952. Translated by Alfred Vig, Il Saggiatore, 1965. [In English see "Aion. Researches into the Phenomenology of the Self" in *Collected Works*. Vol. 9, p. 2. Translated by R.F.C. Hull, Routledge and Paul, 1968, and "Answer to Job" in *Ibid.*, Vol. 11, 1969]. Jung returns on this topic in Paul Radin, Carl G. Jung, Karl Kerényi, *Il briccone divino*, translated by N. Dalmasso and S. Daniele, SE, 1965. [English translation of original version, *The Trickster*, Philosophical Library, 1956]. An interesting interpretation of this motif is made by Pier Aldo Rovatti in "Riflessioni sull'ombra," part of his *L'esercizio del silenzio*, Cortina, 1992, pp. 45–60. But of relevance is also Silvana Sinisi ed., *Le figure dell'ombra*, Officina, 1982.

On the voyage and the writings about the contemporary *flâneur* I would send back to Giampaolo Nuvolati's *Lo sguardo vagabondo. Il flâneur e la città da Baudelaire ai postmoderni*. Il Mulino, 2006, of which I quote p. 21. The list of authors who, with Nuvolati, we could define as "domestic *flâneurs*" would be, however long, quite reductive. It's neither easy nor useful to concoct grids and pigeon-holes within which to place authors profoundly different one from the other, with gazes and literary and artistic products profoundly heterogeneous. Scholars, writers, poets, Calabrians who have experienced the exodus and those who have remained, Italians or Southern Italians, Italian Canadians, with many of which I maintain bonds of friendship and esteem, will certainly be able to appreciate my intense dialogue with their works. Nonetheless it would be good to have at one's disposal an open, fully coloured map of the "narrators" and the sedentary "travellers" and it would be desirable that there be a rethinking, a critical rehabilitation of the sedentary authors of the past. These are authors from various regions of Italy that often have written of little known villages, cities, and places considered peripheral and marginal but who now, in a period such as ours quite responsive to local cultures and local topographies, appear more innovative and original than authors who elèuthera have received greater acclaim.

For comments on the two traditional "types" of narrators—the travelling merchants and the stationary farmers—see Paolo Jedlovsky. *Storie comuni. La narrazione nella vita quotidiana*. Bruno Mondadori, 2000. This same author I would mention here also for his many fundamental works on memory.

With regard to the notion of "the return home" of anthropologists my references are George E. Marcus and Michael M.J. Fischer, *Antropologia come critica culturale*. Translated by Claudio Mussolini, Anabasi, 1994 and James Clifford and George E. Marcus eds., *Scrivere le culture: poetiche e politiche in etnografia*. Translated by Andrea Aureli, Meltemi, 1997. [English original versions George E. Marcus and Michael M.J. Fischer, *Anthropology as Cultural Critique*, University of Chicago P, 1986; James Clifford and George E.Marcus eds., *Writing Culture*, University of California P, 1986].

On ethnographies as literary texts or as works of fiction, to follow Clifford's cue on this, still compelling are Clifford Geertz' reflections in *Interpretazioni di culture*. Translated by Eleonora Bona, Il Mulino, 1987; *Antropologia interpretativa*. Translated by Luisa Leonini, Il Mulino, 1988; *Opere e vite: l'antropologo come autore*. Translated by Silvia Tavelli, Il Mulino, 1990. [English original versions: *The Interpretation of Cultures*, Basic Books, 1973; *Local Knowledge. Further Essays in Interpretive Anthropology*, Basic Books, 1983; *Works and Lives: The Anthropologist as Author*, Stanford UP, 1988].

On the links between literature and anthropology scholarly production has been prolific and multi-faceted, with well-specified trends and positions within the various cultural contexts. Here I point only to a few of the titles that have appeared in Italy, which come with their own rich bibliographical apparatus on the subject: "L'autorità della scrittura," preface to the Italian edition of George E. Marcus and Michael M.J. Fischer, *Anthropology as Cultural Critique*. Anabasi, 1994; Daniel Fabre, "Un'antropologia 'avant la lettre'," in Gigliola De Donato ed., *Carlo Levi. Il tempo e la durata in Cristo si è fermato a Eboli. Fahrenheit 451*, 1999, pp. 269–283; Fabio Dei, "Fatti, finzioni, testi: sul rapporto tra antropologia e letteratura," *Uomo & Cultura*, 45–52, 1993, pp. 58–101; "La libertà di inventare i fatti: antropologia, storia, letteratura." *Il gallo silvestre*, 13, 2000, pp. 180–196 and *La discesa agli inferi. James G. Frazer e la cultura del Novecento*. Argo, 1998; Anna Bellio, "L'ellissi e il cerchio. Contributi francesi tra antropologia e letteratura," in Francesca Sbardella ed., *Antropologia dell'Europa: i testi della riflessione francese*. Patron, 2007, pp. 145–172.

On the theme of the voyage and of the return interesting reflections can be found in Claudio Magris, *L'infinito viaggiare*. Mondadori, 2005. Of Magris I would also mention, for the many indirect references I make to it, *Lontano da dove. Joseph Roth e la tradizione ebraico-orientale*. Einaudi 1977.

By Marc Augé, quoted several times in this volume, I include here *L'etnologo nel metrò*. 1986. Translated by Francesco Lomax, Elèuthera, 1992 [English version: *In the metro*. Translated by Tom Conley, University of Minnesota P, 2002]; *Nonluoghi. Introduzione ad un'antropologia della surmodernità*. 1992. Translated by Dominique Rolland, Elèuthera, 1993 [English version: *Non-places. Introduction to an anthropology of supermodernity*. Translated by John How. Verso, 1995] and *Il metrò rivisitato*. 2008. Translated by Laura Odello, Cortina, 2009.

Of Antonio Prete I have cited his *Trattato della lontananza*. Bollati Boringhieri, 2008, particularly pp. 9–11.

On the journey as salvation, therapy, religious passage—*solvitur ambulando*—my reference is Bruce Chatwin. *Le vie dei canti*. Translated by Silvia Gariglio, Adelphi, 1988 [Original version: *The Songlines*, Viking, 1987]. But of Chatwin see also *Che ci faccio qui?* 1989. Translated by Sandro Mazzone, Adelphi, 1990 [original version, *What Am I doing Here?* Jonathan Cape, 1949]. On the saints who within the various Calabrian folk cultures are also travellers, as well as, within those same cultures, on Christ as one who walks and one who founds truths, see Pasquale Rossi, *Le Rumanze e il Folkore in Calabria*, Tipografia del Riccio, 1903; Luigi Lombardi M. Satriani and Mariano Meligrana. *Un villaggio nella memoria*, Casa del Libro, 1983, pp. 245–305; Maffeo Pretto. *La pietà popolare in Calabria*, Progetto editoriale 2000, 1988. Among the many books about walking, I would especially recall Rebecca Solnit's *Storia del camminare*. 2000. Translated by Gabriella Agrati and Maria Magini. Bruno Mondadori, 2002 [original English version, *Wanderlust. A History of Walking*, Penguin Books, 2001].

In the paragraph on the *nostos* and the *algos* the reference is to Johannes Hofer, "Dissertazione medica sulla nostalgia ovvero *heimwebe*," 1668. In Antonio Prete, ed. *Nostalgia*, pp. 45–61.

The bibliography on nostalgia—in literature, psychiatry, anthropology and sociology—is really boundless but for the perspective I have adopted in this text my sources have been Mircea Eliade. *La Nostalgie des origins. Méthodologie et histoire des religions*. Gallimard, 1971; Fred Davis, "Identity and the Current Nostalgia Wave." *Journal of Popular Culture*, II, 1977, pp. 414–424. Delia Frigessi Castelnuovo and Michele Risso. *A mezza parete. Emigrazione, nostalgia, malattia mentale*. Einaudi, 1982. Jean Starobinski. "Il concetto di nostalgia." In Antonio Prete ed., pp. 85–117; *Storia del trattamento della melanconia dalle origini al 900*. Translated by Franco Paracchini. Guerini e Associati, 1990; Ralph Harper. *Nostalgia: un'esplorazione della brama e della realizzazione nel mondo moderno*. 1966. Translated by Paul Gabriele Weston and Pierfrancesco Callieri. Il Pensiero Scientifico, 1976 [original English version *Nostalgia. An Existential Exploration of Longing and Fulfilment in the Modern Age*, Western Reserve UP, 1966]; Sergio Mellina. *La nostalgia nella valigia. Emigrazione di lavoro e disagio mentale*. Marsilio, 1987; Christopher Lasch. *Il paradiso in terra. Il progresso e la sua critica*. 1991. Translated by Carlo Oliva. Feltrinelli, 1992 [original English version: *The True And Only Heaven. Progress and Its Critics*. Norton, 1991]; Svetlana Boym. *The Future of Nostalgia*. Basic Books, 2001. I point also to the work of Pier Paolo Pasolini, in its entirety, even if here, because of the sense that I have been giving in this book to the term "nostalgia," my allusion is to "8 luglio 1974. Limitatezza della storia e immensità del mondo conta-dino," *Scritti corsari*. 1975. Garzanti, pp. 51–55.

The image of Calabria as a land "in flight" appears in several writings of Corrado Alvaro, particularly in *Calabria*. Jaca Book-Qualecultura, 1990; *Itinerario italiano*. 1941. Bompiani, 1995; *Un treno nel sud*. Ed. Arnaldo Frateili. Bompiani, 1958. The theme of flight and of the voyage is present in almost all Calabrian writers of the 20th century and current time (both when as writers they experi-ence the exodus in person or when they "travel without moving").

On Ernesto De Martino see especially "Angoscia territoriale e riscatto culturale nel mito achilpa delle origini." *Studi e Materiali di Storia delle Religioni*, 23, 1951–52, pp. 51–56; *La terra del rimorso. Contributo ad una storia religiosa del Sud*. Il Saggiatore, 1976; "Note di viaggio," in *Mondo popolare e magia in Lucania*, Roma-Matera, 1975; *La fine del mondo. Contributo all'analisi delle apocalissi culturali*. Clara Gallini, ed., Einaudi, 1977; "L'etnologo e il poeta. Testimonianze ad Albino Pierro," in Albino Pierro. *Il mio villaggio*. Cappelli, 1959, pp. 147–152.

On place and landscape I would flag especially the follow-ing: Gaston Bachelard. *La poetica dello spazio*. 1957. Translated by Ettore Catalano. Dedalo, 1999 [English version: *The Poetics of Space*. Translated by Maria Jolas. Beacon Press, 1969]; Giovanni Ferraro. *Il libro dei luoghi*. Jaca Books, 2001; James Hillman. *L'anima dei luoghi. Conversazione con Carlo Truppi*. Rizzoli, 2004; Lidia Decandia. *Dell'identità. Saggio sui luoghi. Per una critica della razionalità ur-banistica*. Rubbettino, 2000; *Anime di luoghi*. Franco Angeli, 2004; Antonella Tarpino. *Geografia della memoria. Case, rovine, oggetti quotidiani*. Einaudi, 2008; Eugenio Turri. *Antropologia del paesag-gio*. 1974. Marsilio, 2008; Massimo Quaini. *L'ombra del paesaggio. L'orizzonte di un'utopia conviviale*. Diabasis, 200; Luisa Bonesio. *Geofilosofia del paesaggio*. Mimesis, 2001, *Paesaggio, identità e comu-nità tra globale e locale*. Diabasis, 2007.

On "losing one's bearings" and on thinking as locating oneself in space, see Franco La Cecla. *Perdersi. L'uomo senza ambiente*. Laterza, 1988; *Mente locale. Per un'antropologia dell'abitare*. Elèuthera, 1993.

On these topics I owe much, culturally, to Carlo Michelstaedter. *La persuasione e la rettorica*. Edited by Sergio Campailla. Adelphi, 1982.

The verses from the poem "We have to decide" are by Franco Costabile, from his *La rosa nel bicchiere e altre poesie*. Edited by Franco Adornato. Jaca Book-Qualecultura, 1994, p. 101. By Immanuel Kant, I have quoted, here, "Antropologia dal punto di vista prammaticco." 1970. *Scritti morali*. Edited by Pietro Chiodi. Utet, 1970 [English version: *Anthropology from a Pragmatic Point of View*. Translated by Mary J. Gregor. Nijoff, 1974].

The quotation by Mario La Cava can be found in the article by Luigi Malafarina. "Una Domenica con Mario La Cava." *Gazzetta del Sud*, January 2 1988. Similar considerations are voiced by the writer in *Corrispondenze dal Sud d'Italia*. Città del Sole, 2010. Referring to the Calabrian non-urban localities of the 1950s La Cava wrote in this book , pp. 42–43: "So many of the objective conditions [of a decent life] are missing, that the resistance of intellectuals in their native environment often takes on the form of a desperate kind of heroism."

On the themes of the double, of the shadow, of walking, of remaining, of ruins, of nostalgia, also with regard to the latter's relation with melancholy, I have also dwelt in the following: Vito Teti. *Il paese e l'ombra*. Periferia, 1989; *La melanconia del vampiro. Mito, storia, immaginario*. Manifestolibri, 1994; "Il vampiro o del moderno sentimento della melanconia (Vampirismo, eros e melanconia)." *Il vampiro, Don Giovanni e altri seduttori*. Edited by Ada Neiger. Dedalo, 1998, pp. 165–203; "Viaggi religiosi, sentimento dei luoghi, identità. La festa si Maria SS. di Porto Salvo a Melito e a Pentedattilo." *Madonne, pellegrini e santi. Itinerari antropologico-religiosi nella Calabria di fine millennio*. Edited by Luigi M. Lombardi Satriani. Meltemi, 2000, pp. 135–159. "Reliquie, sentimento religioso dei luoghi e identità." *Reliquie e culto dei santi nella Certosa di Serra S. Bruno*. Edited by Tonino Ceravolo e Vito Teti. Centro di Antropologie e Letterature del Mediterraneo-Unical/Museo della Certosa, 2000, pp. 19–37; *Il senso dei luoghi. Memoria e vita dei paesi abbandonati*. Donzelli, 2004; "Abbandoni e ritorni. Nuove feste nei paesi abbandonati della Calabria." *Festa viva. Tradizione, territorio, turismo*. Edited by Laura Bonato. Omega, 2005, pp. 147–169; "Antropologia del terremoto: Rovine, melanconia e mentalità." *La Calabria e i terremoti*. Edited by Luciano Meligrana and Vito Teti. Falzea, 2008, pp. 3–21; "Le rovine: abbandono, memoria, costruzione identitaria." *Cultura materiale, cultura immateriale e passione etnografica*. Edited by Leonardo R. Alario. Rubbettino, 2009, pp. 412–438.

The Road to Vallelonga

The observations by Corrado Alvaro on the Calabrians who move about as a "primitive tribe" can be found in "Calabria in fuga," part of his *Un treno nel Sud*, cit., p. 125. Of pilgrims as "caravans of people that abandon their villages and take everything with them, their traditions, whatever is dearest to them," Alvaro already speaks in his first, youthful text, *Polsi nell'arte, nella leggenda, nella storia*. Tipografia Serafino, 1912, p. 59.

The image of nativity scenes is certainly one of the images that recur most often in Calabrian fiction and in Southern Italian literature. See, for example, Corrado Alvaro. *Gente in Aspromonte*. 1930. Garzanti, 2003 [English translation: *Revolt in Aspromonte*. Translated by Frances Frenaye, New Directions, 1962]; Giuseppe Isnardi. *Frontiera calabrese*. Edizioni Scientifiche Italiane, 1965. For other important reflections see Luigi M. Lombardi Satriani "Paesi e presepi" *in Madonne, pellegrini e santi*, cit., pp. 7–37. On the end of the villages that look like nativity scenes, the depopulation of the Calabrian hinterland, the transformations of the territory and of the landscape I have written in "Un centro di una terra senza centro. Geoantropologia della montagna calabrese." *Meridiana. Rivista di Storia e Scienze Sociali*, 44, 222, pp. 163–194; "Mediterraneum. Geografie dell'interno." *Mediterraneo e cultura europea*, edited by Giuseppe Cacciatore et alii, Rubettino, 2003, pp. 107–128; "La Calabria e il mare." *Spola*, 1, 2006, pp. 18–34; "La Calabria dei paesi," *Spola*, 2, 2007, pp. 8–31; "Dal corpo-paese al corpo frantumato." *Il tessuto del mondo. Immagini e rappresentazioni del corpo*, edited by Francesco Faeta, Laura Faranda,

Mauro Geraci, Lello Mazzacane, Marino Niola, Antonello Ricci e Vito Teti. L'ancora del Mediterraneo, 2007, pp. 195–205. *Il senso dei luoghi*, cit., "Memoria e vita dei paesi abbandonati," cit., "Geografie ed etnografie dell'interno." *I Sud. Conoscere, capire, cambiare*, edited by Marta Petrusewicz, Jane Shneider, Peter Schneider. Il mulino, 2009, pp. 163–182.

On some of the aspects of Calabrian emigration to Canada discussed in this book see Vito Teti. "Canzone popolare ed emigrazione." *Quaderni culturali*. I, 3–4, pp. 14–19. "Beni alimentari: conservazione e innovazione nella comunità calabro-canadese a Toronto." *Beni culturali di Calabria* II, edited by Emilia Zinzi. Gangemi, 1985, pp. 627–649; "New York: mito e specchio della Calabria." *Lo sguardo di New York,* edited by Mauro Mattia and Salvatore Piermarini. La casa Usher, 1990, pp. 121–190; *La razza maledetta. Origini del pregiudizio anti-meridionale.* Manifestolibri, 1993; "Emigrazione, alimentazione e culture popolari." *Storia dell'emigrazione italiana*, edited by Piero Bevilacqua, Andreina De Clementi, Emilio Franzina. Donzelli, 2001, pp. 575–597. I also point to *America dove. Viaggio tra i paesani di Calabria e Toronto.* Directed by Vito Teti. Dipartimento Scuola Educazione. RAI Film. 1983 (eight instalments).

The House of the Thirty-Three Loaves of Bread

By Saverio Strati here I quote *Tibi e Tascia*. Mondadori, 1959, but he has written about the alimentary practices of Calabrian peoples in many of his works. Of Corrado Alvaro see *Un treno nel Sud*, cit., pp. 124–125. Food, bread, water, the ritual aspects of "eating," the sacrality of all victuals are discussed frequently in his novels, short stories, essays, travel journals and notes. But on these aspects see also "La teoria di uomini. Pellegrinaggio a Polsi e viaggio nelle opere di Corrado Alvaro, Fortunato Seminara, Francesco Perri," my contribution to *S. Maria di Polsi. Storia e pietà popolare*. Conference proceedings, 1988. Edited by Pietro Borzomati. Laruffa, 1990, pp. 527–601.

On the hunger of Calabrians speaks Leonida Repaci in *Calabria grande e amara*. Nuova Accademia, 1964, pp. 23–25. Tales, descriptions, bits of history having to do with hunger have been penned by Antonio Familiari, Francesco Perri, Don Luca Asprea, Fortunato Seminara, Raul Maria De Angelis, Sharo Gambino, and Saverio Strati. In the novel of the Calabrian writer Giovanna Gulli entitled *Caterina Marasca*. Cultura Calabrese, 1985, hunger becomes an obsession, a cause of desperation and perdition, an absolute protagonist, as absolute as it is in *Fame*, the much better known and internationally acclaimed novel by Knut Hamsun, translated by Ervino Pocar, Adelphi, 1974 [English version: *Hunger*. 1927. Translated by George Egerton. Duckworth, 1967]. On all of this I have written in "Fame, digiuno, dieta nella storia e nella cultura folklorica della Calabria," in *Salute e malattia nella cultura delle classi subalterne del Mezzogiorno*, edited by Massimo Di Rosa. Guida, 1990, pp. 89–134.

The "horrible bread" with which the hired hands of the Cosenza area feed themselves in the years just after the unification of Italy is made of rye, corn, barley, chestnuts or is a mixture of vetch, lupins and fava beans. See Vincenzo Padula. "Stato delle persone in Calabria. V. I braccianti," *Il Bruzio. Giornale politico letterario*. July 6 1864, p. 2. On bread and the alimentary conditions in the Calabria of the 19th century the more complete Padula source is *Calabria prima e dopo l'unità*. 2 vols. Laterza, 1977.

The quotation by Leopoldo Franchetti comes from "Condizioni economiche e amministrative delle province napoletane, Abruzzi e Molise, Calabrie e Basilicata. Appunti di viaggio (1875)" in the author's *Mezzogiorno e colonie*. La Nuova Italia, 1950. The volume includes an essay by Umberto Zanoni-Bianco. See also Luigi Bodio. "Materiali per l'etnologia italiana raccolti per cura della Società italiana di antropologia ed etnologia, riassunti e commentati da Enrico Raseri." *Annali di Statistica*, s. II, vol. 8 (1879), pp. 125–206, attached to the Report by the honorable Boselli to the Chamber of Members of Parliament with regard to the draft legislation of June 16, 1875 on the inquiry concerning agrarian conditions. Stampati Camera, XII,

1874–75, IV, n. 68A, which are available as well in abstract format: Tipografia Botta, 1879, pp. 184–185; *Inchiesta Jacini*. Proceedings of the Giunta per l'Inchiesta Agraria sulle condizioni della classe agricola. Vol IX, fasc. I-II, which comes with "Relazione di Ascanio Branca sulla II Circoscrizione (province di Potenza, Cosenza, Catanzaro e Reggio Calabria)" and "Monografie Agrarie." Forzani e Tipografie del Senato, 1883, p. 327; Leonello De Nobili. "L'emigrazione," in *La questione agraria e l'emigrazione in Calabria*, edited by Dino Taruffi, Leonello De Nobili, Cesare Lori. G Barbera, 1908, pp. 697–888, particularly p. 773. Severe instances of nutritional discomfort and poor bread quality are pointed out in *Inchiesta parlamentare sulle condizioni dei contadini nelle province meridionali e nella Sicilia*. 8 vols. Tipografia Berterio, 1909–1911. But see also Umberto Zanotti-Bianco. *Tra la perduta gente. Africo*. Le Monnier, 1946, p. 13. On the bread of the village of Africo as well as on the craving for white bread has written Corrado Alvaro, respectively, in *Calabria*, cit., p. 29 and in *Gente in Aspromonte*, cit., as well as in many other writings. See, however, also Nicola Misasi, "In Magna Sila," in his *In Calabria*. Pellegrini. 1976, pp. 121–122, and Ignazio Silone. *Fontamara*. 1933. Mondadori, 1987, pp. 183–84. On the difficult access to wheat in the modern era I would mention Maurice Aymard, "Il sud e i circuiti del grano," in *Storia dell'agricoltura italiana in età contemporanea*. Vol I. *Spazi e paesaggi*. Marsilio, 1989, pp. 755–787.

Interesting information on the craving and the need of bread as well as on the miracles performed by saints can be found in the following: Nicola Ferrante. *Santi italo-greci. Il mondo bizantino in Calabria*. Logos, 1992; Maffeo Pretto. *Santi e santità nella pietà popolare in Calabria*. 2 vols. Progetto 2000, 1993; Tonino Ceravolo. *Gli spirdati. Possessione e purificazione nel culto calabrese di San Bruno di Colonia*. Monteleone, 1994, and *Vita di San Bruno di Colonia. La ricerca di Dio nel silenzio del deserto*. Jaca Book-Qualecultura, 2001; *Profili di santi nella Calabria bizantina*, edited by Domenico Minuto. Giuseppe Pontari, 2002.

On alimentary anthropology, with a special focus on bread, I have dwelt in numerous texts, including *Il pane, la beffa e la festa*.

Alimentazione e ideologia dell'alimentazione nelle classi subalterne. Guaraldi, 1976; "Le culture alimentari del Mezzogiorno continentale in età contemporanea," in *L'alimentazione. Storia d'Italia—Annali 13*, edited by Alberto Capatti, Alberto De Bernardi, Angelo Varni, Einaudi, 1998, pp. 63–165; *Il colore del cibo. Geografia, mito e realtà dell'alimentazione mediterranea*, Meltemi, 1999; *Mangiare meridiano. Culture alimentari del Mediterraneo*, edited by Vito Teti, Abramo, 2002; *Storia del peperoncino. Un protagonista delle culture mediterranee*, Donzelli, 2007.

Fernand Braudel recalls the alimentary anxieties of Mediterranean peoples in *Il Mediterraneo. Lo spazio, la storia, gli uomini, le tradizioni.* 1985. Translated by Elena De Angelis, Bompiani, 1992. But by Braudel see *also Civiltà e imperi del Mediterraneo nell'età di Filippo II.* 1949. 2 vol. Translated by Gaetano Pischedda, Einaudi, 1986 [English translation of original version, *The Mediterranean and the Mediterranean World in the Age of Philip II.* Translated by Siân Reynolds, Harper & Row, 1972].

On the whimsicalities of the climate or on the scarcity or abundance of water, both in their own ways always harmful, my reference is Francesco Saverio Nitti. *Scritti sulla questione meridionale. Vol. IV: Inchiesta sulle condizioni dei contadini in Basilicata e in Calabria.* 1910. Laterza, 1968, pp. 85–86. The quotation from Francesco Perri can be found in his *Emigranti*, Lerici, 1976, p. 47. Corrado Alvaro writes in *Aspromonte*, cit., p. 93: "In this country even the rain is our enemy. Either there's no sign of it for months or it pours out from all cataracts." When in Alvaro's works he talks about torrents or the fountains where pilgrims stop, water becomes the symbol of life or of death (the flood), an element of purification and rebirth: "It was the religion of water. We are part of that population which in war called for 'Water, water,' and this cry that arose during certain nights those who were at the front still remember very well. Anyone who wishes to know us, should look at us when we are travelling and we lean out of the window to observe a jet of water, a stream, a brook. Water flows, water is life," he writes in "L'acqua" in his *Itinerario italiano*, cit., pp. 3–7. By Alvaro see also "Paese d'acque," *Almanacco Calabrese*, IV, 4,

Istituto Grafico Tiberino, 1954. On water as a theme in the works by Alvaro and more generally on the history and the anthropology of water see my "La teoria di uomini. Pellegrinaggio a Polsi e viaggio nelle opere di Corrado Alvaro, Fortunato Seminara, Francesco Perri." *S. Maria di Polsi*, cit., pp. 527–601; "Acque paesi uomini in viaggio. Appunti per un'antropologia dell'acqua in Calabria in epoca moderna e contemporanea." *Miscellanea di Studi Storici*. Università della Calabria, 1987, pp. 75–118; *Storia dell'acqua. Mondi materiali e universi simbolici*, edited by Vito Teti, Donzelli, 2003.

On the changes in the social meaning of bread, see Roland Barthes. "L'alimentazione contemporanea." *Scritti. Società, testo, comunicazione*, edited by Gianfranco Marrone, Einaudi, pp. 31–41 and "Cucina ornamentale." *Miti d'oggi*. Translated by Lidia Lonzi, Einaudi, 1974, pp. 125–126 [English translation of original version, *Mythologies*. Translated by Annette Lavers, Hill and Wing, 1972].

By Pasolini I am citing here the famous "Lettera aperta a Italo Calvino" later published as "Limitatezza della storia e immensità del mondo contadino." *Scritti corsari*, cit, pp. 51–55. See p. 46.

The bibliography on bread, on a global scale, is infinite. Here I would recall the fundamental studies of Arnaldo Luraschi, Piero Camporesi, Massimo Montanari and, more recently, the interesting work by Predrag Matvejević, *Pane nostro*. Preface by Enzo Bianchi, postface by Erri De Luca. Garzanti, 2010. I would like also to recall Enzo Bianchi's beautiful book, *Il pane di ieri*. Einaudi, 2008, in which the quiet, heartfelt nostalgia for the sacredness, the indispensability of bread becomes an occasion for meditation and an appeal for greater "care" towards such a basic element of everyday life. More than from books, I've learned about these aspects of bread from the tales told by my grandmother and by the elders, by my father and by Giotto, by the stories about children who died of hunger and by the story about Giulia who in Toronto likes eating bread with nothing on it just to forget about the bread she wasn't able to eat in her village.

The Shadow and the Sewing Machine

I have borrowed the expression "metahistorical peasant family" from Luigi M. Lombardi Satriani, Mariano Meligrana. *Il ponte di San Giacomo. L'ideologia della morte nelle società contadine del Sud*, Sellerio, 1989 (but the original edition was published by Rizzoli, 1982). On migration as the equivalent of death had also written Ernesto De Martino in *Morte e pianto rituale. Dal lamento funebre antico al pianto di Maria*, Boringhieri, 1975 (first edition 1958, with the title *Morte e pianto rituale: dal lamento pagano al pianto di Maria*). For all these aspects I would send back to my *Il paese e l'ombra*, cit.

On the history and the culture of the Confraternity of the Blessed Crucifix at San Nicola da Crissa see Tommaso Mannacio. *La Confraternita del Crocifisso. Vita e cultura di un sodalizio calabrese (San Nicola da Crissa, dal 1669 ai nostri giorni)*. With a postface by Vito Teti. Mapograf, 1993. I borrow often from the *Statuti e riti della Congregazione del SS. Crocefisso eretta nella Chiesa Madre di S. Nicola*, text in manuscript format, 1669–1680 (a typescript copy, edited by Tommaso Mannacio, is available at the archives of the confraternity in San Nicola da Crissa), with a critical edition edited by me and Domenico Teti now in press. On the Confraternity of the Madonna of the Blessed Rosary, see Domenico Carnovale. *La confraternita del SS. Rosario in San Nicola da Crissa*, 1989.

On the Statutes of the Confraternity of the Crucifix and more generally on the anthropology of confraternities in the modern and contemporary eras I send back to my article "Note per un'antropologia delle confraternite calabresi in età moderna e contemporanea" in *Le confraternite religiose in Calabria e nel Mezzogiorno*. Proceedings of the conference held in San Nicola da Crissa, October 16–18, 1992. Mapograf, 2002, pp. 43–98.

I have also made reference to the first book in print in the counties of Catanzaro and Vibo Valentia, that is, Giovanni Giacomo Martini. *Consiliorum sive responsorum iuris ...* 1635, of which I have edited an anastatic copy: *Introduzione a Consiliorum sive responsorum iuris D. Ion. Jacobi Martini ...* Donzelli, 2003. On this book see my introduction to it, pp. 5–16; as well as my following contributions: "Élites locali, mito delle origini e costruzione dell'identità." *Tra Calabria e Mezzogiorno. Studi in memoria di Tobia Cornacchioli*, edited by Giuseppe Masi, Pellegrini, 2007, pp. 81–109; "Gian Giacomo Martini e Uluccialì alias Kilic Alì Pasha: aspetti della costruzione dell'identità calabrese tra XVI-XVII secolo." *La Calabria del Viceregno spagnolo. Storia arte architettura e urbanistica*, edited by Alessandra Anselmi, Gangemi, 2009, pp. 139–169. On some of the aspects of the urban and social history of the village, see my "Strutture produttive e strutture abitative. San Nicola da Crissa." *Calabria,* edited by Francesco Faeta, Laterza, pp. 119–139. Memories, images, reflections on community can be found in *Le strade di casa. Visioni di un paese di Calabria*, edited by Salvatore Piermarini and Vito Teti, Mazzotta, 1983. The reports of the Jesuit fathers are quoted by Ernesto De Martino. *La terra del rimorso*, cit., p. 22. But see also Pietro Tacchi Venturi. *Storia della Compagnia di Gesù in Italia.* Vol. I, parte I. La Civiltà Cattolica, pp. 324 ff. and part II, p. 93.

The phrase by Joseph Roth is in line with the poetics of his most important novels, such as *Fuga senza fine. Una storia vera.* 1927. Translated by Maria Grazia Mannucci. Adelphi, 1976, or *Tarabas. Un ospite su questa terra.* 1934. Translated by Luciano Fabbri. Adelphi, 1979, or *Giobbe. Romanzo di un uomo semplice.* 1930. Translated by Laura Terreni. Adelphi, 1980 [English original versions respectively *Flight Without End.* Translated by David Le Vay with the collaboration of Beatrice Musgrave. Overlook Press, 1977; *Tarabas. A Guest on Earth.* Translated by Winifred Katzin, Chatto and Windus, 1987; *Job.* Translated by Dorothy Thompson, Overlook Press, 2003]. I have had the opportunity to underscore the analogies between two cataclysmic "ends of the world," the end of the traditional Calabrian way of life and the end of the Austro-Hungarian empire, of the *shtetl,* as they are captured by Roth and Alvaro, two writers that display surprising similarities, in "Tradizione e modernità nell'opera di Corrado Alvaro." *Corrado Alvaro e la letteratura tra le due guerre,* edited by Aldo Maria Morace, Pellegrini, 2005, pp. 515–540.

By Alvaro I would cite also the title of one of his novels, *Tutto è accaduto*, Bompiani, 1962, i.e, in English, *Everything Has Already Happened*.

Worthwhile noting on the idea of home and the shadow, of doubleness, is Pino Stancari. *La Calabria tra il sottoterra e il cielo*, Rubbettino, 1997.

In this chapter I've once again come face to face with clouds. Without me realizing it, clouds have become a basic constituent of my narrations. I would be quite happy to be remembered as one who observes—or even runs after—clouds. Mine is an ancient illness, an incurable vice, a distant art. Clouds, small and large, fogs precede the great plagues; they announce and accompany destruction. It would suffice to recall the descriptions of the 1783 earthquake that flagellated Calabria, or the descriptions of the peasants who interpret the presence of low clouds in the sky as a scourge about to happen, something that will create havoc with their harvest. One could write a kind of dictionary of clouds to see how they have pervaded places, or the fears, the expectations, the desires, the dreams, the visions of peoples. From the clouds of the Big Bang to the clouds of Chernobyl, to those of the World Trade Center Towers, clouds appear at the beginning of the world and warn us of its possible end. The bibliography on this topic is immense. By way of introduction to it I point to the book by Tonino Ceravolo, *Storia delle nuvole. Da Talete a Don De Lillo*. Rubbettino, 2009. I very much loved Jean Baudrillard's *L'America*. Translated by Laura Guarino, Feltrinelli, 1987 [English translation of original version: *America*. Translated by Chris Turner. Verso, 1988] with its exceptional notes on the different clouds of the old world and the new world. "Clouds are a subject of conversation throughout the Mediterranean," writes Predrag Matvejević in his *Mediterraneo. Un nuovo breviario*. 1987. Translated by Silvio Ferrari. Garzanti, 1991, pp. 37–38 [English translation of original version: *Mediterranean. A Cultural landscape*. Translated by Michael Henry Heim. University of California Press, 1999].

During the last thirty years with Salvatore Piermarini we've taken pictures of clouds in places and villages of Calabria and have told their stories in the volume *Le navi che volano. Reportage di viaggio in Calabria 1973–2002*. With comments by Mario Fortunato. Monteleone, 2002. We've also shown the clouds of Ontario and New York and narrated their stories in various other books. Each time, as we looked at our contact prints and the negatives, new clouds that I hadn't imagined and hadn't expected. A paragraph entitled "Clouds" appeared in my book *Il senso dei luoghi*, cit., pp. 270-275. We could consider clouds to be akin to the outdated, immaterial objects of the literary tradition to which Francesco Orlando draws our attention in his *Gli oggetti desueti nelle immagini della letteratura. Rovine, reliquie, rarità, robaccia, luoghi inabitati e tesori nascosti*. Einaudi, 1994.

The Funeral of the Emperor

Apollo Lumini's book on the carnival is *Le farse del Carnevale in Calabria e Sicilia*. Forni, 1977, which is an anastatic reprint of the original, Tipografia Nicotera, 1888.

 Turi's accounts can be found in Salvatore D'Eraclea. *Una memoria del carnevale a San Nicola da Crissa e altre storie*. Mapograf, 1994. On Turi as a character it's useful to compare Luigi M. Lombardi Satriani, Mariano Meligrana. "Emigrazione simbolica: il Carnevale" in their *Un villaggio nella memoria*, cit., pp. 48–53, my "Presentazione" in Salvatore D'Eraclea. Una memoria del carnevale ..., cit., pp. 11–14 and Felicia Malfarà. *I riti e le farse del Carnevale. La tradizione, l'erosione, la fine del carnevale a San Nicola da Crissa*. 2004, a University of Calabria dissertation. Turi is also the protagonist of the documentary *La morte di Carnevale* that I directed for the *Spazio folklore* series of the Calabrian regional branch of the RAI, the Italian national television, in 1979.

 On the Carnival in Calabria I've written also in the following texts, useful, among other things, for the additional bibliographical information they contain: "Comunicazione sul Carnevale in Calabria." *Per un teatro nel Meridione*. Proceedings of the 1st Congress of the Associazione Nazionale Critici di Teatro, edited by Maricla Boggio and Alberto Calogero, Parallelo 38, 1976, pp. 186-201; "Comunicazione sul Carnevale in Calabria." *Per un teatro nel Meridione*. Proceedings of the 2nd congress of the Associazione Nazionale Critici di Teatro, edited by Maricla Boggio and Alberto Calogero, Parallelo 38, 1977, pp. 293–305; "Carnevale è ancora una festa?" *Calabria sconosciuta*, 20, October-December 1982, pp. 27–34; "Carnevale abolito dall'abbondanza." *La gola*, III, 16, 1984, p. 9; "Carnevale e memoria" in Pietro V. Gallo. Carnevale, edited by Antonio Marasco, Mapograf, 1992, pp. 11–43; "Teatro, cultura popolare e letteratura d'élite." *Teatro in Calabria. 1870-1970. Drammaturgia Repertori Compagnie*. Monteleone, 2003, pp. 211–280. But see also these other documentaries I directed: *Carnevale. Gesto riso morte (Monterosso Calabro)*. *Spazio folklore* series. Calabrian regional branch of the RAI. 1980; *Torna Carnevale*. 2nd instalment of *America dove*, cit.

Of the vast literature on Carnival within the European context the following at least deserve to be mentioned: Piero Camporesi. *La maschera di Bertoldo. G. C. Croce e la letteratura carnevalesca*. Einaudi, 1976; Emmanuel Le Roy Ladurie. *Il Carnevale di Romans*. 1979. Translated by Giovanni Bogliolo. Rizzoli, 1981 [English translation of original version, *Carnival in Romans*. Translated by Mary Feeney, Braziler, 1979]; Michail Bachtin. *L'opera di Rabelais e la cultura popolare. Riso, carnevale e festa nella tradizione medievale e rinascimentale*. 1965. Translated by Mili Romano. Einaudi, 1979 [English translation of original version: *Rabelais and His World*. Translated by Hélène Iswolsky. Indiana UP, 1984]; Peter Burke. *Cultura popolare nell'Europa moderna*. 1978. Translated by Federico Canobbio-Codelli. Mondadori, 1980 [Original version: *Popular Culture in Early Modern Europe*. Temple Smith, 1978]; Pietro Clementi et alii. *Per un ripensamento della tematica di Michail Bachtin*. Franco Angeli, 1983; Massimo Montanari. *La fame e l'abbondanza. Storia dell'alimentazione in Europa*. Laterza, 1993. More than to the many, various studies on the topic, I believe, however, that I owe to Turi and to the other farsari, the "farce-masters," the most profound understanding of the ancient carnivalesque spirit.

Afterword

Francesco Loriggio

Stones Into Bread is the first book by Vito Teti to be translated. And it's perhaps fitting that this inaugural translation should be in English and published in Toronto, where his father lived as an immigrant for a number of years and where many other Calabrians from San Nicola da Crissa, his home village, have settled. Were one a Calabrian, as I am, one might even, after reading the book and learning that it's also about migration and about the migration of some of his fellow *sannicolesi* to Toronto, detect in these coincidences something like the hand of fate, and see in them the perfect epilogue. So perfect one might even for a moment ignore some of the questions that arise as we read *Stones Into Bread*. (Why is it only the first of Teti's books to be translated? Would it have been only the first had Teti written in the language of Shakespeare or the language of Molière?) Unfortunately such an epilogue isn't the written afterthought the author has appended to one of his manuscripts. And it doesn't exempt us who have read Teti and think that others should also read him from answering those questions. Or from filling in as many gaps as we can. Starting from scratch or thereabouts.

At present, as of early 2018, Teti's bibliography includes around a dozen major volume-length texts, on topics ranging, among others, from the Mediterranean diet (*Il colore del cibo*) and the past and the future of eating (*Fine pasto*, commissioned for the 2015 World Exposition in Milan) to the history of chilli peppers and their role in Italian cuisine (*Storia del peperoncino*) to the idea of place as it pertains to the effects of the relocation of some of the villages of the Calabrian hinterland which, for one reason or another, had slowly become inhabitable and are now ghost villages (*Il senso dei luoghi, Quel che resta*), to the polemics on anti-Southern discrimination and the role of the South in modern Italian history (*La razza maledetta, Maledetto Sud*), to the linkages between folk attitudes about blood and the figure of the vampire (*La melanconia del vampiro*), to the roaming impulses of Southern Italians, particularly Calabrians (*Terra inquieta*), to the culture of water (*Storia dell'acqua*, as editor), to the contribution of Southern Italian intellectuals to Italian unification (*Il patriota e la maestra*), to Calabrian migration to Canada (*Il paese e l'ombra*, and *Stones Into Bread*, whose Italian title is *Pietre di pane*).

Overall, what Teti does in these works falls most directly within the purview of anthropology, in its multiple manifestations, be it as anthropology itself or ethnology or ethnography. Indeed, it's with the title of ethnologist and anthropologist that Teti has taught—and still teaches—at the University of Calabria. On the other hand, his allegiance to these disciplines, even with regard to their most preliminary demands, has been quite less than typical. Varied as the material he ponders may be, most of the physical research it entails has occurred within the quite limited area of Calabria itself, the region of Italy in which Teti was born and where he has lived all his life. Thus one of the things that would appear to be missing from his work is the fascination with the exotic that has in one way or other, for better or for worse, been generally associated with anthropological practice and has distinguished it from the practice of other social scientists. No direct encounter with non-Western subjects, the West's "others," for Teti. Whence, we could immediately suggest, the diminished appeal, for publishers outside Italy as well as, perhaps, a good portion of the readership of anthropological accounts.

This, circulation-wise, has been the major drawback of much Italian anthropology. Even Ernesto De Martino, the key figure of the discipline in Italy to this day and one of the most original Italian intellectuals of the post-WWII period, is little known outside his country.

Only one of his books has been translated into English and French: not so much, one has to believe, because his work mixed anthropology with ethnography, psychology or philosophy as much as for its particular geographical breadth. De Martino's ultimate aim was to devise criteria through which to accost the so-called primitives and to produce depictions that would do justice to their lore, customs and mores. A Neapolitan by birth, he chose the non-metropolitan areas of the Italian South and its agricultural peasantry, its *contadini,* as his preferred field of study. His expeditions in Lucania and Apulia, in which he enrolled musicologists and psychiatrists as well as ethnographers and folklorists, have remained legendary. And quite ahead of his times, too, was his understanding of the implications of his choice of locale, both with regard to prevailing disciplinary climate and to the political climate of his country. (It's not without interest that his first major monograph was devoted to the problem that the encounter with the "others" of the West or the others of metropolitan culture posed for historicism, for historiography as such and, hence, for a proper grasp of his position as an anthropologist and as a citizen participating in the social debates of the Italy of the period.)

Teti's involvement in the current modulations of those debates, whether disciplinary or socio-political, has been, if anything, more explicit.

Two of his works, *La razza maledetta* and *Maledetto Sud,* engage directly the debate on the interaction—or lack thereof—between Northern and Southern Italy and how it has impinged on the country's self-imaginings. The first does so by showing that many of the negative stereotypes about Italian Southerners, still quite common in Italian society, hark back to 19th-century positivist anthropology, which relied heavily on now long discredited phrenological studies in its classification of individuals. The second picks up on some of the more current tensions between the two regions and its inhabitants to berate both the uppity, self-serving biases fueling the secessionist bombast of the *Lega Nord*, the Northern League, and the revanchism of fringe Southern intellectuals, who in recent decades have begun to re-evaluate positively the policies of the Bourbon monarchy that governed the Kingdom of the Two Sicilies before the unification of Italy.

An intervention on this crucial controversy—built-into the very fabric of Italian social life during the last one hundred and fifty years—can similarly be considered *Il patriota e la maestra*. It traces the relationship between a Southern Italian man of a middle-class family from Teti's own village who partook directly in the struggle to free Italy from foreign occupation and a Northern Italian woman of intellectual temperament (she was a school mistress) who shared his political outlook. The account is an indirect, more discreet response to both poles of the revisionist rehearsals of Italian unification, those of individuals maintaining that it had been achieved primarily through the efforts of the Piedmontese or Lombard social élites, and those by individuals who bemoan its negative impact on the Southern regions.

Other works encroach on other topics that have strong Italian—and as importantly, Calabrian—pendants. Teti's foray into the brouhaha on the Mediterranean diet (in *Il colore del cibo*) under-scores the fact that until the late 20th century for Southern peasants the much-praised centrality of legumes was actually a handicap, a re-minder of their social status, their poverty vis-à-vis the upper classes which could afford meat and fish on a more regular basis. His in-depth revisitation of the meanderings of the chilli pepper from Mexico to Southern Europe (*Storia del peperoncino*) is capped by long chapters on its ubiquitous and highly visible presence in Calabrian cuisine and Calabrian mores.

Of course Teti belongs to a generation which came after De Martino's, and not just chronologically. The career of the Neapolitan master unfolded in the 1950s and 1960s, when for his colleagues the main preoccupation was how to face the "others" beyond the West, how to equip themselves intellectually for such an encounter. The dissemination of Teti's essays would have no doubt benefitted if, be-fore or after that encounter, an anthropology of Europe had managed to impose itself, or at least been pursued more deliberately than it has. Had what has remained a very minor branch of the discipline turned into a full-fledged field of research with a different, more salient standing, had self-knowledge—an assessment of the discipline's unavoidable grounding in European history and European values—been the mandatory first move it should have been, then the overviews of one Europe's non-metropolitan backwater areas would have had greater allure.

The lack of a full-fledged anthropology of Europe notwithstanding, today Teti's Calabria-centred ethnography seems suddenly, very much up-to-date and far from irrelevant. After all, history, European or otherwise, has its own compensatory mechanisms, and it can thrust into the limelight demeanours long relegated off-stage or at the outskirts of the main action. The Mediterranean and its shores, African, Asian *and* European, have been often in the news these last two or three decades. Not simply for the strife they have harboured. They have been one of the places where some of the things that Teti ponders in his works—the movement of peoples, the consequences of the departures on the built and natural environment, on the societies and the individuals left behind—have been constant occurrences, the apparently inexorable rule of thumb of 20th-century and early 21st-century daily life.

But this isn't the only double-edged feature of those works, the feature which has most likely, thus far, hampered their dissemination outside of Italy and which simultaneously enhances their attractiveness, signals them to us. Teti doesn't only abide faithfully by one of the primary tenets of his discipline, whereby anthropologists should endeavour to be participant observers in and of the societies they study. He wears both caps daily, since he was born and still lives in a village in the Calabrian hinterland, a site where his colleagues might choose to conduct their research and which is at the core of his own professional activity. As a result in his writings the line between subjectivity and objectivity is rather thin. The "I" of his books and essays is the "I" of someone who is at once the gatherer of the data and one of the informants, of the sources, an "I" who is author and character and knows it. That doubleness is never out of the picture, even when the second, less official self enters the scene only now and then, in some pages or some excerpts.

Whether Teti tracks the many swerves in the trajectory of the chilli pepper or dwells on the different social implications of some of the ingredients of the Mediterranean diet or zooms in on episodes of the microhistory of the Italian Risorgimento, his analyses—whatever the scale of the topics they address—are always to some extent peppered with autobiographical allusions or with anecdotes about people or events he bore witness to or heard about from individuals he knew. His works are multi-layered texts where pages on his own experience or those of friends and his family can appear side by side with pages on his village or on other villages, on Calabria and Italy as such or on Toronto. Each of these levels straddles the others and interweaves often seamlessly with them, so that we get a perspective in which the personal, the familial, the local, the regional, the national and the international are dimensions which are both distinct and partaking of the same geographical and historical continuum.

All of which brings us back, finally, to *Stones Into Bread*. This book is both the best introduction to Teti's writings and their culmination. Its mixed structure—with short tales preceded by a prologue more straightforwardly essayistic and critical in intent, and interludes and other passages in verse, transcriptions of nursery rhymes and lullabies from his own village—reproposes in highly condensed form, therefore emphatically, most of the content he parlays longhand in the other works and offers an updated and equally trenchant, if equally concentrated, digest of the intellectual and disciplinary concerns he has had to confront.

The pages on the pilgrimages to sanctuaries, on the various protector-saints that populate the religious imagination of the Calabrians, on the nutritional habits and/or aspirations of his co-villagers (with regard to bread and figs especially), on the changing role of women in the families where men were away for long periods, the various outlines of individual destinies (Teti's mother, the village storyteller, the youth apparently doomed to a lackluster future who instead transmogrifies into a highly successful mechanic, the young intellectuals coming back for the summer from the university they attend, *blasé* and estranged), on the church confraternities, on carnival and village *farceurs* are more than enough for an ethnographic overview of a small community and its vicissitudes during the second half of the 20th century. They cover the various aspects of small-town life in the Calabria of the inland, mountainous areas that he grew up in and which he still calls home.

As well, the short-story-collection make-up of *Stones Into Bread* lets stand out equally forcefully the autobiographical references, the many anecdotes about Teti as a boy, as a youth or as an adult. But, like the rest of the narrative portions, these bits of self-descriptions too are pre-empted by the prologue, which superimposes on them the silhouette of the scholar, an image of Teti at his desk, fully committed, as it were, to his vocation, to a way of writing ethnography. Or, to be more precise, by a meditation on the state of the discipline, by what is a sort of meta-text for all of the features of the book.

It's not difficult to assign specific anthropological resonances to the events and the lives Teti limns out for us. The Calabria of *Stones Into Bread* bears little resemblance to the Calabria most frequently in the news these days, the Calabria of organized crime, of the *'ndranghetisti*. Neither is it the Calabria where codes of honour and/or amoral familism are pervasive, as in the past some studies have purported they were, in all Southern Italian or Mediterranean societies. In the tales that unfold in this book women have a much more positive function than these depictions would let us believe. The reality the circumstances of Calabrian villages have thrust upon them, with men continuously working abroad or in other regions of Italy, has meant that women have had to oversee the household, to take fundamental decisions. A status and a freedom they no longer entirely surrender once they join their husbands in their new settings or when their husbands rejoin them. Not by chance Teti recalls in some of the more distinctly personal passages of the book that he was brought up by his mother and his grandmother, and that he had no early childhood memories of his father, who had left to work in Toronto and came back only when the son was already eight years old.

Much the same response, the same images of that "other" Calabria, elicit, in *Stones Into Bread*, the pages on pilgrims and pilgrimages, which bring to mind not violence, strife or competition for resources, but rather the fellowship that is forged when travelling together with other people. And it's also these highly gregarious, convivial, deeply knit attachments that Teti's anecdotes about religious fraternities or about the other non-family-based associations and activities (such as the village feasts, first and foremost the carnival and the accentuated freedom it bestows on the oral verse-makers and the clownesque farce-masters) are keen to record.

There isn't in *Stones Into Bread* as much about the geological and ecological disarray of the region as we might have anticipated, and that Teti's other books have so carefully and poignantly canvassed. Only in "Angelino's Turn," the tale that ushers in the narrative sequence, do we have some kind of adumbration of the hidden menaces Calabrians have to contend with every day. The villages which fall within the anthropologist's compass and constitute his "field" cling to their hillsides or to their mountaintops all too precariously and often have had to be abandoned, due both to the vagaries of human history (a weak economy) and to the congenital environmental fragility (the earthquakes, the bouts of extreme dryness and extreme wetness).

Few other Italian landscapes are so pocked with so many empty houses, so many modern ruins or modern ruins-to-be. With a narrative savvy one doesn't normally expect in social scientists, Teti is quiet about Angelino's last-day scouring of his now deserted burg, never indicating the causes for his family's departure. It's a silence all too eloquent: the Calabria we can infer from the tale is very much, despite (or because of) the unsaid, a *terra inquieta*, as the title of one of its author's books dubs it. The journeys to sanctuaries, the yearning for community underlying the feasts and ceremonies so frequently recurring in the other stories dig deep in the collective psyche: They're the poor person's responses, his or her attempt through which to garner sufficient solidarity and momentarily offset, postpone or conceal the risks and the insecurities inherent to living in the region.

Needless to say, at the core of the social motives of that restlessness—and therefore at the core of almost everything that for the *Calabresi* relates to the realm of history—is migration. *Stones Into Bread* captures as lucidly as can be the parallels between pilgrimages and the transatlantic journeys in search of work and of a different future. In the pages of "The Road to Vallelonga" and then "Figs in Toronto," the salvation that Canada promises, in the guise of the social survival, the social mobility unavailable and unthinkable in Calabria, interlaces with a still unabatedly public, highly ritualistic religiousness. At Midland, Ontario, where the feast of the Madonna of Vallelonga takes place every year, the statue is carried in procession with its face turned towards the Calabrian sanctuary, and the fraternities still exist in Toronto. By the same token, migration injures as much as it redeems, at both ends of the geography.

On this Teti's ethnography is nothing if not complete. In *Stones Into Bread* the money sent back by those who work abroad does keep afloat local economies but in the long run the absence of large fractions of the more productive elements of the citizenry is itself a major cause of the villages' slow drifting towards full demise. The cyclical reappearance of the departees during the summer holidays, when the crowds seem once more to awake the villages from their slumber, to restore some semblance of the lost normality, only renders the awareness of the decline more acute and the clinging to tradition more poignant. That they may have aided and abetted the surging of the changed atmosphere doesn't escape the returnees, from wherever it is they're coming back from.

The younger late-20th century ex-lovers of "Clouds and Back Streets," who have known migration personally only for having left home to study in the more prestigious universities in other Italian regions, are now prey to an unrestrainable, overwhelming *ennui* whenever they meet in their village and start to ponder its future. As for the older migrants, their trips to the former home are less and less frequent and afford less and less release. Equally significant, for some of them (the protagonists of "The Stones of My Cousin Giò" and "The Emperor's Funeral" first and foremost) the village is as much akin to a last stop, the cemetery to go back to when they die, as it is a birthplace or the place where they grew up.

Most importantly, in *Stones Into Bread* the distress of the trans-oceanic travellers is two-pronged. To the Calabria-based, implicit subterranean *angst* they carry with them and which may eventually resurface during the trips back, must be added the *angst* the disloca-tion triggers. The Toronto *Calabresi* whose story Teti narrates allay the apprehension that goes with being in a distant land whose culture, language and values are different from theirs. They survive initially via acts of mimesis, by devising miniaturized varieties of their ori-gins, by creating neighbourhoods that, though imperfect as urban, metropolitan copies of their villages, guarantee at least a modicum of the social cohesion (religious feast and rituals, clubs, associations and so on) of the past, are enough of a buffer between them and the new surroundings to keep full alienation and full strangeness at bay until some adaptation to the society at large kicks in.

But this arrangement is quite provisional; it's a half-measure that can't take the migrants entirely off the hook, and Teti, again careful to ensure that his tales press as far forward as he believes they should go, doesn't let his informer-characters forget it. *Stones Into Bread* fol-lows the *Calabresi* who arrived in Toronto in the early post-WWII decades—friends, family, co-villagers—up to the moment when they begin to acknowledge the changes around them and within them: how their Canadian-born children begin to marry with non-Italians; how returning to Canada is now for them too an urge stronger than going back to the village in Calabria; how the toil that had gone into securing a safe, livable future for themselves and their offspring now begets other histories, other memories, all discontinuous as well as continuous with the history and the memories of the old coun-try. And if the whiffs of existential pathos that emanates from them aren't quite as pungent and irrepressible as they are for those of their children who are writers or artists, they do insinuate themselves in the psyche of the older Italian-born migrants, who, as in "Figs in Toronto," do wonder about the cracks they begin to discern in their own identity.

The overall narrative that can be distilled from the various individual biographies and specific circumstances *Stones Into Bread* unfurls for us is, then, one whose final intent is to reach the present of the *Calabresi* in Calabria and in Toronto. In a period in which "mobility" is the buzz word in cultural circles, one on which the social sciences are erecting their latest paradigms, Teti strives as much to amend the overtones and connotations it comes attached with as he does to confirm them. The migrants whose tales he rehearses for us— the white European migrants of the post WWII years, the migrants of the Western proletariat and the Western peasantry of the 1940s, the 1950s and the 1960s—are individuals on the move, as they have traditionally been, but for them travel can never be perpetual motion, the unending wandering, the nomadism without direction of myth, the Romantic serial novel or some recent philosophers. Italian Canadians are one of the ethnic groups with the highest percentage of home owners. Their journey culminates in some form of settlement, of immobility. And immobility, regardless of how long the stretch, has its injunctions and its inevitable consequences.

In *Stones Into Bread* the rehabilitation of stillness and hence of dwelling reinstates time, that very modern (pre-postmodernist?) dimension, into the overall purview of travel. With migration, as Teti describes it, voyaging acquires a non-spatial *dénouement*, has now the play of generations at its core. Propelled by the desire for movement up the social ladder, it now reveals itself to be ineluctably future-oriented, with the descendants of the migrants situating themselves differently from their parents or grandparents and resembling them less and less, culturally, psychologically and, perhaps, existentially. For much the same reason, its geography is a multi-layered, double-pronged, circular geography, always of greater range than the journey itself. Migration conjoins for long periods, if not forever, departure and arrival. Both can't avoid some sort of mutation. Those who leave will look back nostalgically at the life from which they've severed themselves; those who remain are never without images of the places where the friends and relatives have dispersed and never totally free of the temptation to leave, of the afterwards they might have initiated for themselves.

Like the locations where the migrants have transplanted themselves, the Calabrian villages where the tales of *Stones Into Bread* begin or end also undergo their metamorphoses, often even disappearing altogether. Live outdoor museums of social ruins, as well as, often, of actual ruins, they give the lie to anybody who thinks that only host locations bear the burden of migration, that the migrants' departure disengages one space, one society from the other.

As may be suspected, by now, this doesn't altogether exhaust the breadth of the narrative that reverberates through the book. Macroscopic, reiterated as they are, the tales' crisscrossings between space and time send back only to the more purely field-work, ethnographic side of the enterprise. Through their content they show us how specific social histories—the histories Calabrian villages foster—convert into universal, human experiences. Teti doubles this when in the prologue he affixes to the tales—which he entitles, not insignificantly, "Of Remaining"—he embarks on a defense of immobility in anthropology, of an anthropology that doesn't oblige its practitioners to travel, to seek distant, appropriately non-Western locales in which to act as participant observers and thus prove themselves worthy of membership in the profession. In brief, *Stones Into Bread* is also an ethnography of ethnography, an anthropology of anthropology. Unabashedly, its prologue resuscitates the kind of *pantouflard*, office- or study-based research that reached its apogee in the early, modernist 20th century with Sir James Frazer's *The Golden Bough* and which had been repudiated and/or revised by succeeding waves of its author's colleagues. Revised and re-evaluated so that it could be paired with the more physical, sun-burned, shirt-sleeved field work, the sit-down, couch-bound, mental encounter with the "primitives" can now be also repositioned in the intellectual spectrum.

If it's possible to inquire on the making of lived culture and lived otherness without straying away from home or without putting one foot out of the library or of one's private chambers, if it's possible to do that *before* no less than *after* the advent of computers and the internet, anthropologists may, surely enough, feel free to see kindred spirits also in novelists and poets. At least—and most evidently—in those novelists and poets who travel *sans vapeur et sans voile,* as Baudelaire used to say, or in the various others writers Teti identifies in his prologue.

So how should we deal with all of this, with the intimations we can extract from the self-reflexive, ultra-condensed tale collection *Stones Into Bread* is? Clearly, ethnographies must comply with the precept of descriptiveness and are, hence, more liable to stratify and to privilege "thickness" as an approach. Anthropologists less committed to these principles, to the rationale guiding ethnographic field work or ethnographic accounts might object that the specificity, the singularity of individual cultures should at best be a preliminary preoccupation. Stopping there, without broaching even some basic comparison between the cultural strategies of one society and those of other societies, would preclude the uncovering of laws valid for all places and all peoples, which for some is the ultimate aim of the social sciences.

This, in effect, is one of the built-in limitations of *Stones Into Bread* and of Teti's Calabria-centred works. (Elsewhere, such as in *Storia del peperoncino* and in *Il colore del cibo,* he does cast wider nets.) For example, the mechanism of duplication by which the book's *Sannicolesi* migrants survive, culturally, in Toronto, and which they bring to bear at various levels—alimentary, religious, social, etc.—may not be a fully valid option for those of them who find themselves elsewhere. More assimilationist in attitude than Canada or the United States, the European countries where Teti's cousin Giò was able to make his fortune—Switzerland and France—didn't encourage and haven't encouraged phenomena such as the North American Little Italies, which aren't part of their urban landscape. Any reassessment of modern migration would have to consider all its variations, its histories.

Vice versa, it could be argued that mimesis hasn't been a subterfuge adopted only—or, for that matter, primarily—by migrants. The early Western colonialists also attempted to defuse the strangeness of the territories they had disembarked on via recourse to the memory of the places they had left behind. They did it, among other ways, by affixing tags they were familiar with to the various places they found themselves in, by renaming the new, foreign geography they came across "New England" or "New York" or "Nova Scotia" or "Louisiana" or "New Orleans" or "*La nouvelle France*" or "New Brunswick" or "British Columbia" or with some other such label.

Here collating anthropologically the two ventures on that criterion of the anxiety would have, again, opened up further avenues for research. It might have led to a fuller grasp of the politics of annexation, their psychology and their rhetoric, their undeclared conflation of conquest and heroism or displacement and occupation. (As Italy's belated and misguided efforts at colonialism failed during the post-unification decades and after, Italian government officials began thinking of Italian migrants as *coloni*, as individuals who aided and abetted some of the stronger, more successful Western forays into the "wilderness," and who by their presence there—in the Americas, in Australia—were proof of the thinly veiled desire of Italian élites for expansion and expansionism no less than outposts for the diffusion of Italian goods or opportunities for Italian commerce.) And, once again, on that too it would have deposited the migration the book chronicles smack in the thick of actuality, further corroborating the theorem it proposes in its quick, spur-of-the-moment, un-enlarged-upon observation that "the village is the world and the world is a village."

Teti would most probably answer that, yes, anthropology may have general laws as its final target but the first and foremost duty of ethnographers is to bear witness. Their allegiance goes firstly and foremostly to their "field," to the peculiarities of the communities they have chosen to study, to the eating habits, pilgrimages, religious celebrations, the feasts, the mournings, the "orature" and songs of villages such as San Nicola da Crissa. And if they're able to demonstrate, as he does, that the history of migrant groups can't be dissevered from more blatant, more public, more central and more celebrated histories, that it's embedded in those histories, despite the geographical, social or cultural marginality and *with* the difference it carries, not once it has divested itself of it, they, as ethnographers, have done their job.

The exodus of the *Calabresi* of *Stones Into Bread* had political undertones it shared with the passages of other groups. It also had religious undertones and could be said to be a pilgrimage. But its shrine shining bright on a hill had Catholic, not Protestant, tinges, and what instigated the voyage towards it was the more terrestrial yearning for upward mobility. If all social mimesis is always undertaken to allay some anxiety, Calabrian modulations of it, like the mimesis of all bona fide migrants, didn't require the intervention of armies and legislation: The enclaves inhabited by the huddled masses from the Tyrrhenian or Ionian hinterland were altogether provisional, erasable, not forever inscribed on the territory. And highlighting that difference, Teti would probably conclude, is his primary goal.

Similar arguments, pro and con, will spark some of the critical expostulations *Stones Into Bread* contains or some of the literary qualities of its tales.

For the Teti of the prologue, the psychological discomfort felt by the *calabresi* migrants in their new land can be compared to the loss of a person's shadow, of its self-image, a recurring theme of 19th-century Romantic novels. As he envisages them, once he dons the robes of the intellectual, the miniature reproductions of the village are akin to the attempts of the fictional characters of those books to recover and reconstitute their lost doubles, the replicas of their selves. It's quite an alluring proposition, one which we, recollecting the full scope of social mimesis, could amplify further. In European fiction the preoccupation with the double, the fear of losing one's shadow, does after all emerge in the heyday of colonialism, when explorations and the encounters with non-Western otherness were edging towards their peak and their fallout seeping down into more general sensibilities.

But apart from everything else (here too the goal was to portray Calabrian vicissitudes, their overlaps with European or Western history and culture), restricting the analogies with literature to Calabrian migration allows *Stones Into Bread* to maintain some continuity between the autobiographical episodes that appear in the tales—the paragraphs on Teti as a child or as a youth and as an adult—and the image of Teti as a professional, as a self-conscious ethnographer. One rebounds onto the other: Teti the scholar ruminates on the Teti who is a member of the community being observed and is simultaneously himself—in his capacity as a commentator, as a meta-narrator—caught in the narrative he is glossing.

The educated, learned scribe of the family grew up with the un-vanished, with those who themselves went through their daily lives with the images of friends or relatives now in other lands, who, like him, might have travelled to those places where their father or other stand-ins of themselves had been. How fitting, then, that he would latch on to the very literary narratives of the double and grant them explanatory power over the events of voyaging and remaining he chose to write about.

What differentiates *Stones Into Bread* from the works of other anthropologists who in recent decades have shifted the focus on the textual components of their enterprise is the degree of the complicity with literature and literariness it posits and actualizes. A Clifford Geertz is now recognized as one of the master essayists of our time. Younger members of the discipline (James Clifford et al) zeroed in on the individual rhetorical and formal traits of the reports they were faced with, of the modes and techniques of "writing culture," as they have dubbed it.

The tales of *Stones Into Bread* trump this not only through the type of colloquial, non-specialized language they display or through the personal backdrop against which Teti constantly lines up his narratives. We would be hard put to single out those among his fellow anthropologists who would stand by the note he appends to this book, where he affirms that the villages and the places he describes only resemble the villages and the places he has known, that they "aren't exactly those villages and those places," that the events, the episodes, the people he narrates are "'real' and 'invented' in so far as they're filtered by [his[gaze, by [his] activity as an ethnographer, as a wanderer on foot, as a listener and an idler ... by [his] selection (or the sudden emergence) of [his] recollection or [his] forgetfulness."

In claiming among his prerogatives both the truth of autobiography or ethnography and the truth of the imagination Teti transmutes *Stones Into Bread* into a work that is at once creative non-fiction and historical fiction, a work that applies to anthropological research the rationale traditionally—since Aristotle at least—used to define literature.

Here in these pages that seem at times to be after only a good yarn, anthropological discursiveness can also accommodate the logic and the ontology of the possible, rather than just the logic and the ontology of the factual. It's not only the writerly pitch of the voice, the gracefulness of the slices of life, the non-jargonistic language, the poetic qualities of the imagery. In the end the various levels of enunciation themselves—Teti the individual and Teti the scholar and ethnographer—can't and shouldn't be dissevered: They sustain and supplement each other. Whether "invented" or "real" (here the quotation marks are obligatory) the autobiographical reminiscences, the anecdotes about Teti the person bit by bit construct a character for us. They're at one with the professional other side of the coin that the prologue and the tales outline, which is very much real but is also itself absorbed by and into the narration.

The ethnographer who conducts research in his burg and testifies on its behalf is himself also, finally, when it comes down to it, a rather literary entity. What better ending than the vocation anthropology is—or can be—for the factual and fictional individual who, throughout the years, grows up like the other children, runs after the street vendors, raids the countryside for the early figs, does his part in serenades, as much as in the organization of religious festivities and carnivals, or who, as an adult, stays behind out of loyalty to the the family elders? Isn't the profession Teti has chosen and practices—as he practices it—the crowning narrative closing?

Much the same preordained duality can be discerned in some other features of the book. Clouds, we learn at a certain point, have a role in the culture and the mindset of the people of the region (they make it possible for its heavily agrarian society to predict the weather) but when we first run into them in the tales (particularly "Angelino's Turn" and "Of Clouds and Back Streets") they're more like a poetic image, a recurring literary motif which as Teti reveals in the "Bibliographical Note," is particularly significant for him. Similar double or triple duties have the lullabies and nursery rhymes of the book's interludes, which are at once, as Teti himself observes, information that completes the ethnographic portrayal of the culture of his village, and the "soundtrack" of the narration.

In the bibliography on Southern Italian life and mores only *Christ Stopped at Eboli* can be evoked as an appropriate term of comparison, but Carlo Levi's book was published in the 1940s and although its author is also a primary character in his narration he was an outsider and not a professional anthropologist. Teti updates and complicates that preamble and even if the migration he refers to needs now to be historized, in the wake of current events (which have made Italy and Southern Italy lands of both immigration and of a different type of migration, a migration no longer of people with little education), he still speaks to us, and does so in language and in a manner which opens up vistas on our current reality and invites us to reflect on how we speak about it.

If the gods have had anything to do with the fact that *Stones Into Bread* has appeared in English and in Toronto before anywhere else, their benevolence is well-deserved. And it reaffirms their good taste: it shows that they know a future classic when they see one.

Acknowledgements

THE AUTHOR OF *Pietre di pane* wishes to thank Francesco Loriggio and Damiano Pietropaolo for taking on the daunting task of translation of the texts, but above all for their human and cultural closeness in this journey. Thank you also for the precious collaboration to Anne-Marie Demers, Vincenzo Pietropaolo, Salvatore Piermarini. To my lifelong friend Vincenzo Marchese, a warm and grateful embrace for the cover photo that speaks of our common world of origin. I am grateful to Guernica Editions, publishers of the English version of this book, for their editorial and cultural openness, and to the Department of Humanities of the University of Calabria for its support. My thoughts go to the Italian-Canadian community in general, and in particular to my co-villagers of San Nicola da Crissa. I wish to dedicate this book to the memory of Antonino Mazza, with whom I shared a fraternal closeness in matters of culture.

About the Author

VITO TETI is the founder and current director of the Centre for the Study of the Anthropologies and the Literatures of the Mediterranean at the University of Calabria, where he also holds the chair in cultural anthropology. In his research he has devoted particular attention to the eating habits of the peoples of the Mediterranean area, to the anthropology of travel and migration, to rituals and feasts in traditional and contemporary societies, to the representations of the Italian South. He is the author of various collections of essays, of historical novels, of short stories (which have been translated in English, French and Spanish), as well as of photo reportages and ethnographic documentaries. Among his most recent publications are *Il patriota e la maestra* (2012), *Maledetto Sud* (2013), *Fine pasto. Il cibo che verrà* (2015), *Terra inquieta. Antropologia dell'erranza meridionale* (2015), *Quel che resta. L'Italia dei paesi, tra abbandono e ritorno* (2017).

About the Translators

FRANCESCO LORIGGIO is Professor Emeritus at Carleton University in Ottawa. He has published extensively on both modern Italian literature and Italian Canadian literature. As a translator, he has rendered into English theatre by Achille Campanile (*The Inventor of the Horse and Other Short Plays*, Guernica Editions) and into Italian poetry and prose by Italian Canadian authors. He has also edited various collections of essays and anthologies, among which *Social Pluralism and Literary History. The Literature of the Italian Emigration* (Guernica Editions), *The Last Effort of Dreams. Essays on the Poetry of Pier Giorgio Di Cicco* (WLU Press), and, with Vito Teti, *A doppio filo. Un'antologia di scritture calabro-canadesi* (Donzell Editore).

DAMIANO PIETROPAOLO is an award winning writer/broadcaster, director, translator, and educator. Translations include: selections from Italian Renaissance drama and dramatic theory (*Sources of Dramatic Theory, Volume 1*, Cambridge University Press, 1991); Ugo Betti's *The Queen and the Rebels* (Pro Arte Productions, Toronto, 1997); *The Fellini Radio Plays*, translated and adapted for the stage from radio plays by Federico Fellini (Stratford Festival 2002); a play *Love Letters from the Empty Bed*, adapted from Ovid's *Heroides*, (staged at the Glenn Morris Studio Theatre and the Canadian Opera Company's Bradshaw Amphitheatre, 2012); and the novel *Between Rothko and Three Windows: Murder at the Art Gallery of Ontario* (Quattro books, 2016). Essays, reviews and creative non-fiction have appeared in *Saturday Night Magazine, The Globe and Mail, Grail Magazine, CBC Radio,* and *Il Quotidiano della Calabria.* As editor, director and producer Damiano explored the theme of exile and return and the emergence of a post-national drama in such series as *Where is Here? The Drama of Immigration* (Scirocco Books, 2005), *Little Italies* (2006, CBC Audio Books, 2007). Essays, poetry and short fiction have been translated into Italian and published in *A Filo Doppio,* Ed. By Francesco Loriggio and Vito Teti, Donzelli, Rome 2017.

MIX
Paper from
responsible sources
FSC® C100212

Printed by Imprimerie Gauvin
Gatineau, Québec